OPTIONS TRADING

2 BOOKS IN 1

THE COMPLETE CRASH COURSE.
A BEGINNER'S GUIDE TO INVESTING AND MAKING A PROFIT AND PASSIVE INCOME
+ THE BEST SWING AND DAY STRATEGIES TO MAXIMIZE YOUR PROFIT

Ray Bears

BOOK 1:

OPTIONS TRADING FOR BEGINNERS

The Complete Crash Course to Know All You Need About Investing Strategies and How to Make Profit for a Living. Create a Passive Income Working from Home

Table of Content

BOOK 2:

OPTIONS TRADING

The Best SWING and DAY Investing Strategies on How to Make Money and Maximize Your Profit in The Market, Becoming an intelligent and Profitable Investor. For Beginners

OPTIONS TRADING FOR BEGINNERS

The Complete Crash Course to Know All You Need About Investing Strategies and How to Make Profit for a Living. Create a Passive Income Working from Home

Ray Bears

Introduction

If you were to find an investor and ask to look at their portfolio, you would be able to see that they have a large variety of investments that they are working on. They don't just put all their money on one company all the time. Instead, they have many different types of investments they can work with, such as bonds, stocks, mutual funds, and more. Also, there are times when a portfolio will include options, but it is not as likely to be there as some of the others.

This is like getting a key where once you use that key to open the front door of a house, then it belongs to you. You may not technically own the house because you have the key, but you can use that key whenever you would like, and if you choose, you could purchase the house later on.

Options are set up so that they cost you a certain fixed price for so much time. This length will change based on the option that you are working with. Sometimes you will have an option that only lasts for a day, and then there are some that you may hold onto for a few years. You will know how long the option is going to last before you make the purchase.

Options are nothing new. It is a well-known term in trading, and even though it might be overwhelming for some people to think about, options are not hard to understand. The portfolios of investors are generally composed of different classes of assets, which can be bonds, mutual funds, stocks, or even ETFs. One such asset class are options, and certain advantages are offered by them when used accurately, which other trading stocks and ETFs cannot offer. Like many other asset classes, options too can be purchased with brokerage investment accounts.

Options can be considered as an investment that gives you more "options."

But that doesn't mean that there are no risks involved. Almost every investment entails a multitude of risks. The same goes for options. An investor ought to know of these risks before proceeding with trade.

Options are a part of the group of securities called derivatives. The term derivative is many a time associated with huge risks and volatile performance. Warren Buffett once called derivatives "weapons of mass destruction," which is a little too much.

For a long time, people associated derivatives with high-risk investments. This notion is not true. Options are a kind of derivative because their value derives from an underlying share or security, and for that reason, investors often talk about different derivatives. Options belong to the class of securities known as derivatives.

Derivatives obtain their value from an underlying security. Think about wine, for instance. Wine is produced from grapes. We also have ketchup, which is derived from tomatoes. This is basically how derivatives function.

One can gain a real advantage in the market if they know how options work and can use them properly since you can put the cards in your favor if you can use options correctly. The great thing about options is that you can use them according to your style. If you're a speculative person, earn through speculation. If not, earn without speculating. You should know how options work even if you decide never to use them because other companies you invest in might use options.

Options are an attractive investment tool. They have a risk/reward framework, which is unlike any other. The risk factor involved can be diluted by using these options with other financial instruments or other option contracts, and at the same time, opening more avenues for profits. While many investments have an unbound quantum of risk attached, options' trading, on the other hand, has defined risks, which the buyers know about.

Now, several options will work when you are dealing with options. Some of the ones that you will come across regularly include:

Bonds: A bond is going to be a debt investment where the investor can loan out their money to the government or company. Then this money will be used for a variety of projects by the second party. But at some time, usually determined when the money is given over, the money will be paid back along with some interest. Most of the time, you will work with a government bond, and these bonds are even found on the public exchange.

Commodity: Commodities are another choice that you can make when you are working with options. These will be any basic goods that will be used in commerce and can include some choices like beef, oil, and grain. When you trade these, there will be a minimum of quality that they must meet. These are popular because commodities are considered tangible, which means that they represent something real.

Currency: Currency is going to talk about any type of money that is accepted by the government and can include coins and paper money. Of course, cryptocurrency and Bitcoin are starting to join the market as well. The exchange rate of these currencies, especially when it comes to digital currencies, will change quite a bit in very little time, so it is important to be careful with these.

Futures: These are going to be similar to what you found with commodities, but they have some different guidelines on how they can be delivered, the quantity and quality, and more.

Index: An index is going to be a group of securities that are imaginary and will symbolize the statistical measurement of how those will do in the market.

Stock: You can own a certain percentage of the share, but instead of running that company, you will let other management do that while you make some profits each quarter when the company does well.

Options may sound complex but are pretty easy to understand if you pay keen attention. You will come across numerous traders' profiles with different security types, including bonds, stocks, mutual funds, ETFs, and even options.

Options are another asset class. If applied correctly, they will offer numerous benefits that all other assets on their own cannot. For instance, you can use options to hedge against negative outcomes like a declining stock market or falling oil prices. You can use options to generate recurrent income and for speculative purposes like wagering on the movement of a stock.

When Should You Use Options?

As an investor, you will have several opportunities to use options. However, there is a truly beneficial number. Here is a brief look at them.

Options buy you time if you need to sit back and watch things develop.

You require minimal funds to invest in options compared to buying shares.

Options will offer you protection from losses because they lock in price but without the obligation to buy.

Always keep in mind that options offer no free ride or a free lunch. Trading in options carries some risks due to their predictive nature. Any prediction will turn out one way or another. The good news here is that any losses that you incur will only be equivalent to the cost of setting up the option. This cost is significantly lower than buying the underlying security.

Differentiating Options from Stocks

While there is no expiration date in stocks, the Options contract has one. This expiration period can be as long as a week or months or even years, and it is determined by the kind of options you are practicing and other related regulations.

Stocks are not a part of derivatives, while options are, which means their value is derived from something else.

While stocks are a well-defined numerical quantity, options are not.

One can even profit with a drop in the prices of the underlying stock, which is dependent on the type of strategy they are following.

Stock owners have a right in the company either for dividends or voting or both. Options owners have no such rights.

How option trading works

There are several parties involved in a trade. It isn't possible to trade directly with everyone, and it isn't even practical. This is why, for the sake of convenience, stock exchanges were formed. This is a channel where all the stocks are being traded.

You cannot work directly with the stock exchange, as this would create great confusion. It would mean too many people making deals at the same time. This is where brokers come into play.

Brokers work as mediators, as the channel of communication between you and the exchange. They charge a commission for their service. In the stock exchange industry's early stages, most of the transactions were carried out by the brokers on behalf of their clients. Brokers nowadays still carry out transactions on behalf of their clients, but the clients now have the option to manage their accounts easily. You will have to open a trading account with a broker, and the broker will give you access to that trading account.

Currently, several software programs have been successfully developed where you can directly trade on stock exchanges. The program recommendation, as well as the access credentials, will be provided by the brokerage firm you'll choose.

Like a bond or stock, an option is a tradable security. You can purchase or sell options to a foreign broker or trade them on an exchange within the United States. An option may allow you to leverage your cash, though it may be high risk because it eventually expires (expiration date). For stock options, each option contract represents 100 shares.

An instance of an option is if you want to buy a car/house, but for whatever reason, don't have immediate cash for it but will get the cash next month. You can now buy the asset at the agreed price and sell it for a profit. The value of the asset may also depreciate perhaps when the house develops plumbing problems or other problems or, in the case of a vehicle, gets into an accident. If you decide not to buy the asset and let your purchase option expire, you lose your initial investment, the $2,500 you placed for the option.

This is the general concept of how options trading happens; however, in reality, options trading is a lot more complex and involves more risks.

What kind of investor are you?

Trading has its strategies, its techniques, and its secrets. Different things apply to different people. What works for someone else may not work for you. Why? Because you are two different kinds of investors. Aggressive personalities invest in a completely different manner than conservative personalities. People who are not afraid to take risks are completely different investors than those who are methodical and play it safe. There is no better or worse here. It is just the style of doing business.

There are two major categories of investors:

The active investor those are also called traders. They don't hold on to options for a long time, and their interest lies in making a profit from the volatility of the prices. They trade a lot and as often as possible.

The passive investor these are also called buy-and-hold investors. They are the exact opposite. They are interested in making the maximum gain from each option, and they don't trade often. And when they do, they will trade once or twice.

Chapter 1
What is Options Trading?

Option contracts usually refer to the purchase or sale of certain assets.

An option is a contract between two parties (a buyer and a seller), in which whoever buys the option acquires the right to exercise what the agreement indicates, although he will not have an obligation to do so.

Option contracts commonly refer to the purchase or sale of certain assets, which may be stocks, stock indices, bonds, or others. These contracts also establish that the operation must be carried out on a pre-established date (in the case of the European ones, since those of the US are exercised at any time) and at a fixed price at the time the contract is signed.

To purchase an option to buy or sell it is necessary to make an initial disbursement (called "premium"), whose value depends, fundamentally, on the price that the asset that is the object of the contract has on the market, on the variability of that price and of the period between the date on which the contract is signed and the date on which it expires.

Call and Put

The options that grant the right to buy are called 'Call,' and those that allow the right to sell is called 'Put.' Additionally, it is called European options that can only be exercised on the date of exercise and American Options that can be used at any time during the life of the contract.

When the time comes for the buying party to exercise the option, if it does, two situations occur:

Whoever appears as the seller of the option will be obliged to do what such contract indicates; that is, sell or buy the asset to the counterparty, in case he decides to exercise its right to buy or sell.

Who appears as the option buyer will have the right to buy or sell the asset. However, if it doesn't suit him, he can refrain from making the transaction.

An option contract usually contains the following specifications:

- **Exercise date:** the expiration date of the right included in the option.

- **Exercise price:** agreed price for the purchase/sale of the asset referred to in the contract (called an underlying asset).
- **Option premium or price:** amount paid to the counterparty to acquire the right to buy or sell.
- **Rights acquired with the purchase of an option:** they can be Call (right of purchase) and Put (right of sale).
- **Types of Option:** there may be Europeans, which are only exercised on the date of exercise or American, to be used at any time during the contract. There are, besides, other more complex types of options, the so-called "Exotic Options."

In international financial markets, the types of options that are traded on organized exchanges are typically American and European.

Practical Example

Purchase of a call option by an importing company to secure the Euro price on that day.

To better understand the use of options, this example is presented by an importing company that wants to ensure against increases in the price of the Euro.

To do so, you can buy a European call option today that gives you the right to buy a million euros, within three months, at $ 550 per euro. To acquire that right, the company pays $ 2 per euro, that is, the option premium has a cost of $ 2,000,000.

If on the expiration date of the option, the price of the euro in the market is over $ 550 (for example, at $ 560), the company will exercise the option to buy them, as it will only pay $ 550 per euro.

On the contrary, if on that date the market price of the Euro was below $ 550 (for example at $ 530), the company will not exercise the option, since it makes no sense to pay $ 550 per euro when it can be purchased at the market at $ 530; In this case, the option expires without being exercised.

The cash flows are as follows:

Today (April 10, 20XX).

Buy a European call option, which gives you the right to buy USD 1,000,000 to $ 550 on October 10, 20XX, as the value of the premium is 2 and 1,000,000 contracts are purchased (which means that the notional of the agreement is the US $ 1) there is a cash outlay of $ 2,000,000 for that concept.

Expiration date (October 30, 20XX)

If the Euro is above the exercise price of the option, it would be exercised, and $ 550 per euro will be paid, that is, $ 550,000,000.

Otherwise, the option expires if it is used, and the euros are acquired in the market.

The euros purchased are used to cancel the importation of goods or services:

The following table shows the result of the operation. As can be seen, if on the expiration date of the option contract, the market exchange rate is lower than the exercise price of the call option, the importer will end up paying the market price per euro plus the cost of the premium (in strict rigor, the value of the premium should be updated for the interest that would have been earned if, instead of paying the value of the premium, that money had been deposited); otherwise, the cost of each euro will be equal to the exercise price plus the premium. That is, the importer will have made sure to pay a maximum of $ 552 per euro.

Market exchange rate A	The exercise price of the option B	Prima C	Value of the options (1) D = (A - B)	Result of the options (2) E = D - C	Disbursement for purchase of euros (3) F	Total disbursement G = F + C
530	550	2,000,000	0	-2,000,000	530,000,000	532,000,000
540	550	2,000,000	0	-2,000,000	540,000,000	542,000,000
550	550	2,000,000	0	-2,000,000	550,000,000	552,000,000
560	550	2,000,000	10,000,000	8,000,000	550,000,000	552,000,000
570	550	2,000,000	20,000,000	18,000,000	550,000,000	552,000,000
580	550	2,000,000	30,000,000	28,000,000	550,000,000	552,000,000

Notes:

1. On the expiration date, when the price of the euro in the market is lower than the exercise price, the value of the call option will be zero (as it is not appropriate to exercise the purchase right), whereas, if the opposite occurs, the value of the call option will correspond to the difference between those two prices.
2. That result represents how much money was paid or saved by the fact of coverage.

3. Currencies are acquired in the market when it is not optimal to exercise the option, or by exercising the right of purchase when exercising that right is an optimal decision.

Finally, it should be noted that if a forward-type contract with the same delivery price had been used to perform the same coverage, the importer would have ended up always paying $ 550. However, it would not have had the opportunities (which may appear when hedging with call options) to benefit from declines in the market exchange rate. Also, note that the operation is much simpler to perform: a premium is paid at the time of purchasing the option and on the expiration date (or at any time before that date if the option were of the American type) at least the price that has been agreed.

How the Options Work

Option operators must understand the complexity that surrounds them. The knowledge of the operation of the options allows operators to make the right decisions and offers them more options when executing a transaction.

Indicators:

- The value of an option consists of several elements that go hand in hand with the "Greeks":
- The price of the guaranteed value
- Expiration
- Implied volatility
- The actual exercise price
- Dividends
- Interest rates

The "Greeks" provide valuable information on risk management and help rebalance the portfolios to achieve the desired exposure (e.g., delta coverage). Each Greek measures the reaction of the portfolios to small changes in an underlying factor, which allows the individual risks to be examined:

- The delta measures the rate of change of the value of an option regarding changes in the price of the underlying asset.
- The gamma measures the rate of change in the delta with the changes suffered by the price of the underlying asset.
- Lambda or elasticity refers to the percentage change in the value of an option compared to the percentage change in the price of the underlying

asset, which offers a method of calculating leverage, also known as "indebtedness."

- Theta calculates the sensitivity of the option value over time, a factor known as "temporary wear."
- Vega measures the susceptibility of the option of volatility. Vega measures the value of the option based on the volatility of the underlying asset.
- Rho represents the sensitivity of the value of an option against variations in the interest rate and measures the value of the option based on the risk-free interest rate.

Therefore, the Greeks are reasonably simple to determine if the Black Scholes model (considered the standard option valuation model) is used and is very useful for intraday and derivatives traders. Delta, theta, and Vega are useful tools to measure time, price, and volatility. The value of the option is directly affected by maturity and volatility if:

- For a long period before expiration, the value of the purchase and sale option tends to rise. The opposite situation would occur if, for a short period before expiration, the value of the purchase and sale options is prone to a fall.

- If the volatility increases, so will the value of the purchase and sale options, while if the volatility decreases, the value of the purchase and sale options decreases.
- The price of the guaranteed value causes a different effect on the value of the purchase options than on that of the sale options.
- Usually, as the price of the securities increases, so do the current purchase options that correspond to it, increasing its value while the sale options lose value?
- If the price of the value falls, the opposite happens, and the current purchase options usually experience a drop in value while the value of the sale options increases.

A Bonus of Options

It happens when an operator acquires an option contract and pays an initial amount to the seller of the option contract. The option premium will vary depending on when it was calculated and on which market options its acquisition was made. The premium may be different within the same market based on the following criteria:

What option has been chosen, in-, at-, or out-of-the-money? An in-the-money option will be sold for a higher premium since the contract is already profitable, and the buyer has direct access to the benefits obtained from the contract. Instead, at- or out-of-the-money options can be purchased for a lower premium.

Chapter 2
Trading Basics

This chapter will guide you through the learning curve of options trading that always starts with the most basic move you need to make setting yourself up in a position to be able to trade.

How to Get Started in Options Trading

One thing to know before you pick your firm: times have changed considerably over the last couple of decades when it comes to options trading. Back before the internet became such a regular part of our lives, your brokerage firm—or, at least, your representative at the firm—would make your options trades on your behalf, and you paid a hefty price for their services. Nowadays, however, you'll be doing most of your trades yourself.

Commission for your representative is thus a whole lot lower than it used to be, which means it won't cost you an arm and both legs to rely on your rep in the early days of your experience. While you are learning, feel free to make use of your firm's services to place and confirm your trades, if it helps you feel more comfortable getting to know the process.

With this in mind, there will be sure things to look for when selecting your company:

- Compare commission prices to make sure you are getting a great deal.
- Make sure the firm has up to date software and is capable of setting up trades quickly and reliably to make sure you get those trades you want at the best prices.
- Check out the hours of service to ensure they are compatible with your needs. In these days of online firms, you could be dealing with a firm that's across the ocean from the markets you have an interest in, or you might find that a firm only makes its reps available for the length of the working day, which might not suit your timing.
- Speak personally with the reps at the firm, as these are the people who are going to help you during the process of setting up your strategy. You want someone personable and knowledgeable of the business—and, most importantly, who speaks in terms that you personally find easy to comprehend.

- Take a look at the additional services the firm supplies. Many will offer learning materials, guides, and even classes or webinars to help you hone your strategies. Even if you feel that you know all you need to know already, there's no harm in a refresher course or a little nugget of inspiration every once in a while.

Once you select a firm, you'll then need to consider signing a "margin agreement" with that firm. This agreement allows you to borrow money from the firm to purchase your stocks, which is known as "buying on margin."

Understandably, your brokerage firm is not going to allow you to do that if you don't have the financial status to pay them back. They will, therefore, run a credit check on you and ask you for information about your resources and knowledge.

A margin account is not a necessity for options trading—you don't use margin to purchase an option because it must be paid for in full. However, it can be useful as you graduate to more advanced strategies—in some cases, it will be obligatory. If you opt to sign a margin agreement, discuss it thoroughly with the firm as there are certain restrictions on the type of money you can use that may apply to you.

Next, you'll need to sign an "options agreement"—and, this time, it's a necessary step. This agreement is designed to figure out how much you know about options and how much experience you have in trading them. It also aims to ensure that you are aware of the risks you take by trading and make sure that you are financially able to handle those risks.

By ascertaining these things, your firm can determine what level of options trading you should be aiming for. It will, therefore, approve your "trading level," of which there are five:

- **Level 1:** You may sell covered calls
- **Level 2:** You may buy calls and puts and also buy strangles, straddles and collars. You may also sell puts that are covered by cash and by options on exchange-traded funds and indexes
- **Level 3:** You may utilize credit and debit spreads
- **Level 4:** You may sell "naked puts," straddles and strangles
- **Level 5:** You may sell "naked indexes" and "index spreads."

Don't worry if you're not sure yet what each of these things means. For now, all you need to be aware of is that your firm will determine for you, which level you should be at. As a beginner, don't be surprised if you only reach the first two levels.

Once you've signed the agreement, you'll be handed a booklet that contains a mine of information about risks and rewards within options trading. Right now, if you were to read that booklet, it would seem to be in a foreign language. By the time you finish this crash course, it will be a lot more decipherable—and it's essential for your success that you do read it.

Finally, your firm will present you with a "standardized option contract." It's the same for every trader, which means you stand the same chance of success as every other person out there in the options market.

By trading an option, you are entering into a legal agreement that is insured by the Options Clearing Corporation, which guarantees the contract will be honored in full. Make sure you read that contract to be aware of not only the rights you have as a trader but also the obligations you must follow in the same role.

Congratulations, you have an options account. This is the conduit through which you will create and implement your strategies and begin your adventure in options trading.

Learning the Lingo

Options traders speak their language—it's not meant to confuse you, it's just the natural process of creating a shorthand by which one trader can converse with another more easily and thoroughly.

Of course, it does make it difficult to plunge into the waters of trading if you can't speak that language. A lot like trying to decipher road signs in a foreign country, it makes it hard to know the right direction—or even where you're standing right now.

We're going to take a look at the standard terms you'll be dealing with as you enter the world of options trading before we begin taking a more in-depth look at your strategies.

Don't worry about trying to learn them by rote—they will all become clear as you forge onwards. This glossary will always be available to you to check on meaning if you need to:

- **Strike Price:** A price per share agreed upon before an option is traded. At this price, the stock may be bought or sold under the terms of your options contract. Also known as the "exercise price."
- **Bid/Ask:** The latest price that a market maker has offered for an option is its "ask" price. In other words, it's what the seller is willing to accept for the trade. The latest amount that a buyer has offered for an option is the "bid" price.
- **Premium:** The premium is a per-share amount paid to the seller to procure an option. The seller will keep this premium no matter whether the buyer exercises their right to buy or sell the stock at the deadline.
- **In-the-Money:** Often shortened to ITM, this means that the stock price is above the strike price for a call or below the strike price for a put. In other words, it is now at the right price to be traded.
- **Out-of-the-Money:** Often shortened to OTM, this means the price is below the strike price for a call or above it for a put. Such an option is priced according to "time value."
- **At-the-Money:** The strike price is equal to the stock price.

- **Long:** In this context, "long" is used to imply ownership. Once you purchase a stock or option, you are "long" that item in your account.
- **Short:** If you sell an option or stock that you don't own, you are "short" that security in your account.
- **Exercise:** The owner of the option takes advantage of the right to buy or sell what they purchased by "exercising" it.
- **Assigned:** When the owner exercises their option, the seller is "assigned" and must make good on the trade. In other words, they must fulfill their obligation to buy or sell.
- **Intrinsic Value/Time Value:** The intrinsic value of an option refers to how much it is ITM. Most options also include time value, which refers to how long left until its expiry. This time has value because, during that time, the stock can still change in price. An OTM option has no intrinsic value because it is a loss, but it does have time value because that loss might change.
- **Time Decay:** Linked to time value, this term refers to the fact that, as time ticks on, the amount of time value slowly decreases. At the expiration date of the options contract, the contract has NO time value and is worth only its intrinsic value.

- **Index Options/Equity Options:** Index options are settled by cash, whereas equity options involve trading stock. The main difference between these two types of options is that an index option usually cannot be exercised before the expiry date, while an equity option usually can.
- **Stop-Loss Order:** This is an order to sell either an option or a stock when it reaches a particular price. Its purpose is to set a point at which you, as the trader, would like to get out of your position. At this price, your stop order is activated as a market order; in other words, by looking for the best available price at that moment to close out your position.

These are the most common terms you will hear when you enter the world of options trading. It's worth mentioning that, as you extend your understanding, you'll encounter more. However, these are plenty to help you decipher your first trades and get stuck in.

Chapter 3
Basic Options Strategies

If you were first to open your contract by selling, we say that you are "short." If you buy to open a position, we say that you are "long." The simplest way to trade options is to take a long position on a call or a put. Although when buying and selling stocks, we say that someone "shorts" the stock when they are hoping to profit off a decline in share price, you can be expecting to profit from a decline in share price, but you are "long" concerning the put option.

The strategy for profiting from going long on a call or put option is simple. You are hoping the price of the stock would move in your favor so that you will earn a profit. The industry is full of naysayers that downplay this basic strategy; however, the reality is you can earn profits in this way. That is buying or selling individual options, be they the call or put variety. The key to success when doing this type of trading is to stay on top of it and don't buy options on a whim. You need a good reason to buy a call or a put option by itself, and that means paying attention to the financial news surrounding the company, earnings reports, and looking at simple market trends to determine when you have a reasonable probability of earning a profit.

Day Trading and Options

This is just an aside, but watching the movement of a stock price over a single day can provide opportunities to ride a short-term trend in price and profit handsomely. Rising and falling share prices are magnified in the price of the option, so when the share price goes up a few tens of cents, you might profit by $65 or $75 in a single day.

But be aware that the rules for day trading apply to options as well. To be a day trader approved by your broker in the United States, you need to have a margin account, and it needs to have $25,000 deposited in the account. Since options trading often takes place on the level of tens or hundreds of dollars at a time, the vast majority of beginning options traders are not going to be looking to be a day trader. But you are going to be tempted to get out of some trades on the same day that you enter the trade because you might have ridden a trend in one direction or the other to significant profits.

The trend might not continue the following day, and you don't want to eat some of your profits from the theta or time decay.

The rule you need to be aware of is if you make four-day trades over five days, which means you will be labeled a pattern day trader. To keep your account open, you'd have to fund it with $25,000. So, this is a situation that you are probably going to want to avoid. To avoid being pulled under by this, simply limit the number of day trades to 3 per week.

Remember that the five-day rule means five consecutive trading days, so weekends don't count. If you made a day trade on Friday, the following Monday, that day, trade still counts against you.

Call Options Basic Strategy

The basic strategy behind making profits with call options is to buy low and sell high. You can profit from this strategy riding a single day's price movements or by "swing trading" the option over one or more days, meaning that you will hold the option overnight. You are not going to hold the option until expiration unless you have the intention of buying the stock.

The time to sell the option is the point at which you have made an acceptable level of profits. You should set this level beforehand so that you are not letting the emotions of the moment rule your decisions. It's not uncommon to make $50 or $100 profits in a few days or even in a single day off of one option contract, but many traders get dollar signs in their eyes—they get overcome with greed—and as a result, they hold their positions too long. That can mean lost profits, defeat by time decay, or even seeing the option wiped out.

One lesson that you are going to learn is that options prices can fluctuate dramatically. This is because the underlying stock is 100 shares. So a small change in the stock price is magnified by 100 for your investment in the option. Using a one-to-one pricing relationship for the sake of simplicity, if the price of the stock moves up by a mere 45 cents, the price of the option will go up by $45. On the other hand, if it drops by 30 cents, the price of the option would drop by $30.

Although the situation of using one-to-one pricing is not realistic, it is pretty clear that small price changes in stock mean significant price changes in your investment.

The key to success with trading options is to have a trading plan that you follow, and which has specific rules.

One skill you are going to need to develop when it comes to calling options is the ability to read stock charts. There are three necessary skills that I recommend you have:

- Learn how to read and interpret candlestick charts.
- Learn how to use moving averages.
- Learn how to use and interpret Bollinger bands.

A candlestick chart divides a stock chart into time intervals that you specify. The time interval you are going to use is going to depend on the time frame over which you are hoping to trade. I have had some success trading call options using a buy to open strategy. I can't say what the situation is in all cases, but what I will tell you is that I don't stay in these trades very long. What I do is I check the early morning financial news for any surprises, and then when the market opens, I look for early indicators of how it is going to move.

If the other aspects of the stock look good—that is, I can buy options with a high level of open interest—then I will enter a position if it looks like there is going to be a strong move over the day or the next few days.

Let's give a few specific examples so that you will have some practical advice for the situation. You can trade index funds like the Dow Jones Industrial Average (trade options on DIA), the S & P 500 (trade options on SPY), or the NASDAQ (trade options on QQQ). These index funds are susceptible to general economic and political news. So, if you see that a good jobs report has come out, that is a good signal to get in on one or more of these funds. It's often worth the risk to get in on options for these index funds the day before. Then you can wake up and see the results. It's going to be possible to double an investment overnight. Since you are not day trading, in that case, it's a simple matter to exit your positions for a profit. But keep in mind, there is a risk as well if it works against you. If you buy a call, but the early indication is a market sell-off, then get rid of the put first thing when the market opens.

This is an excellent example of why open interest is essential to look at. If you were to buy an option on something with a small level of open interest, you might not be able to get rid of your options before the put lost a lot of money. With something that is very heavily traded like SPY, however, it is a sure bet that you can unload the put quickly.

You also want to pay attention to news about specific companies. For example, if there is news coming out in the early morning hours that the government is going to investigate the social media companies that is a good indication that going long on a put option would be a reasonable strategy. Conversely, recently, the FTC announced a settlement with Facebook, and this sent the stock soaring.

You are not going to be getting the news "first" as an individual retail investor, but the good news is that with options trading if you are staying on top of things, you are going to be able to get in and out of your trades and take profits if you are careful about it.

Reading the Charts

As an options trader, you are going to have to learn how to read charts. The first thing to do is look up candlestick patterns so that you can recognize when a trend reversal might becoming. Candlestick patterns are not absolute rules or truth-tellers; they are an indicator. So, you consider the candlestick charts and use the entirety of the information that you have available to make your decisions.

As we said earlier, a candlestick can be divided into different timeframes. If you are looking to ride a trend over a single day, a five-minute timeframe is reasonable to use. In this case, each candlestick is going to tell you what the price action was over five minutes.

The candlesticks are going to be colored green or red. If a candlestick is green, it's a "bullish" candlestick. That means that throughout interest, the closing price had risen to a more considerable higher than the opening price. By itself, it doesn't tell you where the price is headed. For a bullish candlestick, the top of the candle is the price at the end of the trading session, and the bottom of the body is the price at the start.

Chapter 4
Variety of Options and Their Styles

Call Options

These options provide you with the right to buy stock labeled as an underlying one. With Call Options, you can buy not only stocks but also commodities, bonds, or any other instrument that has a specified price, otherwise known as the strike price, within a specific timeframe. Call Options contract gives you the right to buy, but you don't have an obligation to do so. A person who is bullish on the stock is usually the investor who expects the value of the stock to increase shortly. This kind of investor buys call options and manages them in the specified time frame. Again, let's take an example.

Let's say that the investor we will name Mr. B thinks that next month CCC Company will have more significant earnings for the stock, and the stock will have a higher value. In this case, Mr. B buys a call option for the CCC Company's stock for 20 dollars, for example. The contract of the option has a term that Mr. B can buy up to 100 shares from CCC Company within the next two months. The strike price for these shares within this time frame is

100 dollars. So, if the value of the stock goes 100 dollars in the next period, Mr. B won't exercise his option, which means that he will lose his first 20 dollars of investment (remember, if the option is not exercised within the specific time frame, or two months in this particular case, the contract expires and becomes worthless).

On the other hand, if the value of the stock goes over 100 dollars, and the next price is 130 dollars, for example, Mr. B can exercise his option. He can now buy the stock for 100 dollars and sell it for 130 dollars on the market. The risk that Mr. B took paid off, and he earned a significant profit.

Put Options

These options have opposite traits from the Call Options. Put Options represent the contract in which the purchaser has the right to sell his or her stocks. These stocks, like all others, must be sold for the strike price (a price that's been specified for a specific time). Put Options, like Call Options, give the right to sell, but they are not obligatory. Now we can return to Mr. B and observe him as an investor who is bearish on a particular stock.

In this example, Mr. B thinks that the price of the stock he is interested in will decrease, and, in that case, he will purchase a put option. According to Mr. B, the stock that CCC Company has is overpriced, and its value will go lower in the next two months. Let's say that Mr. B buys a Put Option on this stock for 20 dollars again. Contract of the Put Option gives Mr. B a chance to sell the stock he bought from CCC Company for 120 dollars in the next 60 days. So if the stock value increases more than 120 dollars per share, Mr. B won't have to exercise his Put Option, the time frame will pass, and the option will become worthless, which means that he would lose only his initial capital of 20 dollars. However, if the value of the stock goes down and the price goes from 120 dollars to 90 dollars, for example, the Put Option will be exercised, and Mr. B can sell this stock for 120 dollars per share. Once again, he judged correctly, and he has made a considerable profit.

How to Make a Profit Using Call Options and Put Options

There are many ways for a trader to use Call Options and Put Options and be successful in the process. The best way to show some of the most efficient ways to use these options is by using real numbers. Imagine you want to buy shares from US Bank. Let's suppose that the bank currently sells them for the price of 200 dollars per share and that you conclude that this number is going to go up since the shares are underpriced. Let's also suppose that the predicted amount of time that the shares will need to increase their value is a few months from now. At the moment, you don't have enough capital to buy 100 shares from the US Bank. However, you still want to make some profit from the stock that will rise in value according to your estimation. If this is the case, you can use Call Option and buy it for the stock. This way, you reduce the cost, and you pay only a fraction of the original stock price. Once that you purchased the Call Option, you gained the right to buy 100 shares of US Bank stock for 200 dollars per share in the next two months. One of your doubts might immediately be how you are supposed to buy that stock for 200 dollars per share in the next 60 days when you don't have the initial amount of money for that in the first place? Well, the thing is that you are not under obligation actually to buy the stock if you want to make money. If your estimation is correct, and in the next period, the value of the stock goes over 200 dollars per share, the Call Option that you bought would increase in value too. In other words, your option contract value rises with the value of the stock price. Keeping this in mind, you get the opportunity to sell your Call Options contract to make money, not the shares. That is the real connection because once when the stock price rises, your contract is worth a lot more than the money you invested in buying it.

A similar thing happens if you purchase the Put Options contract. The only difference is that your estimation has to be decreased in the stock value rather than prices going higher. Once when the underlying security price goes down, the price of your Put Option will go up. The more that the stock price falls, the more expensive your contract becomes. Using options in both cases means that you can make a profit regardless of the rise or fall of the stock prices.

Option Styles

There are various styles of options used in the trader's market, and it is essential to understand them. However, most of the options that are used in everyday trading belong to one of the main styles—American style or European style. These two categories are often called vanilla options, and their main difference is the time of execration for both types of options.

American Options

The first style of options that we will introduce is also one of the two that are used most often. These options are called American Options, and their main characteristic is that they can be exercised at any point as long as the option hasn't reached its expiration date. American Options are also considered to be the most frequent type of contract traded on the market when it comes to future exchanges.

European Options

European Options has a different excretion policy. The expiration date of the option has to be defined in the contract, which means that the option can be exercised only during that specific period. The type of market called 'over the counter' or OTC for short is the market in which European Options are traded the most.

However, the value of American and European Options is calculated differently. Additionally, the expiration date is also different for each of these styles. For American Options, the expiration date is pre-determined before the investor purchases the contract. The American Option always expires on the third Saturday of the following month. Contrarily, the European Option becomes worthless on Friday—a day before the third Saturday of the specified month. There are a few similarities between these so-called vanilla options too. They both have the rule of buying and selling at the strike price, and they both include pay-off. Furthermore, whether you calculate pay off for the Call or Put Options, the process is the same, and it usually means that the strike price for these options is the same most of the time.

Exotic Options

As we already mentioned, vanilla options are the two main styles that investors use while trading. However, many other option styles should be aware of. These other styles that are not that frequent are called Exotic Options.

Bermuda Options

In this case, are a style of option that qualifies as something in between American and European versions? The critical difference is that Bermuda Options can be exercised on more than a few dates as long as the contract is valid.

Barrier Options

On the other hand, there are Barrier Options. These options are the most different ones so far, and the reason is that there is a border that needs to be passed to get the payoff for the underlying security price. This is the case for both Call and Put Options. Barrier Options are divided into four categories:

- **"Down and Out" Barrier Options –** the purchaser of this option has the right (but like in every other case, no obligation) to buy or sell shares, depending on the type of option that he chooses. The condition is that whether these underlying assets are bought or sold, it has to be done using the already determined strike price. The strike price, however, mustn't go lower than a barrier that is pre-determined with the option contract until the expiration date. If by any chance the price of the owner's shares goes below this barrier, the option loses every value, and that is why it was named "down and out."

- **"Down and In" Barrier Options –** this option is the total opposite of the "down and out" category. An investor who has this option should know that the only time when the "down and in barrier" has value is when the price of all assets that are underlying and allowed to be purchased by the contract goes below the barrier that was pre-determined for that particular option until it expires. The purchaser has the right to sell or buy shares (again, depending on the type of purchased option) if the barrier was crossed. This trade also has to be done before the expiration date is due and at the strike price.

- **"Up and Out" Barrier Options** – this category of Barrier Options is similar to "down and out". The main distinction is the fact that the barrier itself is placed differently. In this case, "up and out" means that if the price of any underlying asset being purchased increases above the barrier predetermined by the contract, the option will lose its value.

- **"Up and In" Barrier Options –** Unlike "up and out", this category has similarities with "down and in" options rather than "down and out". The barrier, in this case, is set above the current value of any underlying asset purchased by the investor. The only time that this kind of option carries value is when the price of the stock reaches the placed barrier before the contract expires.

Chapter 5
Risk Management

Excellent risk management can save the worst trading strategy, but horrible risk management will sink even the best strategy. This is a lesson that many traders learn painfully over time, and I suggest you learn this by heart and install it deep within you even if you can't fully comprehend that statement.

Risk management has many different elements to both quantitative and qualitative. When it comes to options trading, the quantitative side is minimal thanks to the nature of options limiting risk by themselves. However, the qualitative side deserves much attention.

Risk

What is risk at any rate? Logically, it is the probability of you losing all of your money. In trading terms, you can think of it as being the probability of your actions, putting you on a path to losing all of your capital. An excellent way to think about the need for proper risk management is to ask yourself what a lousy trader would do. Forget trading, what would a lousy business person do with their capital?

Well, they would spend it on useless stuff that adds nothing to the bottom line. Thcy would also increase expenses, market poorly, not take care of their employees, and be undisciplined with regards to their processes. While trading, you don't have employees or marketing needs, so you don't need to worry about that.

Do you have suppliers and costs? Well, yes, you do. Your supplier is your broker, and you pay fees to execute your trades. That is the cost of access. In directional trading, you have high costs as well because taking losses is a necessary part of trading. With market neutral or non-directional trading, your losses are going to be minimal, but you should still seek to minimize them.

What about discipline? Do you think you can trade and analyze the market thoroughly if you've just returned home from your job and are tired? If you didn't sleep properly last night, or if you've argued with your spouse or partner? The point I'm making is that the more you behave like a terrible business owner, the more you increase your risk of failure.

Odds and Averages

Trading requires you to think a bit differently about profitability. I spoke about minimizing costs, and your first thought must have been to seek to reduce losses and maximize wins. This is a natural product of linear or ordered thinking. The market, however, is chaotic, and linear thinking is going to get you nowhere.

Instead, you need to think in terms of averages and odds. Averages imply that you need to worry about your average loss size and your average win size. Seek to decrease the former and increase the latter. Notice that when we talk about averages, we're not necessarily talking about reducing the total number of losses. You can reduce the average by either reducing the sum of your losses or by increasing the number of losing trades while keeping the sum of the losses constant. This is a shift in thinking you must make.

Thinking in this way sets you up nicely to think in terms of odds because, in chaotic systems, all you can bank on are odds playing out in the long run. For example, if you flip a coin, do you know in advance whether it's going to be heads or tails? Probably not. But if someone asked you to predict the distribution of heads versus tails over 10,000 flips, you could reasonably guess that it'll be 5000 heads and 5000 tails. You might be off by a few flips either way, but you'll be pretty close percentage-wise.

The greater the number of flips, the lesser your error percentage will be. This is because the odds inherent in a pattern that occurs in a chaotic system express themselves best over the long run. Your trading strategy is precisely such a pattern. The market is a chaotic system. Hence, you should focus on executing your strategy as it is meant to be executed over and over again and worry about profitability only in the long run.

Contrast this with the usual attitude of traders who seek to win every single trade. This is impossible to accomplish since no trading strategy or pattern is correct 100% of the time.

This is because you don't have to do much when trading options. You enter and then monitor the trade. Sure, it helps to have some directional bias, but even if you get it wrong, your losses will be extremely limited, and you're more likely to hit winners than losers.

Despite this, always think of your strategy in terms of its odds. There are two basic metrics to measure this. The first is the win rate of your system. This is simply the percentage of winners you have. The second is your payout ratio, which is the average win size divided by the average loss size.

Together, these two metrics will determine how profitable your system is. Both of them play off one another, and a decrease in another usually meets an increase in one. It takes an extremely skillful trader to increase both simultaneously.

Risk per Trade

The quantitative side of risk management when it comes to options trading is lesser than what you need to take care of when trading directionally. However, this doesn't mean there's nothing to worry about. Perhaps the most important metric of them all is your risk per trade. The risk per trade is what ultimately governs your profitability.

How much should you risk per trade? Common wisdom says that you should restrict this to 2% of your capital. For options trading purposes, this is perfectly fine. Once you build your skill and can see opportunities better, I'd suggest increasing it to a higher level.

A point that you must understand here is that you must keep your risk per trade consistent for it to have any effect. You might see an excellent setup and think that it has no chance of failure, but the truth is that you don't know how things will turn out. Even the prettiest setup has every chance of failing, and the ugliest setup you can think of may result in a profit. So never adjust your position size based on how something looks.

Calculating your position size for a trade is a pretty straightforward task. Every option's strategy will have a fixed maximum risk amount. Divide the capital risk by this amount, and that gives you your position size. Round that down to the nearest whole number since you can only buy whole number lots when it comes to contract sizes.

For example, let's say your maximum risk is $50 per lot on the trade. Your capital is $10,000. Your risk per trade is 2%. So, the amount you're risking on that trade is 2% of 10,000, which is $200. Divide this by 50, and you get 4. Hence, your position size is four contracts or 400 shares. (You'll buy the contracts, not the shares.)

Why is it important to keep your risk per trade consistent? Well, recall that your average win and loss size is important when it comes to determining your profitability. These, in conjunction with your strategy's success rate, determine how much money you'll make. If you keep shifting your risk amount per trade, you'll shift your win and loss sizes. You might argue that since it's an average, you can always adjust amounts to reflect an average.

My counter to that is, how would you know which trades to adjust in advance? You won't know which ones are going to be a win or a loss, so you won't know which trade sizes to adjust to meet the average. Hence, keep it consistent across all trades and let the math work for you.

Aside from risk per trade, there are some simple metrics you should keep track of as part of your quantitative risk management plan.

Drawdown

A drawdown refers to the reduction in capital your account experiences. Drawdowns by themselves always occur. The metrics you should be measuring are the maximum drawdown and recovery period. If you think of your account's balance as a curve, the maximum drawdown is the biggest peak to trough distance in dollars. The recovery period is the subsequent time it took for your account to make new equity high.

If your risk per trade is far too high, your max drawdown will be unacceptably high. For example, if you risk 10%

per trade and lose two in a row, which is very likely, your drawdown is going to be 20%. This is an absurdly large hole to dig your way out. Consider that your capital has decreased by 20%, and the subsequent climb back up needs to be done on lesser capital.

This is why you need to keep your risk per trade low and in line with your strategy's success rate. The best way to manage drawdowns and limit the damage they cause is to put in place risk limits per day, week, and month. Even professional athletes who train to do one thing all the time have bad days, so it's unfair to expect yourself to be at 100% all the time.

These risk limits will take you out of the game when you're playing poorly. A daily risk limit is to prevent you from getting into a spiral of revenge trading. A good limit to stick to when starting is to stop trading if you experience three losses in a row. This is pretty unlikely with options trades to be honest unless you screw up badly, but it's good to have a limit in place from a perspective of the discipline.

Next, aim for a maximum weekly drawdown limit of 5% and a monthly drawdown limit of 6-8%. These are pretty high limits, to be honest, and if you are a directional trader, these limits don't apply to you. Directional traders need to be a lot more conservative than options traders when it comes to risk.

Understand that these are hard stop limits. So if your account has hit its monthly drawdown level within the first week, you need to take the rest of the month off. Overtrading and a lack of reflection on progress can cause a lot of damage, and a drawdown is simply a reflection of that.

Qualitative Risk

Quantitative metrics aside, your ability to properly manage qualitative things in your life and trading will dictate a lot of your success. Prepare well, and you're likely to see progress. You need to see preparation as your responsibility. I mean, no one else can prepare for you, can they?

There are different elements to tracking your level of preparation, so let's look at them one by one.

Chapter 6
Pitfalls to Avoid

You will encounter downturns from time to time, especially during trading. If not dealt with, you may end up burnt out and extremely frustrated. You must learn how to handle yourself in these cases to avoid further despair. For making the best out of a bad situation, the following pointers may be of help to you:

- Embrace your failure and accept it
- Do not avoid addressing your shortcomings, no matter how embarrassing they may be
- Take personal responsibility and avoid blaming others
- Analyze your actions and identify where you went wrong
- Consider whether you would have handled the situation differently
- Listen to the opinions and advice of your colleagues
- Learn from the situation and rectify your relevant behavioral aspect
- Avoid repeating the error or mistake in a similar situation in the future

The Misconceptions and Pitfalls of Options Trading

A long call option is useful when you expect a stock price to rise in the future. You engage in long call options whenever you feel very bullish about a particular stock. This strategy is aggressive and relies on your confidence in rising future stock prices. Your potential for profits is unlimited since the expected upward trend maintains a trajectory assuming all factors remain the same. However, your risk is limited to the premium since you make losses when the stock price remains or falls below the strike price.

A short call option is strategically opposite to a long call option. In this case, you are hoping and predicting that stock prices will fall in the future. You have to be particularly bearish to engage in short call options. If the stock price follows your predicted downward trend, you make a profit. Short calls are risky since your profit margin is limited to the premium while your risk exposure is unlimited. You may end up with substantial losses should the stock prices reverse direction and start rising in value.

Tips you can apply to succeed in options trading

You need abundant knowledge and experience to trade in options successfully. However, since it will take time for you to gain the relevant experience, you may apply the following tips during trading:

Evaluate your choices

Evaluating your choices before delving into options trading is akin to conducting due diligence. You want to have all pertinent information available to you before investing in options. Such due diligence will put you on a path to eventual profitability in the end.

Failure in conducting this evaluation might lead you to unimaginable losses due to unforeseen pitfalls associated with options trading. Trading in options primarily involves buying and selling of options. You need to have a grasp of all the available options from which to choose. Having a keen eye for profitability will serve you well in the long run. You will soon realize that trading options is quite different from outright buying and selling a stock. You should never confuse these two different investment strategies.

A proper evaluation of available investment strategies will clear this confusion for you. You should first have the knowledge related to options trading and understand all the terminologies involved. You need not just identify the lingo, but learn the meaning of every term in options trading. You will be wise to consult an experienced professional or brokerage firm to get a full understanding of both the advantages and downsides of trading options.

Set your objectives

What do you aim to achieve from trading options? You must clearly state and write down your goal at the beginning of options trading. Your stated purpose should be specific, time-bound, measurable, and transparent. Don't set out with abstract goals that don't have any specificity. Such poor objectives include statements like I want to make much money at the end of my options trade.

This goal is not specific enough. A better explanation of the objective should sound something like 'I will make a profit of X dollars within a Y time frame.' Your goal is then specific to the amount of money you will be aiming to make and is time-bound within a specified period. In addition to having a set-out objective, you must develop your investment policy statement. This policy will provide you with strict guidelines to follow during your trading. It protects you from deviating from the laid down course of actions.

Besides, your policy statement needs to identify the potential pitfalls that may hamper your path towards success and provide ways of tackling challenges. You need to promptly devise a way to either avoid or address such challenges according to your policy guidelines. Every investment strategy faces risks, and options trading will be no different. You must assess your risks against your objectives and adjust accordingly. Once you have a clear goal, your decision-making should be focused on achieving your overall objective by the end of your set expiry period.

Identify profitable options

Your main aim for investing in options is to make profits. Therefore, you need to have an eye or a killer instinct for identifying opportunities that have a high potential for returns. Options trading deals with the potential future stock price movements in a particular direction. You need to be able to predict the next price trend of a given stock correctly based on current factors available to you. It is a test of your speculative ability.

Your ability to identify this trend typically develops with experience. The more you trade-in options, the more your knack to define valuable options will improve. Remember, your options become profitable only if the stock trend follows your earlier prediction. This prediction is also time-bound; hence, your forecast has to come true within a specific period. In direct stock trading, you make profits from increased stock value over time. An options trade makes money from a correct trajectory of the stock price over the same period.

You could predict a downward trend and make a profit if the stock price correspondingly trends downwards over the specified period. However, in a direct stock trade, a downward trend would indicate a loss of value in your particular stock. To increase your chances of identifying profitable options, you need a keen eye for the market trends and any associated factors affecting volatility. Stock volatility is directly related to options profitability. Such a stock guarantees you future price movements, and the only unknown is the kind of trajectory.

Conduct intelligent trades

Now that you have identified your potentially profitable options, it is time to make your entry into the options market. During trading, follow this straightforward rule: You should always make a habit of buying options contracts that are underpriced while selling the overpriced contracts. Also, you should know when to make your move rather than the number of steps you make. Your timing is more valuable than the quantity.

This way, you end up gaining overall value from your particular option. The historical volatility of a given stock will influence your predictability of the future price movements of that particular stock. Therefore, having available data on this volatility is vital for the profitability potential of your trades. You should not spend a lot of time feeling the market and trying to make your decisions based on your market emotions. When you do this, you will certainly lose your investment. Also, wasting time in overanalyzing the minor underlying factors affecting stock prices will take too much of your time.

Remember, your options contract is time-bound, and it depreciates, the closer you approach your expiry date. Intelligent trading is a well-informed piece of business when it comes to trading options. Here are some examples of call and put options that explain the value of smart trading. When you deal with call options, you should buy your option contract at a lower strike price than your projected future value of the associated stock.

When the worth of the stock goes up as you intended, the value of your option also rises. Your option contract is in the money and, most importantly, is profitable. Once the stock price has gained the maximum amount it possibly can during the period, your best move is to sell your call option. This way, you will have made a significant profit since the only way the stock can move from here onwards is to trend downwards.

When you keep waiting for a more extended gain momentum, your option starts losing value since the stock price starts falling. In this case, you either let the option expire and make a loss or exercise its time value and gain some benefit, albeit a small amount. This option roll out would be preferable from your depreciating option.

On the other hand, you own a put option that you are considering to sell. First, you need to buy put options at a much higher strike price than your projected future minimum stock value. Since you expect the stock price to fall over the particular period, your put option remains profitable during this duration. Your intelligent move would be to exercise the option at the minimum stock value.

After the downward trend, the only way the stock can go from here is a trend upwards. When you sell your put option at the stock's minimum value point, then you will have made a significant profit from that trade. However, if you delay exercising your option contract, your contract's value will start falling since the stock price will be trending upwards. Just like the call option, a put option depreciates as you approach its expiry date. In this case, you may avoid a total loss by exercising the option's time value instead of letting it expire.

Chapter 7

Calls Spread

If the prospect of implementing the long stock leg of the strategies intimidated, you. This is because call spreads don't need you to establish a stock position. Instead, you will be playing one strike price against another. The downside is that you need to have a definite market bias, so they aren't fully market neutral from a strategy perspective.

None of the strategies is 100% market neutral. However, from a risk perspective, they insulate you from the gyrations of the market, and this is the context in which you should understand these strategies. So let's take a look at how call spreads work.

Bull Call Spread Strategy

The bull call spread assumes that you have a bullish view of the market based on your technical analysis. The beauty of this strategy is that it can be adjusted, just like a collar, but without the need for establishing a long stock position. Indeed, all spread strategies have this inherent advantage to them.

This strategy works best in markets that are titled bullish but not explicitly so. What I mean is that often the market heads in a particular direction, but you'll find that it meanders about, diving as often as it rises with a small net push upwards. This sort of see-saw movement is perfect for the bull call spread.

It works even in strong bull markets, although I recommend simply going long on a call to capture the full movement. Mind you, such strong bullish movements happen very infrequently, so you need to pick and choose carefully. Let's take a deeper look at how this strategy works.

Execution

The bull call spread has two legs to it:

1. Along at or in the money call
2. A short out of the money call

The primary profit generator in this strategy is the long call. This is what captures the upward movement of the stock and enables you to earn the increased premium via the increased intrinsic value of the option. The short call is effectively your profit target or slightly beyond it and improves your overall profit, and you earn income from the premium upon writing it.

Let's look at how the math works out using good old AMZN. Our market price is still $1833.51, so to establish the first leg of this trade, let's choose an in the money or at the money option, from the near month contracts. The closest we can get is 1835, which is being offered at $63.65 per share.

Next, what would be an appropriate target price? Well, this depends on how you read the market. If it is ranging sideways, but with a slightly bullish title, placing your target at the range boundary is a good idea. Your short call will need to be beyond this limit. Let's say our target is $1862. This makes writing the 1865 strike call an attractive option. The premium we will receive on writing the option is $44.55 per share.

So how does the math work out?

Cost of trade entry = Cost of long call - Premium from short call = 63.65-44.55 = $19.10 per share.

Maximum gain = Short call strike price - long call strike price = 1865-1835 = $30 per share.

Maximum loss = cost of trade entry.

Your trade entry equals the maximum possible loss because if the price of the stock decreases, as a worst-case scenario, your long call expires worthless and you get to keep the full premium from the short call. Your maximum profit is capped by the strike price of the short call.

Note that you need not be worried about the short call moving into the money. This is because you have the lower long call covering this position. In such a scenario, you simply exercise the lower call and use that to fulfill the higher call's exercise. The reward to risk ratio of this particular example is pretty decent if not amazing.

Remember that this strategy takes advantage of sluggish markets or non-committal markets with a slight bullish tilt to them. In such markets, a directional trader stands a very high chance of being wiped out. Viewed in this light, the advantage of this strategy is obvious.

Adjustment

It is possible to adjust the bull call spread. Again, this depends on how confident you are in your analysis, and if you believe that the market is faking traders out before going in its intended direction. The adjustment is the same as with a collar. First, you cover your short call position for a profit, since its premium would have decreased.

Next, you close out the long call for a loss since it will now be out of the money. All things being equal, the loss from the long call will be offset by the gain from closing the short call. So on a net basis, you're still in the trade. You reestablish a long call from the new market level and can decide whether you wish to keep the same target price or change it.

Notice how, unlike the collar, there is no absolute need for price to hit its target. This is because you don't have the long stock component in the trade, which will carry an unrealized loss when the market dips. You simply square out your calls and reestablish the trade. If you feel you made a bad call, you eat the maximum loss and move on.

Risk management underpins the success of this strategy. You should evaluate your ability to read the markets beforehand, and I'll give you a framework within which you can improve and analyze your skills. Once you've established your success rate, you can then work out how much you need to risk, given the reward on offer.

You can always use leverage to finance this trade, but it doesn't make it easier to enter the trade as it does with the collar. As with all things leverage, be careful and check that it squares with your risk math. With this strategy, the most obvious advantage is the lack of upfront margin needed. This makes it a much more approachable and realistic strategy for those traders who don't have large amounts of capital to risk trading.

In case you turn out to be completely wrong about the market direction, you can always adapt and turn the strategy around to account for this. The way to do this is to establish a bear call spread.

Bear Call Spread Strategy

Just like the bull call spread takes advantage of sluggish bull markets, strategy takes advantage of sluggish bear markets. The best time to put both of these strategies into action is towards the end of trends where counter-trend participation is getting higher by the minute. The market is about to move into an accumulative or distributive phase in preparation for a trend change.

This happens to be the state of the market, for the most part, so you can rest assured that both of these strategies will work wonders for you. The bear call spread also works in a sideways market with the best place of implementing it is near the top end of a sideways range. For now, let's dive in and break this down.

Execution

The bear call spread contains two legs within it:

1. An at the money or near the money short call
2. An out of the money long call

The primary instrument of profit is the short call, which takes advantage of the price decreasing while the long call caps the downside. The primary earning factor in this trade is the premium you will earn on writing the short call. Similar to the bull call, your maximum profit and loss are capped, and this gives you a great view of your trade's probabilities right off the bat.

Let's look at how this would work with the current levels of AMZN. With a market price of $1833.50, the closest at the money call in the far month is the 1835 strike call. Writing this earns us a premium of $60.15 per share (the bid price of the contract). When it comes to deciding the strike price of the long call, you want to place this beyond the closest relevant resistance level. Let's say this happens to be the 1840 level. The premium for this happens to be $58.10 per share.

So let's look at how the math will work out:

Cost of trade entry = Cost of long call - Premium earned from short call = 58.1-60.15 = -$2.05 (you earn this amount on entry)

Maximum loss = Strike price of long call - Strike price of short call = 1840- 1835 = $5 per share.

Maximum gain = cost of trade entry.

The maximum gain you can earn on this trade is from the premium of the short call. However, your long call will decrease in price simultaneously so that they will offset one another. As you can see, the reward/risk profile is skewed for this strategy, with the risk being greater than the reward.

So why should you pursue this? Well, first of all, you must understand that the success rate of this strategy depends a lot on how well you can read market conditions. If the market is strongly bearish, you're better off buying a put instead of using the bear call spread. Again, it is the fact that you can produce profits in sluggish markets that make it so attractive.

Most directional trades get wiped out in the sideways market or stay out entirely because if the market doesn't go anywhere, how can they make money. This is not the case with options, so an inverted reward to risk profile is a small price to pay. As always, your risk management is paramount, and you should work out your numbers well in advance.

Adjustment

Can you adjust this trade? Sure. Just like the bull call spread, if the market goes against you, you move the spread higher and have your initial legs offset one another by closing them out or exercising them. Or you could absorb the maximum loss and move on.

The real question here is whether you should adjust a bear spread to a bull spread and vice versa.

Chapter 8
Understanding of Options

To get an understanding of the meaning of stock options, we first must know the meaning of the two words independently.

Stock refers to the total money a company has from selling shares to individuals.

Option (finance) refers to a portion of the ownership of the company that can be sold to members of the public.

Now that we know the meaning of both stocks and options, we can easily define stock options. We can define the term in the following ways:

Stock options provide an investor with the right to sell or buy a stock at a set price and date.

The stock option can also refer to an advantage in the form of an opportunity provided by a company to any employee to buy shares in a company at an agreed-upon fixed price or a discount.

Stock options have been a topic of interest in recent years. We are having more and more people engaging in options trading. The profitability of stock options has resulted in a lot of debates. Some say it has a scam; others claim that it is not a worthy investment, while others say that they are minting millions from it. All these speculations draw us to one question, which is what stock options are? For us to accurately answer this question, we will have to go through stock options keenly. We will be required to know all about it and what it entails. This information makes it easy to make judgments with facts as opposed to using assumptions. You will get to say something that you can back up. Knowing gives you an added advantage and places you in a powerful position.

As a novice trader, acquiring information will transform your trading abilities. Having the necessary skills and knowledge will make you an expert in trading within a matter of time. This will provide you with the knowledge you need before engaging in a stock option. It is a good thing that you have taken the first step in getting this. It indicates that you are ready and will learn, and that is a major move. Asides from acquiring knowledge, it is crucial that you learn to implement it. This will mean practically doing that which you have learned. Some people acquire knowledge, but they are unable to utilize it for their benefit effectively. I hope that after you go through this, you will have the courage to trade a stock option. This mainly addresses the beginners, and it is written to make a difference in their life. I will proceed to take you through stock options and make you aware of what it entails.

Understanding Stock Options

For us to understand stock options, we consider the following:

Styles

There are two main option styles. These are European and American options styles. If you intend to engage in options trading, it is advisable to equip yourself with knowledge of the various styles. As you analyze the styles, you will identify those that work for you and those that don't. You will also find that some styles are easier to learn and handle as opposed to others. You can decide to engage in the convenient one for you and avoid engaging in the style that you have difficulties understanding.

The American style option allows one to exercise a trade any period between the time of purchase and the time a contract expires. Most traders engage in this style due to its convenience. It allows one to carry out a trade any period within which a contract is valid. The European style option is not commonly used as compared to the American style. In the European option style, a trader can only exercise their options during the expiration date. If you are not an expert in options trading, I would advise you to avoid using the European style.

Expiration date

An expiration date refers to the period in which a contract is regarded as worthless. Stocks have expiration dates—the period between when they were purchased and the expiry date, indicate the validity of an option. As a trader, you are expected to utilize the contracts to your advantage within this time frame. You can trade as much as you can and get high returns within the period of buying and the period of expiry. Learn to utilize the time provided adequately. If you are not careful, the option may expire before you get a chance to exercise it.

We have beginners who assume this factor and end up making heavy losses. You will be required to be keen while engaging in the stock market. Forgetting to investigate the expiry date may result in your stocks being regarded as worthless without getting a chance of investing in them. In some rare cases, the stocks are exercised during the expiry date. This is common in the European option. I would not encourage a beginner to engage in this type of option. It is tricky and could lead to a loss if you are not careful while carrying out the trade.

Contracts

Contracts refer to the number of shares an investor intends to purchase. One hundred shares of an underlying asset are equal to one contract—contracts aid in establishing the value of a stock. Also, contracts tend to be valuable before the expiry date. After the expiry date, a contract can be regarded as worthless. Knowing this will help you discover the best time to exercise a contract. In a case where a trader purchases ten contracts, he or she gets to 10 $ 350 calls. When the stock prices go above $ 350, at the expiry trade, the trader gets the chance to buy or sell 1000 shares of their stock at $350. This happens regardless of the stock price at that time. In an event whereby the stock is lower than $350, the option will expire worthlessly. This will result in making a complete loss as an investor. You will lose the whole amount you used to purchase options, and there is no way of getting it back. If you intend to invest in options trading, it is good to become aware of the contracts and how you can exercise them for a profitable options trading outcome.

Premium

The premium refers to the money used to purchase options. You can obtain the premium by multiplying the call price and the number of contracts by 100. The '100' is the number of shares per contract. This is more like the investment made by the trader expecting great returns. While investing, you will expect that the investment you chose to engage in will result in a profitable outcome. No one gets in business anticipating a loss. You find that one is always hopeful that the investment they have chosen to engage in will be beneficial. You will constantly look forward to getting the best out of a trade.

The above factors tell us more about stocks. In case you were stuck and did not fully understand what stocks entail, now you have a better understanding. You will come across numerous terms when you decide to engage in stocks. Don't let the terms scare you; they are mostly things you knew, but just did not know that they go by those terms. We have many people who are quite investing in stocks just because they could not understand the various terms being used. This should not be the case. You can take some time to go through the terms and understand what they entail carefully.

Options in the Stock Market

Stock options are not as hard as people make them appear. At times people try to make them seem difficult, yet it is an easy thing that can be grasped by almost everyone. As a beginner, don't be discouraged into thinking that options trading is a difficult investment. You will be surprised how easy it is, and you will wonder why you never invested in it sooner. When engaging in stock options, there are four factors the investors will have to consider. Putting these factors into consideration will have a positive impact on their trade.

The Right, But Not the Obligation

What comes to your mind when you read this statement? Well, when we talk or rights, we mean that you have the freedom to purchase a certain type of option. When we talk of obligation, we are referring to the fact that one does not have a legal authority to exercise a duty. Options don't give traders a legal authority to carry out a duty. This means that there is the freedom to trade, but it is not legally mandated.

Buying or Selling

As a trader, you are given the right to purchase or trade an option. There are two types of stock that one can choose from. We have the put option and the call option. Both differ and have their pros and cons. If you intend to trade in options, it is important that you equip yourself with adequate knowledge before trading or purchasing stocks. This information will have an impact on your expected income. The stocks you choose to buy or sell will dictate if you will earn high returns or if you will end up making a loss.

Set Price

There is a certain price that has been set to exercise the option. The price will vary depending on the option type. Some stock options tend to be valued more than other options. Several factors will influence the price of options. As you continue reading this, you will come across those factors. Knowing them will help you know when to carry out a trade and when not to carry out a trade, depending on the influence of the factors; a trade may generate a high income or end up resulting in a loss.

Expiry Date

The expiry date is when a contract will be considered useless. Stock options have an expiry date. The date is set to determine the value of an option. Any period before the expiration date, contact is regarded as being valid. This means that it can be utilized to generate income at any point before the expiry date. When it gets to the expiry date, a trader has no power to exercise the option. This is as a result of the contract being regarded as worthless. As an investor, it is good to constantly ensure that your investment is within the duration of its validity.

Chapter 9
Stock Picking

Stay Away from Penny Stocks

Beginners must stay away from penny stocks. Penny stocks can be treacherous and deceptive for new traders. I have nothing against penny stocks. Many people like to trade in penny stocks as they are cheap, and they can give great momentum. These two qualities make them a darling of most small budget traders. However, these are the very qualities due to which every trader must stay away from penny stocks. It's very hard to tell which way the stock would move, and most of the companies that penny stocks are trading in are shady.

As a beginner, your focus should remain to trade in solid stocks that have a proven track record of performance. Therefore, whosoever may push them to you, stay away from the penny stocks.

Qualities to Look for

Liquidity

Many things in the market can make the life of a trader difficult, and poor liquidity would easily top the list among them. Liquidity in the stocks means the volume or the number of shares getting traded in a day. If a stock has poor liquidity, then selling the stocks or squaring off your position in that stock would become difficult.

Stocks with poor liquidity are also easy to manipulate. Even a limited number of big traders can create fake momentum in such stocks, and you might fall into that trap.

Another big issue with low liquidity stocks is a wider spread. The difference between the bid price and the asking price is so high that most traders are not able to close their positions profitably.

In the beginning, you must only choose stocks with good liquidity.

Mind the Volatility

Volatility in the stock market isn't a bad thing. A certain level of volatility is desirable in good stocks so that you can make money trading them in a round-trip within one session. However, if the whole market is highly volatile, or a certain stock has become very unstable due to certain news, result declaration, litigation, or any other positive or negative information, you must avoid trading in such a stock. Certain strategies can help you in making money through options trade, but when a stock is highly volatile, trading can be hazardous.

Most of the action in a highly volatile stock is within a few minutes, and by the time most day traders enter into that stock, it starts to move in the opposite direction. Therefore, it is better to avoid such mayhem and let the market settle down a bit before you place your trade. As a beginner, your focus must remain on making normal trades in a normal market.

Good Correlation Stocks

Although the stock market runs on uncertainty, yet every trader likes to lean on dependable stocks. Stocks that don't perform erratically. These stocks always have a better scope for a day trader, as mapping them becomes easier. These are called correlative stocks because they have a very strong correlation with the movement of specific sectors, indices, and segments.

As a new trader, your focus should also be on such stocks that are not very unpredictable. You may not see very sudden or erratic moves in them, but that would also save you from several unpleasant surprises.

Stocks That Follow the Market Trend

We have always been taught to be different and swim against the tide. We have been told that winners who don't follow the league create one of their own. Well, when it comes to the stock market, you wouldn't want to bet on such winners to start with.

Such stocks can give you an excellent start, but there is no way in the world that you will be able to predict them. They are rocky and risky.

It is always better to find the stocks which follow the market trend. This simply means that look for those stocks that run as the market runs. If the markets are bullish, these stocks will rise with the market. If the market sentiment is bearish, they will show a negative trend. Such stocks will give you a chance to earn money both in the bull runs as well as bear runs.

Most of the stable stocks show such movements. You can rely on them, and taking a position and getting out of it on the same day in such stocks is comparatively easy. You wouldn't want to get into a stock that's rising when the market is falling, and as soon as you put your money in it, the movement stops or takes an opposite turn. Such stocks are very dangerous, and there are plenty of them out there. Sticking with the big and reliable ones can help you in preventing such issues.

Good Fundamentals

Although many experts would say that fundamental analysis doesn't play an important role in day trading, don't get sold on that completely. When the market's mood is bad, only these kinds of stocks survive. The reason is simple when the tide is over, and the traders like to go with safer options.

Stocks with good fundamentals will always be more reliable and dependable. The market trusts them. Even small news about their profits and expansion can bring big moves in such stocks. You may not find such movement in smaller stocks even with big news because most traders don't trust them.

Initially, only trade with stocks that have good fundamentals. They will help you understand the way the market functions, and once you feel you are ready, you can also start trying others.

Ownership Pattern

This is another critical point that usually gets ignored. Stocks are held by retail investors and traders like me and you and also by institutional investors. Both types of investors have different buying and selling patterns.

A retail investor can dump all the held shares with the drop of a hat. As soon as a piece of bad news comes, the retail investors are the first to exit. However, institutional investors can't do that. They maintain very large portfolios, and their decision-makers need to have approval at several levels. This means a stock in which institutional investors also have a good stake will be more reliable as they'll have a lot of volatility even after a major news event. The slow response of the institutional investors also ensures that there is no panic or crisis like situation suddenly because many stocks are locked with them.

Looking at the ownership pattern of stocks can help you in understanding the risk involved with the stock. If a stock is primarily held by retail investors, there can be no definite knowledge about the people who hold them. It can be just a group of certain individuals who can start creating momentum in the stock artificially. They can also dump all the shares all of a sudden. Institutional investors simply can't do that.

As a new trader, trade in the stocks in which institutional investors like mutual funds, hedge funds, etc., have a good stake. Such trading will keep your risk contained.

Understandable Chart Patterns

Once you start reading the technical charts, you'll find that some stocks make real sense on the charts. They follow patterns. Their movements are somewhat predictable. They aren't very jumpy or choppy. While doing this, you'll also come across stocks that don't follow any pattern. They don't correlate to the indices or segments. They are vagabonds. Such stocks are risky for day trading.

Every day, traders have to impress their minds that you don't want to be stuck with one stock forever. It doesn't matter how good or bad it is. You want to get in and out of that action fast. Stocks that don't follow an understandable pattern can get trapped. Once you buy them, understanding or predicting their movement will be difficult and you will not find a way out.

The best way out is to look for stocks that have an understandable chart pattern. The stocks that are moving in a definite pattern are always a better bet.

Sensibility to the New Flow

Last but not least, sensibility to the news flow can be a big asset for an intraday stock. Some stocks react great to news events and give a good trading opportunity. However, some stocks would remain dormant, no matter what kind of news pours in. They are thick-skinned and become unpredictable as far as trading is concerned. You should avoid such stocks.

Look for stocks that show a great movement and sensibility to news events and give you trading opportunities.

High Volume

No matter how good the stock looks, if it doesn't have the volume, it is not fit for intraday trading. Don't fall for such stocks as the risk of getting caught in them will be very high. This is the first and foremost quality you must look for while picking your stock of the day for trading.

Testing Support and Resistance Levels

Look for stocks that are testing their support or resistance levels. These stocks can give a breakout, and you will have an excellent opportunity to earn from such stocks. You must sift out their levels carefully and study their historical patterns. If they have done that even in the past, it can be a great sign.

Near 52 Weeks Low or High

Stocks that are near their 52 weeks low or high can also give you a good opportunity to trade. Such traders can make a breakout and set new targets, and hence if you can correlate that with the fundamentals of these stocks, you can build an opportunity to trade.

Gainers or Losers of the Week

These stocks will be in the news and, therefore, trading in these stocks can be a good idea. However, you'll have to remain cautious as a stock that has been continuously gaining for some time can't continue to do so. You'll have to study whether the stock is already overbought or underbought as consolidation and profit booking can take place. While you look at these factors, you would also like to consider the fact whether the stock is undervalued or overvalued as that would also have an impact on its escalation and fall.

Stocks with High Market Anticipation

These stocks are the newsmakers, and they would be riding a wave. Their movements are hard to predict as more than the fundamentals and technical aspects; they are running on the market sentiments. However, these stocks can also give you short trading opportunities. However, you must keep in mind that quick in and out of such stocks is always the best. Don't try to hold your position for too long as they can take a serious turn on any side, and you can get locked in them.

From Your Niche

Finally, pick the stocks from your niche. As a new trader, it always feels better to have an open field. However, as you grow in the stock market, you'll realize that having a niche is always a better and more reliable option. Look for all these qualities in the stocks from your field, and you will have very few things to worry about.

Chapter 10
How Prices are Determined

Options prices are determined in part by the price of the underlying stock. But options prices are also influenced by the time left to expiration and some other factors. We are going to go over all the different ways that the price of a given option can change and what will be behind the changes. It's important to have a firm grasp of these concepts so that you don't go into options as a naïve beginning trader.

The Market Price of Shares

The most significant factor that impacts the price of an option is the price of the investment known as the stock that is behind the option. However, it's not a 1-1 relationship. The amount of influence from the underlying stock is going to change with time. Furthermore, it depends on whether the option is in the money, at the money, or out of the money. The fraction of the options price due to the price of the underlying stock is called the intrinsic option's value.

If an option can be the same as the market pricing or not be comparatively favored, it has zero intrinsic value. An option would have to be priced in the money to have any intrinsic value.

- For a call option, if the market price is lower than the strike price or the same, the option will have no pricing at all from the intrinsic value. If the share price is higher than the price used to trade shares via the option, the option will have intrinsic value.
- For a put option, if the share price is at or above the strike price, the option will have zero intrinsic value. If the share price is below the strike price, then the option will have some value from the stock. This is called intrinsic value.

Notwithstanding, to confuse matters, even when an option is at or out of the money, the As time goes on, though the underlying stock price has certain influence that can change the value of the option. The amount of influence that the item's market price known as the stock has on the price of the option is given by a quantity called delta. You can read the value for delta by looking at the data for any option you are interested in trading. It is given as a decimal value ranging from 0 to 1 for call options, and it's given as a negative value for put options.

It's given as a negative value for put options because this reflects the fact that if the stock price is found to increase, the price of a put option will be reduced. In contrast, if the stock price declines, the value of the put option will increase. It's an inverse relationship, and thus, the delta is negative for put options.

To understand how this will play out, let's look at a specific example. Suppose that we have a $100 option. That is, the strike price is set to $100. If the price of the underlying stock is $105, the delta for the call option is 0.77.

That means that if the dollar value of the stock increases by $1, the value of the option will rise by approximately 77 cents. This is a per-share price change. So, for the option that you are trading, there are 100 underlying shares. So, a 77 cent price rise would increase the value of the option by $77.

For a put option with the same strike price, the option would be out of the money, because the share price is higher than the strike price. In this case, for the put option, the delta is given as -0.23. That means that the put option would lose approximately $23 if the share price went up by $1. On the other hand, if the share price dropped by $1, the put option would gain $23.

The intrinsic value of the call option described in this theoretical exercise would be $5 per share. The total cost of the option would be $6.06 per share, reflecting the fact that the call option has $1.06 in extrinsic value. In contrast, the put option has zero intrinsic value. It has almost the same extrinsic value, however, at $1.03.

I have used a 45–day time frame before expiration for this exercise. Options prices are governed by mathematical formulas, so it's possible to make estimates of what the option price is going to be ahead of time. Some many calculators and spreadsheets are available free online for this purpose.

Now, let's say that instead, the share price was $95, so that the call option was out of the money, and the put option was in the money. In this case, the call option has zero intrinsic value, and it has a $0.94 extrinsic value so that the option would be worth $94. Delta has switched, but not exactly. In this case, for the call option, the delta is 0.25. If the share price rose to $96, with everything else unchanged, the price of the call option would rise to $1.21 per share. This illustrates that you can still earn profits from cheaper out of the money options.

If the share price stayed at $95, the put option would have a delta of -0.75. Notice that if we take the absolute value and add the delta for the call and the put option, they sum up to 1.0.

So, if you see an option of the call type that has a strike that is lower than the market price, with a delta given by say 0.8, which means the put option with the same strike price and expiration date will have a delta of -0.20.

Delta does more than give you the prediction of changes in the underlying share price and price movements of the option. It also gives you a (rough) estimate of the probability to expire in the money for the contract known as an option.

If you sell to open, you don't want the option to expire in the money. Therefore, you are probably going to sell options that have a small delta. On the other hand, if you buy to open, you want the option to go in the money, if it isn't already. So, you would buy an option with a higher delta.

If we say that a given call option has a delta of 0.66, this indicates if we see changes such that the underlying stock price rises by $1, the price of the option on a per-share basis will rise by $0.66. But it also tells us that there is a 66% chance that this option will expire in a positive condition, that is, it will be in the money.

Something else you need to know is that delta is dynamic. If the price of a share increases on the market, the delta rises for the call option and gets smaller in magnitude for the put option. A declining share price will have the opposite effect.

The amount that delta will change is given by another "Greek"—gamma. Most beginning traders probably aren't going to be too worried about gamma; what we've described so far is all you need to know to enter into effective options trades. But gamma will tell you the variation in the value of the delta with a change in stock price. So, if gamma is 0.03, this means that a $1 rise in the stock price will increase delta by 0.03 for a call option. The inverse relationship holds for a put option.

If an option is at the money, the delta is going to be about 0.50 for a call option and -0.50 for a put option. That makes sense, if the strike price is equal to the share price on the market, there is a 50% probability that the market price will move below the strike price, and there is a 50% probability that the market cost of shares will move above the strike price.

Implied Volatility

One of the most important characteristics of options after considering delta and time decay is the amount a stock price varies with time. Volatility will give you an idea of how the price swings of stock will are. If you look at a stock chart, I am sure that you are used to seeing the price go up and down a lot, giving a largely jagged curve. The more that it fluctuates, and the bigger the fluctuations in price, the higher the volatility. Of course, everything is relative, and so you can't say that any stock has an "absolute" level of volatility. What is done is the volatility for the entire market is calculated, and then the volatility of a stock is compared to the volatility of the market as a whole. When looking at the stocks themselves, this is given by a quantity called beta.

If the stock generally moves with the stock market at large, beta is positive. If beta is 1.0, that means that it has the same volatility as the entire market. That is a stock with average volatility.

If beta is less than 1.0, then the stock doesn't have much volatility. The amount below 1.0 tells you how much less volatile the stock is in comparison to the market as a whole. So, if the beta is given as 0.7, this means that the stock is 30% less volatile than the market average.

If beta is greater than 1.0, then the stock is more volatile than the average. If you see a stock with a beta of 1.42, which means the stock is 42% more volatile than the average for the market.

If beta is negative, that means the stock, on average, moves against the market. When the market goes up, it goes down and vice versa. Most stocks don't have a negative beta, but they are not hard to find either.

Volatility is a dynamic quantity, so when you look it up, you are looking at a snapshot of the volatility at that given moment. Of course, under most circumstances, it's not likely to change very much over short periods like a few weeks or a month. There are exceptions to this, including earnings season.

Implied volatility is a quantity that is given for options. Implied volatility is a measure of the coming volatility that the stock price is expected to see over the lifetime of the option (that is until the expiration date).

One of the things that make options valuable is the probability that the price of the stock will move in a direction that is favorable to the strike price. When an option goes in the money, or deeper in the money (that is the share price moves even higher relative to the strike price of a call, or lower relative to the strike price of a put), the value of the option can increase by a large margin.

If a stock is more volatile, there is more chance of this happening, since the price is going to be going through larger price swings. Therefore, the higher the implied volatility, the higher the price of the option.

Chapter 11
Volatility in the Markets

While the stock market has long term trends that investors rely on fairly well as the years and decades go by, over the short term, the stock market is highly volatile. By that, we mean that prices are fluctuating up and down and doing so over short periods. Volatility is something that long-term investors ignore. It's why you will hear people that promote conservative investment strategies suggesting that buyers use dollar-cost averaging. What this does is it averages out the volatility in the market. That way you don't risk making the mistake of buying stocks when the price is a bit higher than it should be, because you'll average that out by buying shares when it's a bit lower than it should be.

In a sense, over the short term, the stock market can be considered as a chaotic system. So from one day to the next, unless there is something specific on offer, like Apple introducing a new gadget that investors are going to think will be a significant hit, you can't be sure what the stock price is going to be tomorrow or the day after that. An increase in one day doesn't mean more increases are coming; it might be followed by a major dip the following day.

For example, at the time of writing, checking Apple's stock price, on a Friday, it bottomed out at $196. Over the following days, it went up and down several times, and on the most recent close, it was $203. The movements over a short-term period appear random, and to a certain extent, they are. It's only over the long term that we see the actual direction that Apple is heading.

Certainly, Apple is at the end of a ten-year run that began with the introduction of the iPhone and iPad. It's a reasonable bet that while it's a solid long-term investment, the stock probably isn't going to be moving enough to make good profits over the short term from trades on call options (not to mention the per-share price is relatively high).

The truth is that volatility is a friend of the trader who buys call options. But it's a friend you have to be wary of because you can benefit from volatility while also getting in big trouble from it.

The reason stocks with more volatility are the friend of the options trader that the options trader, in part, is playing a probability game. In other words, you're looking for stocks that have a chance of beating the strike price you need to make profits. A volatile stock that has large movements has a greater probability of not only passing your strike price but doing so in such a fashion that it far exceeds your strike price enabling you to make a large profit.

Of course, the alternative problem exists—that the stock price will suddenly drop. That is why care needs to be a part of your trader's toolkit. A stock with a high level of volatility is just as likely to suddenly drop in price as it is to skip right past your strike price.

Moreover, while you're a beginner and might get caught with your pants down, volatile stocks are going to attract experienced options traders. That means that the stock will be in high demand when it comes to options contracts. What happens when there is a high demand for something? The price shoots up. In the case of call options, that means the stock will come with a higher premium. You will need to take the higher premium into account when exercising your options at the right time and making sure the price is high enough above your strike price that you don't end up losing money.

Traders take some time to examine the volatility of a given stock over the recent past, but they also look into what's known as implied volatility. This is a kind of weather forecast for stocks. It's an estimate of the future price movements of a stock, and it has a considerable influence on the pricing of options. Implied volatility is denoted by the Greek symbol σ, implied volatility increases in bear markets, and it decreases when investors are bullish. Implied volatility is a tool that can provide insight into the option's future value.

For options traders, more volatility is a good thing. A stock that doesn't have much volatility will be a stable stock whose price isn't going to change very much over the lifetime of a contract. So, while you may want to sell a covered call for a stock with low volatility, you're probably not going to want to buy one if you're buying call options because that means there will be a lower probability that the stock will change enough to exceed the strike price so you can earn a profit on a trade. Also, remember that highly volatile stocks will attract much interest from options traders and command higher premiums. You will have to do some balancing in picking stocks that are of interest.

Being able to pick stocks that will have the right amount of volatility so that you can be sure of getting one that will earn profits on short term trades is something you're only going to get from experience. You should spend some time practicing before actually investing large amounts of money. That is, pick stocks you are interested in and make your bets, but don't make the trades. Then follow them throughout the contract and see what happens. In the meantime, you can purchase safer call options, and so using this two-pronged approach gain experience that will lead to more surefire success down the road.

One thing that volatility means for everyone is that predicting the future is an impossible exercise. You're going to have some misses, no matter how much knowledge and experience you gain. The only thing to aim for is to beat the market more often than you lose. The biggest mistake you can make is putting your life savings into a single stock that you think is a sure thing and then losing it all.

Options to pursue if your options aren't working

At this point, you may think that if the underlying stock for your option doesn't go anywhere or it tanks that you have no choice but to wait out the expiration date and count the money you spend on your premiums as a loss.

That isn't the case. The truth is you can sell a call option you have purchased to other traders in the event it is not working for you. Certainly, you're not going to make a profit-taking this approach in the vast majority of cases. But it will give you a chance to recoup some of your losses. If you have invested in a large number of call options for a specific stock and it's causing you problems, you need to recoup at least some of your losses may be more acute. In fact, the right course of action in these cases is rarely certain, especially if the expiration date for the contract is relatively far off in the future, which could mean that the stock has many chances to turn around and beat your strike price. Remember, in all bad scenarios, actually buying the shares of stock is an option—you're not required to do it. In all cases, the biggest loss you're facing is losing the entire premium. You'll also want to keep the following rule of thumb in mind at all times—the more time value an option has, the higher the price you can sell the option for. If there isn't much time value left, then you're probably going to have to sell the option at a discount. If there is a lot of time value, you may be able to recoup most of your losses on the premium.

Let's look at some specific scenarios:

- The stock is languishing. If the stock is losing time value (that is getting closer to the expiration date) and doesn't seem to be going anywhere, you can consider selling the call option to recoup some of your losses related to the premium. The more time value, the less likely it is that selling the option is a good idea. Of course, the less time value, the harder it's going to be to sell your option. Or put another way, to sell it you're going to have to take a lower price.
- Suppose the stock isn't stagnant, but it's tanking. If there is a lot of time value left and there is some reason to believe that the company is going to make moves before the expiration date of your contract that will improve the fortunes of the stock when you can still profit from it, then you may want to ride out the downturn. This is a risky judgment call, and it's going to be impossible to know for sure what the right answer is, but you can make an educated guess. Besides, if the stock is tanking and there is no good news about the company on the horizon, you are pretty much facing the certainty that you're not going to be able to exercise your options to buy the shares. In that case, you should

probably look at selling the option contract to someone more willing to take the risk. At least you can get some of the money back that you paid for the premium.

Now let's briefly consider the positive scenario. Buying options and then trading the stocks can feel like a roller coaster ride, and that rush is what attracts a lot of people to options trading besides the possibilities of making short term profits. Let's consider an example where the stock keeps rising in price? How long do you wait before selling?

There are two risks here. The first risk is that you're too anxious to sell, and so do it at the first opportunity. That isn't a huge downside; you're going to make some profits in that case. On the other hand, it's going to be disconcerting when you sit back and watch the stock continuing to rise. That said, this is better than some of the alternatives.

One of the alternatives is waiting too long to buy and sell the shares. You might wait and see the stock apparently reaching a peak and then get a little greedy, hoping that it's going to keep increasing so you can make even more profits. But then you keep waiting, and suddenly the stock starts dropping. Maybe you wait a little more, hoping it's going to start rebounding and going up again, but it doesn't, and you're forced to buy and sell at a lower price than you could have gotten. Maybe it's even dropping enough so that you lose your opportunity altogether. A really volatile stock might suddenly crash, leaving you with a lost opportunity.

Chapter 12
Candlesticks

When you are engaging in options trading, you don't have to become an expert on stock charts how a day trader of stocks needs to be. However, it is a good idea to get some familiarity with the trading tools so that you can make reasonably sound estimates of where a stock price is moving, which will translate into more winning trades for the options trader.

Also, as an options trader, as we mentioned above, you don't necessarily need to dive deeply into this subject, and you also don't need to be sitting at your computer staring at graphs and charts all day long. Most options traders are simply going to go with the flow of where stock prices are moving, rather than trying to get into the weeds of every last detail.

One reason for this is that changes in share prices are magnified through options. A change of a few tens of cents or dollars is big for the options trader but less significant for a stock trader. Second, a day trader is looking to make their profits over a few hours, so they have to sit there staring at their computer screens waiting for the exact moment to enter and exit a trade, and they can't risk holding the kinds of positions they take overnight. As an options trader, despite the reputation for risk and complexity that comes with options, you will not be trading with the same constraints.

So, knowing something about the technical analysis can help you be a more successful options trader. It will help you spot changing trends in prices and recognize the right times to enter and exit trades. Of course, this is more art than science, and there is no exact right time to do anything in the stock market; you are just playing your odds. That said, having the knowledge to recognize likely shifts in pricing trends can help you make better trades.

The first main tool used by traders to understand and predict changes in pricing trends is the candlestick chart. We are going to look at candlestick chart basics and give you enough information so that you can read candlestick charts and understand them fairly well, and so that you can recognize likely changes in pricing trends. But don't get fooled into magical thinking by candlestick charts; they are not scientific or foolproof. Use them as a guide, not as something absolute that you must follow.

We are also going to look at some of the main tools used in so-called technical analysis. These are mathematical tools built to help traders get more information out of pricing trends in the markets. The technical analysis tools should be viewed as aids as well, and far too many people get fooled into thinking they are infallible, rather than recognizing them for what they are, which is to assist, not absolute, and "true" answers.

The best approach to be taken is to combine a few tools. What most traders do is look for an indication in one of their main ways to track stock market price changes, and then they will use another tool to either confirm or deny what they saw in the first place. Only when two or three different tools or indicators confirm the same pricing trend, do they take action in the markets.

As an options trader, you will be applying these tools to the pricing of the underlying stock and not to the option itself. So, if you are interested in trading options on Facebook, you are going to be studying the trading behavior of the Facebook stock, and not the options. When you see favorable changes in the Facebook stock, then you will go ahead and make moves with your options trades.

Candlestick Charts

A candlestick chart is a method of plotting financial data that tells you how prices moved over a given trading session. Rather than having a continuous curve, the price data is broken down into different time frames. There is not a specific time frame that is used; you can create candlestick charts using various time frames. For example, you can have a chart break up a trading day into fifteen-minute increments. Then, the candlesticks will be created for each fifteen-minute increment throughout each trading day, and it will give you pricing information for each of those increments. You can break prices down by the minute, by five-minutes, by an hour, by four hours, and so on.

When you are looking for the right time to enter and exit trades once you have decided that it is about the right time to do so, you might use one minute or five-minute intervals. This will also depend on how active trading is. If a stock is moving by a lot, over a few minutes, options prices can change drastically. So if you have a call option on Netflix in your portfolio, and you are looking to sell it, if prices of the underlying stock are moving by a significant amount, you are going to want to keep close tabs on short-term pricing changes. So you might use a five-minute candlestick chart for this purpose.

Candlestick charts are quite general in their application. They can be used for any financial asset that is traded in real-time. They were originally developed in Japan, to track changes in the price of rice. So, they can be used for commodities, stocks, bonds, Forex, or any other asset. Naturally, they are used for stocks.

Looking at the basic unit of a candlestick chart, which is a trading session of the selected time length, the first thing to look at is the color. At a glance, the color of a candlestick tells you the direction of price movement in that trading session. There are different color schemes used on charts, but it is typical to use a white background for stocks. If the stock price went up over the period, then the color will be green. If the price of the stock dropped over the period, the color is going to be red.

The candlestick is going to have a "body" and "wicks" coming out of it (in some treatments, the wicks are referred to as "shadows"). The length of the body tells you how much the price moved throughout the entire trading session. This information is to be taken in conjunction with the color of the candlestick.

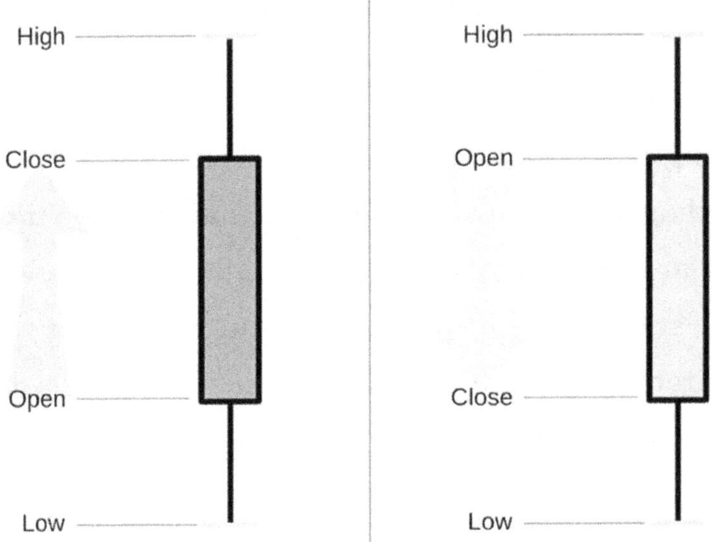

If the candlestick is green, then the candlestick's bottom is the opening price for the trading session (low in value), and the top of the candlestick is the closing price of the trading session (high in value—so the price rose over the trading session).

If the candlestick is red, the relationships are reversed. In this case, the top of the candlestick is the opening price for the trading session. Then, the bottom of the candlestick is going to be the lower closing price of the trading session, reflecting that the stock lost value over the period.

Red and green candlesticks are also referred to by the mood they represent. If a candlestick is red, the mood is "bearish" since people are getting out of the stock, and so it can be referred to as a bearish candlestick. Conversely, if the mood is bullish, prices are rising, and people are trying to buy into the stock, and so, a green candlestick is bullish.

The wicks on a candlestick have the same meaning regardless of color. The top wick is the high price attained during the trading session, and the bottom wick is the low price seen during the trading session.

Candlesticks can help you determine the momentum of trading. If the wicks are long, but the body is short, that helps you determine that there was a large push of the price in one direction or another. Still, there was not enough momentum to sustain it, and prices ended up moving back to where they were when the trading session opened, or at least relatively close by.

Remember that pricing is related to supply and demand. So, if prices are rising, there is more demand for the stock. If prices are dropping, people are dumping the stock (increasing the supply), and demand is decreasing.

Candlesticks and Trends

The main way that candlesticks are used is to spot changes in price trends. So, you want to be paying close attention to candlesticks when the stock price has been dropping or rising for some time, and you are looking for signals that a reversal in the price trend is about to occur.

A sudden shift from selling to buying or vice versa is one way that a trend reversal can be noted. This is indicated by an "enveloping" candlestick. That is, you have a candlestick of one type that is larger than the preceding candlestick of the opposite type, then you have a situation where a trend reversal is indicated.

Take, for example, the situation where stock prices have been declining. You are going to see some fluctuation, but there is going to be largely a trend of red candlesticks reflecting the trend of dropping prices. When you see a small red candlestick followed by a bullish candlestick that has a body that is large enough to completely engulf the body of the bearish or red candlestick that preceded it, this is usually a sign that the sell-off is over, and prices are going to start rising. So, this is an indication that you want to buy a call option (or sell a put option) on the stock at this point. When prices are rising, you look for a bearish candlestick to engulf a bullish candlestick to indicate that peak price has been reached, and people are going to start selling off the stock.

Another indicator of a change in trend is when you have seen a trend in one direction, and then you see three candlesticks in a row of the opposite type. Let's consider a downward trend in prices first. If prices have been dropping, then you see three green or bullish candlesticks in a row, particularly when each succeeding candlestick has a higher closing price, this is a solid indication that prices are going to reverse, and the stock is entering an upward price trend. On the other hand, if you are at the top of an uptrend, and you see three bearish candlesticks in a row, each with lower closing prices than the preceding candlestick, that tells you that the stock price is probably going to start dropping.

Of course, these are rules of thumb; they are not exact or guaranteed to lead to the results described. They often or usually do, but you should confirm these signals using another tool before making major trading decisions.

Chapter 13
Market Trends

A market is a chaotic place, with several traders vying for dominance over one another. There is a countless number of strategies and time frames in play, and at any point, it is close to impossible to determine who will emerge with the upper hand. In such an environment, how is it then possible to make any money? After all, if everything is unpredictable, how can you get your picks, right?

Well, this is where thinking in terms of probabilities comes into play. While you cannot get every single bet right, as long as you get enough right and make enough money on those to offset your losses, you will make money in the long run.

It's not about getting one or two right. It's about executing the strategy with the best odds of winning over and over again and ensuring that your math works out with regards to the relationship between your win rate and average win.

So, it comes down to finding patterns that repeat themselves over time in the markets. What causes these patterns? Well, the other traders, of course! To put it more accurately, the orders that the other traders place in the market create patterns that repeat themselves over time.

The first step in understanding these patterns is understanding what trends and ranges are. Identifying them and learning how to spot them when they transition to each other will give you a huge advantage, not only with options trading but also with directional trading.

Trends

In theory, spotting a trend is simple enough. Look left to right, and if the price is headed up or down, it's a trend. Well, sometimes it is that simple. However, for the majority of the time, you have both with and counter-trend forces operating in the market. It is possible to have long counter-trend reactions within a larger trend, and sometimes, depending on the time frame you're in, these counter-trend reactions take up the majority of your screen space.

Trend vs. Range

This is a chart of the UK100 CFD, which mimics the FTSE 100, on the four-hour time frame. Three-quarters of the chart is a downtrend, and the last quarter is a wild uptrend. Using the looking left to the right guideline, we'd conclude that this instrument is in a range. But, is that true?

Just looking at that chart, you can see that short-term momentum is bullish. So, if you were considering taking a trade on this, would you implement a range strategy or a trending one? This is exactly the sort of thing that catches traders up.

The key to deciphering trends is to watch for two things: counter-trend participation quality and turning points. Let's tackle counter-trend participation first.

Counter-Trend Participation

When a new trend begins, the market experiences an extremely imbalanced order flow, which is tilted towards one side. There's not much counter-trend participation against this seeming tidal wave of trend orders. Price marches on without any opposition and experiences only a few hiccups.

As time goes on, though, the trend forces run out of steam and have to take breaks to gather themselves. This is where counter-trend traders start testing the trend and trying to see how far back into the trend they can go. While it is unrealistic to expect a full reversal at this point, the quality of the correction or pushback tells us a lot about the strength distribution between the with and counter-trend forces.

Eventually, the counter-trend players manage to push so far back against the trend of stalemate results in the market. The with and counter-trend forces are equally balanced, and thus, the trend comes to an end. After all, you need an imbalance for the market to tip one way or another, and balanced order flow will only result in a sideways market.

While all this is going on behind the scenes, the price chart is what records the push and pull between these two forces. Using the price chart, we can not only anticipate when a trend is coming to an end but also how long it could potentially take before it does. This second factor, which helps us estimate the time it could take, is invaluable from an options perspective, especially if you're using a horizontal spread strategy.

In all cases, the greater the number of them, the greater the counter-trend participation in the market. The closer a trend is to end, the greater the counter-trend participation. Thus, the minute you begin to see price move into a large, sideways move with an equal number of buyers and sellers in it, you can be sure that some form of redistribution is going on.

Mind you, and the trend might continue or reverse. Either way, it doesn't matter. What matters is that you know the trend is weak and that now is probably not the time to be banking on-trend strategies.

Starting from the left, we can see that there is close to no counter-trend bars, bearish in this case, and the bulls make easy progress. Note the angle with which the bulls proceed upwards.

Then comes the first major correction, and the counter-trend players push back against the last third of the bull move. Notice how strong the bearish bars are and note their character compared to the bullish bars.

The bulls recover and push the price higher at the original angle and without any bearish presence, which seems odd. This is soon explained as the bears' slam price back down, and for a while, it looks as if they've managed to form a V top reversal in the trend, which is an extremely rare occurrence.

The price action that follows is a more accurate reflection of the market's power, with both bulls and bears sharing chunks of the order flow, with overall order flow in the bull's favor but only just. Price here is certainly in an uptrend, but looking at the extent of the bearish pushbacks, perhaps we should be on our guard for a bearish reversal. After all, the order flow is looking pretty sideways at this point.

So how would we approach an options strategy with the chart in the state it is in at the extreme, right? Well, for one, any strategy that requires an option beyond the near month is out of the question, given the probability of it turning. Secondly, looking at the order flow, it does seem to be following a channel, doesn't it?

While the channel isn't very clean if you were aggressive enough, you could consider deploying a collar with the strike prices above and below this channel to take advantage of the price movement. You could also employ some moderately bullish strategies as price approaches the bottom of this channel, and figuring out the extent of the bull move is easier thanks to you being able to reference the top of the channel.

As the price moves in this channel, it's all well and good. Eventually, though, we know that the trend has to flip. How do we know when this happens?

Turning Points

As bulls and bears struggle over who can control the order flow, the price swings up and down. You will notice that every time price comes back into the 6427-6349 zone, the bulls seem to step in masse and repulse the bears.

This tells us that the bulls are willing to defend this level in large numbers and strongly. Given the number of times the bears have tested this level, we can safely assume that above this level, bullish strength is a bit weak. However, at this level, it is as if the bulls have retreated and are treating this as a sort of last resort, for the trend to be maintained. You can see where I'm going with this.

If this level were to be breached by the bears, it is a good bet that a large number of bulls will be taken out. In martial terms, the largest army of bulls has been marshaled at this level. If this force is defeated, it is unlikely that there's going to be too much resistance to the bears below this level.

This zone, in short, is a turning point. If price breaches this zone decisively, we can safely assume that the bears have moved in and control the majority of the order flow.

Turning Point Breached

The decisive inflection point zone is marked by the two horizontal lines, the price touches this level two more times and is rejected by the bulls. Notice how the last bounce before the level breaks produces an extremely weak bullish bounce, and the price just gives in through this. Now, watch the force with which the bears advance.

The FTSE was in a longer uptrend on the weekly chart, so the bulls aren't completely done yet. However, as far as the daily timeframe is concerned, notice how price retests that same level, but this time around, it acts as resistance instead of support.

For now, we can conclude that as long as the price remains below the turning point, we are bearishly biased. You can see this by looking at the angle with which bulls push back as well as the lack of strong bearish participation on the push upwards.

This doesn't mean we go ahead and pencil in a bull move and start implementing strategies that take advantage of the upcoming bullish move. Remember, nothing is for certain in the markets. Don't change your bias or strategy until the turning point decisively breaks.

Some key things to note here are that a turning point is always a major S/R level. It is usually a swing point where a large number of trend forces gather to support the trend. This will not always be the case, so don't make the mistake of hanging on to older turning points.

The current order flow and price action are what matters the most, so pay attention to that above all else. Also, note how the candles that test this level all have wicks on top of them.

This indicates that the bears are quite strong here and that any subsequent attack will be handled the same way until the level breaks. Do we know when the level will break? Well, we can't say with any accuracy. However, we can estimate the probability of it breaking.

The latest upswing has seen very little bearish pushback, comparatively speaking, and the push into the level is strong. Instinct would say that there's one more rejection left here. However, who knows? Until the level breaks, we stay bearish. When the level breaks, we switch to the bullish side.

Putting it all Together

So now we're ready to put all of this together into one coherent package. Your analysis should always begin with determining the current state of the market. Ranges are pretty straightforward to spot, and they occur either within big pullbacks in trends or at the end of trends.

Trends vary in strength, depending on the amount of counter-trend participation they have. The way to determine counter-trend participation levels is to simply look at the price bars and compare the counter-trend ones to the trendy ones. The angle with which the trend progresses is a great gauge as well, for its strength, with steeper angles being stronger.

Chapter 14
Options Strategies

Strangles and Straddles

This type of strategy is used when the stock is expected to make a large pricing move, but you don't know the direction that the stock will move. It involves buying a call and put option together in a single trade. A strangle involves setting an abounding range for the expected stock movement, using different strike prices for the put and call option. A lower strike price is used for the put option, while a higher strike price is used for the call option. The breakeven price is the breakeven price for the call option if the stock rises, or the breakeven price for the put option if the stock drops.

As an example, if the share price of the stock were $100 but it was expected to make a big move, you could set up a strangle with a $105 call option and a $95 put option. If the stock prices fail to move either above the call option strike price or below the put option strike price, you will lose money on the trade. The maximum possible loss is the cost of buying the options.

The strategy is considered neutral because it will make profits if the stock moves up (strongly) or down (strongly). You will invest in this type of strategy when you expect a large move in the stock, so, for example, many traders buy strangles before an earnings call. Most earnings call result in big price movements of the stock, but before the call, you are not sure which direction it will move.

The strike prices selected for the call and put option will be out of the money. Both options will have the same expiration date.

The maximum profit on the upside is theoretically unlimited, but it will depend on how far the stock price moves above the strike of the call option. If that happens, the put option expires worthless, and your profit selling the call option less the cost of buying the put option is your net profit. If the stock price drops, the maximum profit will occur in the extremely unlikely case that it dropped to zero, less the cost of the call option. If the stock price moves to any level below the breakeven price of the put option, you can earn a profit.

A straddle is used for the same purpose, but in this case, we set the strike prices of the call and the put option to the same value, and both options will have the same expiration date. With a straddle, you want the stock price to move off the strike price used in either direction.

Iron Condor

An iron condor is one of the most popular options strategies. An iron condor is an options strategy created with four options consisting of two puts (one long and one short) and two calls (one long and one short), and four strike prices, all with the same expiration date. The goal is to profit from low volatility in the underlying asset. This is an income-producing strategy, and it is sold for a net credit (keep this in mind, there is a lot of misinformation about iron condors). An iron condor is sold using a call credit spread and a put credit spread, all in the same trade. The two options with inner strike prices will be sold. So, for example, suppose that a stock is trading at $200 a share. You could sell a call option with a strike price of $205 and buy a call option with a strike price of $210. Simultaneously, you would sell a put option with a $195 strike price and buy a put option with a $190 strike price.

As long as the stock price stays in between the inner strike prices—ranging between $195 and $205 in our example—you will make a profit. So, an iron condor is used when you expect the stock price is not going to change very much over the lifetime of the options. All options used in an iron condor have the same expiration date.

To pick your strike prices, determine where support and resistance are. You want to set the strike price of the put option you sell a little bit above the support price and set the strike price of the call option you sell a little bit below the resistance price. Then set the outer strike prices slightly above the resistance price level for the purchased call option and below the support price level for the purchased put option.

Many traders make a full-time living strictly selling iron condors. The chart has the following form:

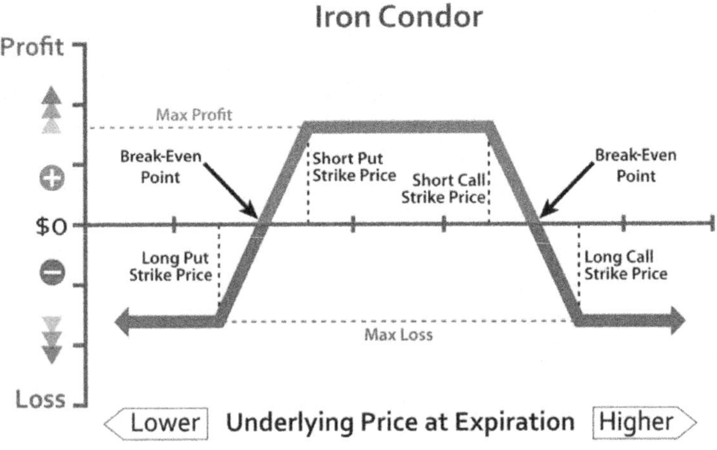

You will receive a net credit for the call credit spread, and a net credit for the put credit spread. The total credit received is your maximum profit. If the stock remains in between the inner strike prices, this is when you will earn profits.

One advantage of the iron condor is that losses are also capped. The maximum loss, should the stock move to the upside, is the difference in strike prices of the two call options. If the stock moves lower, the maximum loss is the difference between the strike prices of the put options. Using our example here would be a $5 loss (per share – total $500) if the stock moved below $190, or above $210.

Iron Butterfly

An iron butterfly is a less popular way to set this up since it creates a narrow range for the stock. An iron butterfly is an options trade that uses four different contracts as part of a strategy to benefit from stocks or futures prices that move within a defined range. The trade is also constructed to benefit from a decline in implied volatility. In the case of an iron butterfly, you set your inner strike prices the same. For example, using a stock trading at $200, we could sell a call option and a put option with a

$200 strike price, and then buy a call option with a $205 strike price, and buy a put option with a $195 strike price. Losses will be incurred if the stock price goes above the $205 strike of the upper call or below the $195 strike of the put.

Equity Collar

This is a strategy used to hedge risk. It is used on a long stock position that you have, and this is used by large traders. So, to use this strategy, you would have a large number of shares of some stock. If you are uncertain about the direction of the stock that you own, you could set up an equity collar to hedge your risk with put and call options. You set it up by buying an equal number of put and call options with strike prices above the share price for the call options and strike prices below the share price for put options. The options will all have the same expiration date. If the share price moves above the call strike price, you will earn profits on the call options, and the put options will expire worthlessly. If the stock price moves below the put options, the call options will expire worthlessly. You can exercise the put options and sell your stock at a price that is higher than the market price or sell the put options for a profit and keep your stock.

Short Gut

A short gut is a less popular options strategy that involves selling a call and a put option simultaneously. You sell the two options with the same expiration month, but not necessarily the same expiration date. First, you sell a call option at a certain strike price and then you sell a put option with a higher strike price. Maximum losses are uncapped if the stock price moves in either direction, so you are hoping the stock price will stay the same. Maximum profit is equal to the premiums received from selling the options. This is a little-used strategy; you must be a level 4 options trader to use it and you must have enough cash in your account to cover selling the two options (cash as collateral).

Long Gut

A long gut involves buying a call option and buying a put option with a higher strike price. In this case, you are hoping to make a profit from the stock moving in either direction, so it is someone analogous to a strangle, but you are doing it with the strike prices of the call and put reversed. If the stock price moves up, you will make money from the call but lose money on the put, and if the strike price moves down, you will make money on the put and lose on the call.

Synthetic Strategies

Synthetic strategies are obscure and rarely used by small traders. To make a synthetic put, you must have a large margin account. To set it up, you will have to short the stock, so you will borrow shares of stock from the broker and sell them on the market, hoping to buy them back at a lower price. Then you will buy a call option on the same stock. If the stock price rises, you will make a profit on the call option to help offset the loss of having to buy the shares back at a higher price (if you borrow shares from the broker, you have to buy them back and return them to the broker at some point). If the stock price drops as expected, you will lose money on the call option, which will expire worthlessly, but you will make the expected profit from shorting the stock. You can buy it back at the lower share price, return the shares to the broker and then the profit from doing that less the cost of the call option is your net profit. So, this involves shorting stock using a call option as insurance.

Chapter 15

The Basics of Technical Analysis

Technical analysis is the method of using charts and other recording methods to analyze various data in options trading. Using these visual instruments, you have the chance to determine the direction of the market because they give you a trend.

This method focuses on studying the supply and demand of a market. The price will be seen to arise when the investor realizes the market is undervalued, and this leads to buying. If they think that the market is overvalued, the prices will start falling, and this is deemed the perfect time to sell.

You need to understand the movement of the various indicators to make the perfect decision. This method works on the premise that history usually repeats itself—a huge change in the prices affects the investors in any situation.

History

Technical analysis has been used over the years in trades. The technical analysis methods have been used for over a hundred years to come up with deductions regarding the market.

In Asia, the use of technical analysis led to the development of candlestick techniques, and it forms the main charting techniques.

Over time, more tools and techniques have come up to help traders come up with predictions of the prices in various markets.

There are many indicators that you can use to determine the direction of the market, but only a few are valuable to your course. Let us look at the various indicators and how to use them.

Support and Resistance

These levels occur at points where both the buyer and the seller are not dormant. These levels are displayed on the chart using a horizontal line extended from the past to the future. The different prices reach the support and resistance points in the future.

How to Apply Support and Resistance:

- Using these points allows you to know when to call or put.
- Support and resistance give you a way to determine the entry point to use for a directional trade.

The Significance of Trends in Option Trading

Technical analysis works on the premise of the trend. These trends come by due to the interaction of the buyer and the seller. The aggressiveness of one of the parties in the market will determine how steep the trend becomes. To make a profit, you have to take advantage of the changes in the price movement.

To understand the direction of the trend, you ought to look at the troughs and peaks and how they relate to each other.

When looking for money in options trading, you ought to trade with a trend. The trend is what determines the decision you make when faced with a situation—whether to buy or to sell. You need to know the various signs that a prevailing trend is soon ending so that you can manage the risks and exit the trades the right way.

Characteristics of Technical Analysis

This analysis makes use of models and trading rules using different price and volume changes. These include the volume, price, and other different market info.

Technical analysis is applied among financial professionals and traders and is used by many option traders.

The Principles of Technical analysis

Many traders on the market use the price to come up with information that ultimately affects the decision you make. The analysis looks at the trading pattern and what information it offers you rather than looking at drivers such as news events, economic and fundamental events.

Price action usually tends to change every time because the investor leans towards a certain pattern, which in turn predicts trends and conditions.

Prices Determine Trends

Technical analysts know that the price in the market determines the trend of the market. The trend can be up, down, or move sideways.

History Usually Repeats Itself

Analysts believe that an investor repeats the behavior of the people that traded before them. The investor sentiment usually repeats itself. Since the behavior repeats itself, traders know that using a price pattern can lead to predictions.

The investor uses the research to determine if the trend will continue or if the reversal will stop eventually and will anticipate a change when the charts show a lot of investor sentiment.

Combination with Other Analysis Methods

To make the most out of the technical analysis, you need to combine it with other charting methods on the market. You also need to use secondary data, such as sentiment analysis and indicators.

To achieve this, you need to go beyond pure technical analysis and combine other market forecast methods in line with technical work. You can use technical analysis along with fundamental analysis to improve the performance of your portfolio.

You can also combine technical analysis with economics and quantitative analysis. For instance, you can use neural networks along with technical analysis to identify the relationships in the market. Other traders make use of technical analysis with astrology.

Other traders go for newspaper polls, sentiment indicators to come with deductions.

The Different Types of Charts Used in Technical Analysis

Candlestick Chart

This is a charting method that came from the Japanese. The method fills the interval between opening and closing prices to show a relationship. These candles use color-coding to show the closing points. You will come across black, red, white, blue, or green candles to represent the closing point at any time.

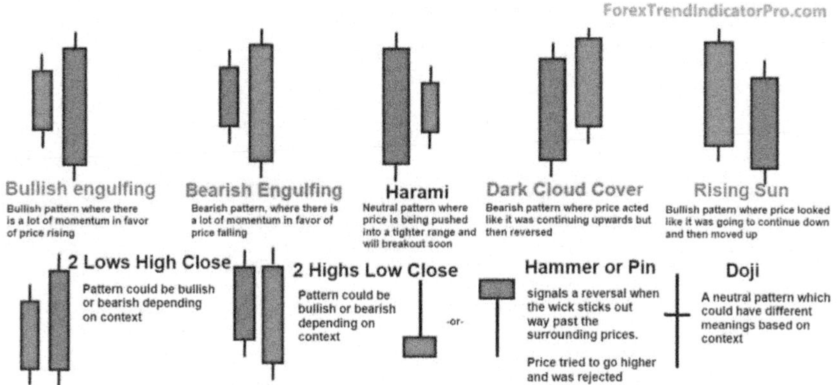

Open-high-low-close Chart (OHLC)

These are also referred to as bar charts, and they give you a connection between the maximum and minimum prices in a trading period. They usually feature a tick on the left side to show the open price and one on the right to show the closing price.

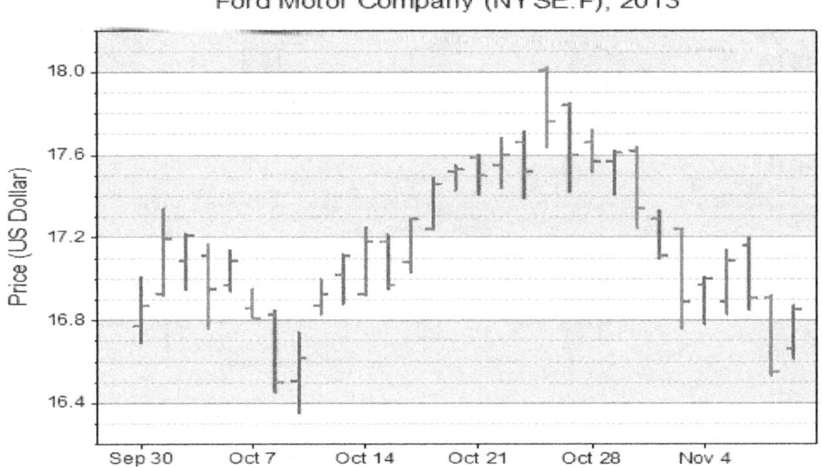

Line Chart

This is a chart that maps the closing price values using a line segment.

Point and Figure Chart

This employs numerical filters that reference times without fully using the time to construct the chart.

Overlays

These are usually used on the main price charts and come in different ways:

- **Resistance** – refers to a price level that acts as the maximum level above the usual price

- **Support** – the opposite of resistance, and it shows as the lowest value of the price
- **Trend line** - this is a line that connects two troughs or peaks.
- **Channel** – refers to two trend lines that are parallel to each other
- **Moving average** – a kind of dynamic trend line that looks at the average price in the market
- **Bollinger bands** - these are charts that show the rate of volatility in a market.
- **Pivot point** – this refers to the average of the high, low, and closing price averages for a certain stock or currency.

Price-based Indicators

These analyze the price values of the market. These include:

- **Advance decline line** – this is an indicator of the market breadth
- **Average directional index** – shows the strength of a trend in the market
- **Commodity channel index** – helps you to identify cyclical trends in the market

- **Relative strength index** – this is a chart that shows you the strength of the price
- **Moving average convergence (MACD)** – this shows the point where two trend line converges or diverge.
- **Stochastic oscillator** – this shows the close position that has happened within the recent trading range
- **Momentum** – this is a chart that tells you how fast the price changes

The Benefits of Technical Analysis in Options Trading

There are a variety of benefits that you enjoy when you use technical analysis in trading options. The benefits arise from the fact that traders are usually asking many questions touching on the price of the market and entry points. While the forecast for prices is a huge task, the use of technical analysis makes it easier to handle.

The major advantages of technical analysis include:

Expert Trend Analysis

This is the biggest advantage of technical analysis in any market. With this method, you can predict the direction of the market at any time. You can determine whether the market will move up, down, or sideways easily.

Entry and Exit Points

As a trader, you need to know when to place a trade and when to opt-out. The entry point is all about knowing the right time to enter the trade for good returns. Exiting a trade is also vital because it allows you to reduce losses.

Leverage Early Signals

Every trader looks for ways to get early signals to assist them in making decisions. Technical analysis gives you signals to trigger a decision on your part. This is usually ideal when you suspect that a trend will reverse soon. Remember the time the trend reverses are when you need to make crucial decisions.

It Is Quick

In options trading, you need to go with techniques that give you fast results. Additionally, getting technical analysis data is cheaper than other fundamental analysis techniques, with some companies offering free charting programs. If you are in the market to use short time intervals such as 1-minute, 5-minute, 30 minute, or 1-hour charts, you can get this using technical analysis.

It Gives You A Lot of Information

Technical analysis gives you much information that you can use to make trading decisions. You can easily build a position depending on the information you get then take or exit trades. You have access to information such as chart patterns, trends, support, resistance, market momentum, and other information.

The current price of an asset usually reflects every known information of an asset. While the market might be rife with rumors that the prices might surge or plummet, the current price represents the final point for all information. As the traders and investors change their bearing from one part to another, the changes in assets reflect the current value perception.

If all this turns out to be true, then the only info you require is a price chart that gives all the price reflections and predictions. There isn't any need for you to worry about the reasons why the price is rising or falling when you can use a chart to determine everything.

With the right technical analysis information, you can make trading easier and faster because you make decisions based not on hearsay but facts. You don't have to spend your time reading and trying to make headway in financial news. All you need is to check what the chart tells you.

You Understand Trends

If the prices on the market were to gyrate randomly without any direction, you would find it hard to make money. While these trends run in all directions, the prices always move in trends. Directional bias allows you to leverage the benefits of making money. Technical analysis allows you to determine when a trend occurs and when it doesn't occur, or when it is in reversal.

Many of the profitable techniques that are used by traders to make money follow trends. This means that you find the right trend and then look for opportunities that allow you to enter the market in the same direction as the trend. This helps you to capitalize on the price movement.

Trends run in various degrees. The degree of the trend determines how much money you make, whether in the short term or long-term trading. Technical analysis gives you all the tools that make it possible for you to do this.

Chapter 16

Tips and Tricks in Stocks

A Stock Price Can Move in 3 Directions

When starting, most traders forget that stock prices don't just go up or down. They can also stay the same; that's the third option. Beginners often forget about this third direction and subsequently lose money. Sometimes stock prices remain in a narrow range or just don't move at all.

Buying a call option means betting on the rise of the stock price. This means that if the pricc goes up, you will make a profitable trade, but if it doesn't, you won't. The price might not go down, but it might not go up either. If you bought an OOTM call and the price doesn't go up, you will lose all your money, as the option will be worthless after expiry. For an ITM call, you can at least get back your intrinsic value in case the price doesn't change.

One of the most aggravating things as a trader is seeing your call option expire just a few days before the price skyrockets. This teaches you an important lesson: sometimes you need to give your strategies more time. It's common to see traders buying short-term call options hoping the stock price would rise quickly, but it stays flat the entire time. Then it goes up the next month when your option has expired. Near month options always carry this inherent risk, and this is also why longer-term options tend to be costlier as well.

The consensus in the market is that out of all the long call and put options, about 70% tend to lose money. This is supported by the concept that there are three directions the stock price could move in, not two. For sellers, this is good news. It means that 70% of them will make money, and this is also why many of the conservative traders move away from buying a call and put options and start writing or selling covered calls or puts.

So, remember this when you make your next trade. Beginners often make this same mistake over and over, so it's in your interest to learn to break this bad habit.

Study the Chart

Before you make any trade, there's one thing you must always do and I mean always. You need to look at the chart of the underlying stock and study it well. This is done to find trends, patterns, resistances, etc. So, you study the one-month chart first, then the three-month chart and then for the whole year. You will be able to see whether there are any trends in the chart.

Do you notice that the stock price is climbing slowly but steadily? Or maybe it is slowly declining over a long period that might not have been visible in a short-term chart? Maybe it's just stuck in a narrow range and doesn't look like it will be moving soon. When you notice these things, you must question whether these patterns are consistent with your starting strategy. See the general direction of the price, then draw a line through the middle of these stock prices. To see the channel it's trading in, simply draw two more lines—one at the top and one at the bottom.

Whenever you want to buy a new call, first ask yourself one simple question: why do you believe the price will rise? There is not much reason for a stock's price to go up to a certain point if it hasn't been trading there recently. That can change, of course, if some new information turns up or a new event takes place. These include things like upcoming shareholder meetings, upcoming earnings announcements and new product/version releases.

Using Support Levels

Let's talk about support levels. Support level, often called just "support," is a certain price level below which an asset doesn't fall for a certain time. This happens because whenever an asset's price dips low enough, new buyers enter the market.

While studying a stock's chart, if you notice that there is strong support at a particular price point and the current stock price has dipped that low, you can consider bouncing off that support level and make a profit. The call options will be cheaper, and the probability that the stock price will go back up is higher.

Using Resistance Levels

Resistance levels or resistance is similar to support levels in concept but the exact opposite in meaning. Unlike support, resistance is the price point above, in which the asset's price struggles to rise. Whenever an asset's price reaches a certain point, there is a big influx of sellers who are willing to sell at a price. This leads to a price ceiling of a sort. However, it can be short-lived if some new information enters the market, changing the whole attitude of the market toward the stock.

So, if you notice solid resistance at high prices while studying the stock's chart, and you see that the current price is reaching that point soon, it's worth considering buying a put option. The chance that the price will fall off is high, and put options are cheaper during the time.

Using Stock Chart Channels

We can use the support and resistance levels to draw trendlines, and this gives us the trading channel. It's nothing but the section between these two trendlines. They're important because the market considers channels important, and traders generally believe that stock prices don't usually go outside of these trading channels.

If the stock's price is currently at the lower level of the range, you can use it to make a small profit, because the price will most probably move back up. So, you can take advantage of this movement by buying a call when the price is low and selling it a short while later to make a profit.

That's how you identify the support, resistance, and channel of a stock price, and then use it to base future decisions on. It helps you make better predictions about the stock price.

Study the Option Chain

Okay, so let's talk about Option Chains now, something you should always be looking out for. On any decent stock quotes page, you will see a button that either says "Option Chain" or just "Options." This is where you can see the full list of calls and puts that are available on that particular stock, and this list is generally divided into two separate columns. Call options are usually on the left, and put options are usually on the right. The expiration dates and stock prices of all the call and put options are also shown in the option chain.

The thing you need to take note of first is the expiration date. Earlier, options used to have a fixed expiration date. They all expired on the third Friday of every month, without question. But in recent years, options exchanges have changed things a lot, and now most of the active stocks have options with weekly expiration dates. It's become really important now to take note of the exact date your options are expiring.

Once that has been taken care of, you need to look at the strike prices available. Most stocks have strike prices in $5 increments, while some also have $2.50 or $1 increments.

Next, you need to look up the volume of the contracts being traded. In the volume column, you can see which ones are the most actively traded contracts. If you notice that there's much volume on a certain strike price and expiration month, maybe that option is worth considering. You'd do well to avoid the contracts with very little or zero volume.

Finally, what you need to do is look at the spread between the asking price and the bid price of the options contracts that are being traded most heavily. If the spread is less than or equal to 10 cents, it's safe to trade it. A spread larger than 10 cents, however, signifies potential liquidity problems. You should not trade such options without careful consideration. So, try to avoid thinly traded calls and puts that have high spreads.

Sometimes, it is much easier to go where the smart money is instead of trying to find your path. This is why starting with a high-volume option is a good idea. Start by asking yourself why you think so many people are trading that particular contract. You can also get a feel for the liquidity of the contracts and the incoming buy/sell orders if you have a streaming option chain. With streaming options chains, you can immediately see price movements because they refresh every second. Take note of how frequently and by how much the asks and bids change.

For beginners, it is often recommended that you start with a highly liquid stock like Apple or Google. It is very volatile, especially during the opening and closing hours of the day. So, take notes of this during the first and last 15 minutes of a trading day, which is from 9:30 am to 4:00 pm ET. That's the time of most volatility generally. You will also notice the market activity going dull around noon when everyone goes for lunch, and then when they come back, the diminished volumes pick up again after about 1:00 pm ET.

Calculate the Break-Even Point

Once you've settled on a call or put option to buy, the next thing you should do is calculate its break-even point. For this, you need to take notes of both the bid-ask spread and the commission charged on the buy and sell trade. To make a profit, you need to have full confidence that the option price will move more than the break-even point. And for this, the underlying stock needs to even more than that.

Break-Even Point Calculation

There are two break-even points that you need to calculate when trading options. For short term traders, the break-even point is calculated by using the bid-ask spread and commission charges. For long term traders who plan to hold the option until the expiration date, the break-even point is calculated by calculating where the underlying stock's price needs to be at the date of expiration.

Let's talk about short term trades first. Calculate the difference between the bid and ask prices, the bid-ask spread. Now, let's say your commission is $10, and the spread is 10 cents. So, for one contract, you have to overcome a spread of $10. You're also paying a $10 commission when buying and a $10 commission when selling the option. This means you start with a net loss of $30 already. To recover this and break-even, your options bid price must increase at least 30 cents. If you buy two contracts, though, the bid price only needs to go up by 15 cents. This is because the spread will be divided among the two contracts, and the commission will remain the same. For three contracts, it becomes even smaller. The option's bid price need only increases by 10 cents for you to break even.

Chapter 17
How to Trade in Stocks

The Advantages of the Options Trading System

By opening a part of the position (half, for example), we avoid losing a lot of money if we make a mistake on the meaning of the market. In a way, the trader tests the market. We only strengthen our position when the market gives us the reason. In this case, we expect confirmation or a new low point (in a bull market) or high point (in a bear market) in the current trend. For example, if we are buyers, it is possible to strengthen one's position when the RSI lands on the neutrality zone. The placement of the stop will be slightly below the base, which has been broken to strengthen the position.

This technique allows the trader to avoid the classic mistake of getting out of a winning position too early and hesitating to cut a losing position. If the position results in a loss, it will not be too big, and therefore the trader will not hesitate to cut it. Indeed, when the loss is heavy, it is often painful, and traders prefer to go into hope mode rather than face it. Besides, this approach allows the trader to play the movement in all its amplitude since it will strengthen its position, which will prevent it from going out quickly.

Besides, the trader who strictly applies his plan will avoid downward averaging. This serious fault is often fatal. From now on, with this method, the trader will strengthen his position only when the market evolves in his direction and will not cut it too fast or with a small gain. Finally, the last advantage of this method is that it allows testing the market. If the stock doesn't react as expected, the loss will be only 50% of the loss that would have been incurred if the entire position had been opened at the very beginning. Thus, this method allows the trader to strictly adhere to the stock market adage: "Cut your losses and ride your winners."

The Limits of the Options Trading System

This method presents the risk of strengthening a position while a market reversal is emerging. It is not effective in a market without a trend because the trader will strengthen its position on an extreme level (high point or low point). He must, therefore, be convinced that there is a tendency to apply this approach. This method adapts badly to a market without trend, but even in this case, it presents limited risks.

The Classic System: Open Its Position in One Time

The classic method is to fully open its position and then take profits during the upward movement (for a purchase) or downward movement (for sale).

The Limits of the Classical System

This system is mainly adapted to a market without a trend. It should be noted that the losses are much greater than for the options trading system and that the performance is not necessarily greater. Nevertheless, when the market is volatile, this system is the most efficient. The trader will have to focus on carefully selecting his positions (thus increasing his probability of success) and taking profits faster.

A Pragmatic Method to Maximize Trading

One of the main attractions of technical analysis is that it doesn't present huge barriers to entry. It is less demanding than the fundamental analysis in terms of knowledge to acquire. Fundamental analysis generally requires long and solid academic training in economic and financial analysis. This training is usually difficult to acquire, which can discourage more than one.

The researcher Olivier Godechot conducted a sociological study on traders operating in a Paris trading room. This research found that traders and other financial operators had little control over economic reasoning. The author even goes ahead to say that the market economist was merely popularizing the economy and did not push his analyzes very far.

Moreover, even with this method of analysis, investors are not necessarily well equipped to understand the significant and persistent discrepancies in the price of a financial asset compared to its fundamental value. The tests conducted by Meese & Rogoff (1983) have shown that fundamental analysis can't predict the evolution of exchange rates. They even go so far as to argue that a naive model was often more efficient than a model based on fundamental analysis.

The frequent and large discrepancies between the price of a financial asset and its fundamental value (assessed by financial analysts) are hardly explained by the fundamentals, or they are posterior. Finally, the technical analysis is not reduced in the short term, as many experts say. This method offers reliability in the forecasts made, and this as well in the short term as in the medium and long term, as we will see it after that.

Equal Treatment for All Stakeholders

For the Orthodox school, an efficient market is characterized by the transparency of information. But many insiders (employees of a company, business bankers, family, friends, financial analysts, etc.) have some privileged information, which they can take advantage of. Everyone is not equal in the phase of information.

For the proponents of technical analysis, all the information available at a given moment is integrated into the courses. If a company intends to report poor results, this information is likely visible on the price, and the technical analysis offers the opportunity to anticipate this negative news. Very often, insiders will seek to get rid of their securities, which cause a decline in stock prices (no apparent news) and are a sure sign for seasoned operators.

The role of the technical analyst is to detect the moments when a title will shift without valid reason and, therefore, to be alert all the time. The graph contains all the information investors need, which puts them on an equal footing. Some economists even go so far as to say that technical analysis doesn't necessarily contradict market efficiency because it is based on the same assumptions. This approach is attractive and reassures private investors, who have the same information as professionals.

With technical analysis, performance will be primarily a function of personal discipline and experience. Indeed, having the same information doesn't mean that its use will be the same for everyone. Some people will know how to exploit it better than others and will react appropriately. Implicitly, this means that using the same analysis tool doesn't necessarily imply consistency in decision making. The psychological dimension that explains the effectiveness of technical analysis also makes it possible to understand why individuals don't make the same decisions while basing themselves on the same information.

Technical Analysis Is Better Accepted by the Academic World

Considered originally as a naive model by the academic world, technical analysis is increasingly accepted today.

Indeed, the assumption of the efficiency of the markets, dominant yesterday, is more and more questioned. The work done by behaviorists and conventionalists supports the idea that prices can strongly and durably shift their fundamental value for no good reason.

A. Orlean defends the idea of self-referential rationality, at the origin of rational speculative bubbles that can be formed even in the presence of perfectly rational individuals. Stakeholders will rationally use the dominant convention to make their decisions because they believe that it is better to follow the market than to refer to fundamental value.

Better yet, the work of the behaviorists gives an almost scientific character to the technical analysis. H. Krow likened technical analysis to behavioral analysis. According to Krow, technical analysis is the counterpart of behavioral analysis.

Closer to home, an article in The Economist in 1993 establishes a link between behavioral finance and technical analysis. This is only fair because technical analysis has focused on the behavior of individuals well before the emergence of the behaviorist approach. Moreover, this pragmatic approach had highlighted the existence of recurrent errors, the peculiarity of human nature. Thus, the famous: "Let your profits run and cut your losses quickly" is symptomatic of market reality. Indeed, stakeholders would tend to cut their winning positions too quickly and hesitated for a long time before closing their losing positions. This stock market adage, which cannot be dated precisely, has been demonstrated by the experiments of Kahneman and Tversky.

An Approach Acclaimed By Major Traders

A method is judged by its success. Pragmatically, the success of technical analysis can be explained simply by the spectacular performance of some of its users.

The problem of technical analysis is that it can be of formidable efficiency in the hands of a great trader and represent an extreme danger for a novice trader. O. Godechot quotes in his work a trader who explains the reason for the success of the technical analysis in his trading room:

"The chief economist of the trading room makes many mistakes or justifies an economic event posterior while the chartist of the room is right in nearly 70% of cases."

On many traders surveyed by high-flying J. Schwager, over 80% said they only use technical analysis or fundamental analysis. Ed Seykota is a perfect example: a graduate engineer from MIT. This trader has achieved a performance of 25,000% over sixteen years. He doesn't hesitate to say that he doesn't touch fundamentals—which he even calls "funnymentals"—and only uses models that use technical analysis.

According to him, "a good surfer doesn't have to master fluid physics and resonance to get a good wave. The goal is to feel when the wave will take shape and have the courage to seize it at the right time." The famous trader Bruce Kovner goes in this direction when he explains the effectiveness of this method:

"I use a lot of technical analysis, and it's a fabulous method. It helps to clarify the fundamental analysis. Technical analysis is like a barometer. Fundamentalists who say that graphs are useless are like the doctor who feels it's pointless to take the temperature of his patient. That doesn't make sense. If you are a serious trader, you need to know where the market is, whether euphoria is dominant or whether pessimism prevails. The trader must know everything about the markets if he wants to have an advantage."

The approach of Kovner is rich in information. Indeed, according to this manager, technical analysis should not be considered as an exact science, but rather as a market barometer. It allows us to know the forces involved and to guess the dominant feeling of the market. It is, as for the doctor, to take the temperature of the market, to make a diagnosis before recommending a remedy. However, Kovner being an exceptional trader, it is difficult to generalize his approach. It is true that operators often use technical analysis without real control and rarely operate as strategists.

These non-standard traders are an excellent ad for technical analysis. This method, which may seem esoteric and unscientific, draws its credibility and quasi-scientific character from the success of "some" of its users. What better argument for market efficiency than a person who has regular earnings over a long period and consistently uses the same method of analysis?

Nevertheless, these remarks must be nuanced. The success of these traders is not only explained by the method of analysis. Strong market experience, iron discipline and personal talent have probably played a significant role in their success. It is important to note that many traders have been ruined several times before accumulating considerable fortunes, and that experience plays a fundamental role in the success of a trader.

Chapter 18
Trading Techniques

Even with its numerous benefits, options trading exposes the trader to the risk of losing their capital, and it is known to be naturally speculative. Not everybody has the ability to become an intelligent options trader. This is because smart options trading requires a trader to have a specific set of skills, attitude as well as personality type. For that reason, in this chapter, we will discuss some of the ways you can trade-in options intelligently:

Exercise Active Learning

A report from the Chicago board of trade indicated that 90% of traders who venture into options trading incur significant losses. What barricades the intelligent traders from the average ones is that smart options traders ensure that they learn from their misdoings and, consequently, the lessons they acquire in their trading strategies. Smart options traders have practiced and practiced even more over time until they fully understood the lessons behind every loss they incurred; they grasped the economics that steers the market, as well as how the market behaves on different occasions.

Financial markets are in a state of continuous change and evolution; a smart trader has to clearly comprehend what is taking place and how the entire system works. By exercising active learning, you will not only have the ability to execute your current strategies, but you will equally have the ability to spot opportunities that other people may bypass or not see.

Consider the Key Elements in an Options Trade

When you decide to take out an option, you are acquiring a contract to sell or buy a stock, normally one hundred shares of the stock for every contract, at a pre-arranged price by a given date. You must make three critical choices before you place the trade:

1. Determining What Direction, You Think the Stock Will Move

This greatly affects the kind of options contract you adopt. If you feel like the stock prices will go up, you will choose to buy a call option. A call option refers to a contract that allows you to buy but doesn't obligate you to purchase a stock at a prearranged price (usually referred to as the strike price) in a given period.

If you are of the idea that the price of stocks will decrease you will purchase a put option. This kind of option allows you but doesn't obligate you to trade in shares at a stated amount of money before the expiry of the contract.

2. Foresee How Low or High the Price of the Stock Will Move from Its Price at the Moment

It is advisable to purchase an option that will show where you expect the stock will be located during the lifetime of the option.

For instance, if you feel like the price of shares of a company that is presently trading at $100 will go up to $120 sometime in the future, you will purchase a call option that has a price that is lower than $120. In this scenario, you will hypothetically opt for a strike price that is not greater than $120 subtracted from the option's cost, in that the option still rakes in profits at $120. If it happens that the stock actually rises beyond the strike price, then your option is in the funds.

In the same way, if you believe that the share price of the company will go down to $80, you would opt to purchase a put option (allowing you to sell shares) at a strike price that is higher than $80 (preferably a strike price that is not below $80 in addition to the option's cost in such a way that the option still rakes in profit at $80). If the stock dips under the strike price, your option lies in the money.

It is important to note that you cannot just choose whichever strike price you want. Option quotes – professionally referred to as option chains – have a variety of strike prices within easy reach. The accretion during strike prices are regulated throughout the industry and usually depend on the price of the stock.

The amount you pay for an option, usually referred to as the premium, contains two elements: time value and intrinsic value. Time Value refers to whatever remains, and it includes how turbulent the stock is, interest rates, the time left before it expires among other components. On the other hand, intrinsic value refers to the disparity between the share price and the strike price, on the condition that the stock price is higher than that of the strike. For instance, let us say you have a call option worth $100 whereas the price of the stocks is $110. Let us assume that the option is at a premium of $15. This time value will be $5 whereas the intrinsic value amounts to $10 ($110 subtracted from 100).

3. Predict the Time Frame within Which the Stock Is Expected to Move

All the options contract that you purchase have an expiry date that shows the final day you can use the option. It is also important to note that in this case, you cannot simply generate a date out of nowhere. The choice of a date is determined by the ones that are given whenever you bring forward an options chain.

Expiry dates range from years to months or even days. Weekly and daily options tend to be extremely risky and are set aside for experienced traders. For investors who have been in the trade for a long time, annual and monthly expiry dates are preferred. Prolonged dates of expiry give the stock ample time to move and wait for your investment proposition to play out.

A prolonged expiry date is also important because it gives the option enough time to add value, regardless of whether the price of stocks is lower than the strike price. The time value of an option decays as the expiry date comes closer, and option purchasers don't desire to see the options they bought reduce in value, possibly expiring without any value if the stock turns out to be below the strike price at the end of the period.

Chapter 19

Important Trading Rules to Follow

Trading in Derivatives is Risky and Time Sensitive

This is the first rule that every trader must understand clearly. The money in your trading account is not an investment. You will be trading from it, and all your trades will be short-term and time-sensitive.

This means that you will not be able to make long-term positions through options trading, and this shouldn't even be your goal. Your objective should remain to get into viable trades for as little time as possible and get out of them as early as possible.

Every option trade will be losing its time value with each passing day. The longer you keep it, the higher would be the time decay, and hence to make a profit, you must get out of the trade as early as you have reached your estimated target. In case your trade is making a loss, getting out of the trade on time will become even more important as it will even lose the time value soon and become worthless in value.

Your view about options trade should be of short-term profit, and you must not try to remain in the trade till the expiry and, in most of the cases, that will bring down your profit potential.

Do not Try to Convert Your Trades into Long-Term Positions

This is a trend seen in many traders. When they are making a profit in their trades, they try to convert their trades into positions by exercising their right to buy the stocks.

This is unnecessary and unwise. Even if a trade is making a profit today, there is no surety that it will keep doing that in the long-term. You will be better off booking your profit and closing your position so that you have free capital to make further trades. Most people try to do this to get the dividend income to be received in that trade or for various other such reasons. You must understand that the market already calculates all such factors, and that would get reflected in the increase in the premium. You don't have to keep your money stuck in that trade to get that benefit.

Moreover, this becomes a mentality that starts affecting even the negative trades as people start taking positions in the trades going in loss.

You must keep your priorities straight. If you want to invest in some stock, then look at it through investing potential. Always treat your trades as simple profit-earning potential. This simple thing will help you in keeping the trading capital free, and even your trading decisions will not get affected by your impulses.

Invest Your Time and Labor in Research

Always remember that it is your hard-earned cash that is at stake. If you start putting your money into everything that you hear, then you will simply become a tool of market manipulation. All the experts sitting on various business news panels and brokerage firms have their interests in mind and not yours. The people writing long reports on the performance of various firms and giving sure-shot predictions are trying to swing the market for their benefit. If there is someone who can find the true potential in a trade, it is you.

This will not happen until and unless you do your research. Invest your time and labor in finding the right trades and the reasons for those trades. You don't have to focus on a whole lot of things. Simply pick a few and then narrow down your search. You can initially take the experts' help initially to find the news making stocks, but after that, the real research has to come from you because only that would be in your interest.

Never fall prey to the predictions made by the experts. Remember, if they were so sure, they would put their own money into it and not advise you to do it. Their attempts are directed towards selling your subscriptions, courses, tips and insider news, and all of that is practically worthless from the perspective of an individual trader.

Learn from Your Losses

Every loss would allow you to learn. Don't feel aggravated by losses. They will be a part of your journey, but you shouldn't start making them a habit.

Learn from the mistake you made. Find out that vital thing you missed and put that into your next strategy. Learn from the mistake of others.

Trading is a widely researched and published field. Remember that you can't make all the mistakes to learn everything in the market. That would make your journey a bit too painful. Try to learn even from the mistakes made by others and incorporate those learnings into your strategies.

Always keep in mind that you will not earn profit from every trade, but every trade will give you a learning opportunity.

Always enter the market with a long-term goal and start slow with smaller trades. Learn the things every trade teaches you.

If you have had five consecutive good trades in a row that doesn't make you an expert or a pro, try to analyze whether it was your research, sudden market swing, or any other factor and add them to your strategy. Remember that the same factors that helped you make these winning trades could have led to fate in another way as well.

You must test your strategy and risk-abilities after every trade so that you don't get complacent.

Get Over Your Fears

Markets can become intimidating at times. You will see the markets moving rapidly while you are even unable to decide where you should begin with. At this stage, call down.

FOMO or the fear of missing out is a real phenomenon that people experience in the market. They place limit trades, and they don't get them. They feel that they are missing out on golden opportunities, and if they don't take any action now, they will get left behind. This is one mistake that you must never make.

The market is a much bigger place than you can imagine. There are innumerable trades taking place every moment. You will get plenty of opportunities to find a good trade, and you are not missing out on anything. Before anything else, you must get over your anxiety and feeling of inadequacy.

In the market, the worse thing than not doing anything is to do something that you don't understand. Never be that person who is simply trying to know the market and loses all the capital on poor trades.

Simply watch the market for a few days and try to find one good trade that clicks you the most. Then, simply observe the movement of that trade as if you had invested in that trade. Repeat this process several times over with other trades to test your understanding of the market.

Don't fear the pace of the market or your anxiety that you aren't able to do anything in it. The market will give you plenty of chances when you are ready for it, or else it will take away all the capital you have.

Follow Your Research and Not The Crowd

You must understand that every individual in the market is trading with a different objective. There is no way you will be able to predict the actual mind of the market ever. Some people are simply trading in options for hedging. Then there will be people who will be buying opposite trades for a balance. Some traders will be simply trying their beginner's luck in the market. There is no point in following the crowd endlessly without having any idea of their real motives.

The best way to not follow the herd is to have your understanding and research of the trade. Look into every trade you are interested in closely. Look at its historical performance, fundamentals, technical, financials, volatility, volume, open interest, and all such parameters so that you can understand the reason for the interest of the people in that contract.

You must find out whether the option contract is overbought or oversold. Find out if there is any declaration going to come from that company. All these things will better equip you to deal with the market trend and your chances of making negative trades would go down.

Begin with a Stop-Loss in Mind

One major mistake many traders make is that they are never able to ascertain a point at which they should surrender their hopes from a trade. This is a very risky thing. Such people take the loss-making trades to their very end, where they inevitably expire as worthless. This can be prevented to a great extent most of the time if traders keep a stop-loss in their minds.

You must have a clear understanding of the amount of loss you are ready to bear on that trade and that should be the complete amount. Fix a percentage in your mind depending upon your risk appetite and the volatility in that trade. If you see that trade going south, it is prudent to close that trade and get out of it. If you don't do that, you will be at risk of greater loss.

Don't treat options as the final bargain. They are continuous trades, and hence you should have no hesitation in getting in and out of those trades. Some trades might perform well after exiting them but never worry about them as their percentage would always remain minuscule.

One very important thing is that this stop-loss figure should be clear in your mind even before you begin your trade. Don't buy and contract and then begin thinking about it as some trades may not give you the chance to do so. Furthermore, once you have a trade, you may want to give it a try for a bit longer and that is dangerous thinking.

As soon as a trade gets toxic or loss-making for you, get out of it at the first chance you get.

Don't Run Only After the News

Mostly news is broken just to create a stir in the market, and most of it is planted for the vested interest of a few individuals. If you look closely, you'll find that such newsbreaks bring temporary movement, and then things get back to normal. However, these short news-driven moments are enough to lure in unsuspecting victims in the form of news traders, newcomers, and the ones who are not doing their research on the fundamentals of the company.

If you want to become a successful trader in the market, you must be good with your numbers. Look at all the data present about the company. Find the real news through the numbers. All your positions and biases about the trend in the company should be based on your understanding of the fundamental and technical analysis of the company and not just the news.

Even in this strategy, you may sometimes miss some vital news trends, which may make you lose an opportunity. But it will prevent you from hundreds of fake news planted just to lure the traders into a contract.

These are some basic rules in the market that will make you trade more sensibly. It will help you in maintaining strong control over your sanity, and you would be able to survive in the market much longer.

You must never forget that the market is ruthless and unforgiving. There is no pardon for making financial mistakes in the market, and if you continue making many of them without learning the lessons, the market won't let you do that for too long.

These rules will help you in navigating the market with better control and precision.

Chapter 20
Advanced Strategies in Options Trading

The goal in options trading is to earn profits by analyzing stock charts and trends in the securities market. Once you are good at analyzing the market and finding the right time to enter and exit, you will be earning money as well as gaining experience. More skill, knowledge and experience will then limit the amount of risk you bear when making your options trading activities.

While advanced trading strategies are good, you need to make sure that you understand the strategy before applying it. If you are a beginner options trader, starting with the basics is very important. Seek to gain mastery over the market when you are feeling bullish, bearish, and neutral about the stock price movements in the market.

It is also very important that you expand your brokerage account to be able to use some of these advanced trading strategies while trading in options. A demo trading level is good to seek trial before signing up for a brokerage account. Once you are okay with how the brokerage account, sign up for the basic level. Success at using the basic trading strategies to make money should then take you to the next level in your options trading plan: advanced options trading.

When it comes to using advanced trading strategies, one of the most important things to consider is analysis. Your analysis is what determines the kind of strategy to use. Through technical and fundamental analysis, you can make predictions in the market to determine when things will be bullish, bearish, and neutral. These forecasts come with their corresponding plans, which should go to build upon your trading.

Combining Fundamental and Technical Analysis for Advanced Trading

While you may choose to prefer one method of analysis much more than the other, the most important thing is always to learn how to blend or combine the two analytical approaches on the stock market to make a good trading decision.

Maybe you have been looking at a stable and liquid stock that has not been experiencing much volatility in the stock market. All of a sudden, the stock begins to fluctuate in the market. Instead of jumping and making your trading decisions, you must stay objective and adopt both a technical and fundamental analysis to make a well-informed decision.

In some cases, volatility in a stock market can be influenced by changes in the micro and macro-economic conditions of the company. When these factors change, they tend to impact revenue, stock per earnings, dividends, interest rates, and certainly stock movement. This is the reason some schools of thought say you should never take any real money position in the market if you have not used technical and fundamental analysis to make an informed forecast in the stock market.

How Fundamental and Technical Analysis Complements Each Other

There are different kinds of traders in the market. The information required from each trader to decide on the market may vary from one to another. That means looking at what the market forecasts and financial news media are saying and then checking whether the information agrees with each other.

The goal is to make a bullish technical analysis that has a strong confirmation from a fundamental analysis perspective. If the stock appears bullish from a technical perspective, but then weak from the technical analysis, you might want to watch and consider your decision and forecasts. To generate profitable trades and to ensure that the tides are moving in your favor, you have to ensure that there is an agreement between your technical analysis forecasts and fundamental analysis forecasts.

This will help increase the probability of your decisions being correct and earning you revenue with each trading activity. A good 50/50 outlook from a technical analysis and fundamental analysis perspective can help increase your winning trades and ensure your trading capital has not been wiped out. Therefore, always learn to pair or combine the analytic reports of both sides when making your options trading decision.

Analytical Trading Example

A. Revenue Earning Seasons

At the end of every quarter, all publicly traded companies are required by law to provide a report on their quarterly performance. Before their reports, there is some level of market predictions based on their performance for the past quarter. This quarterly information provided by the company gives a deep insight into the status of the company financially, and their capability to yield profit and increase earnings per share.

When the final quarterly financial reports are provided by the company, and the market realizes that the results have beaten market expectations, the difference in expectation tends to lead to an increase in stock prices, causing a change in the financial charts. As a seasoned trader looking to excel in capital gains, you have to analyze the financial reports of the company and the market reactions to help determine whether stock prices will move upward or downward. This can help you know whether to feel bullish, bearish or neutral about the market.

B. Catastrophic Events

The stock price of a company can be affected by catastrophic events occurring in the company. Assuming a publicly-traded company has been poorly managed by the directors and officers of the company leading some of their subsidiaries going bankrupt or closing, it will affect their stock price. The stock price of a company is likely to go down if they have a huge lawsuit that has resulted in the company being fined for hundreds and millions of dollars by the court system.

As a technician, you need to keep watch over this information and use it to make your trading decisions. Bankruptcies, lawsuits, mismanagement, and many other internal events that were happening in a company greatly affected the earnings per share and the overall stock price of the company. This is why an advanced trading strategy involves blinding both fundamental and technical investing to trade.

C. Global Economic Uncertainty

During times of global uncertainty, people tend to move their money from one financial instrument to another. In this case, the price of gold is inclined to rise when the global economy is uncertain. When companies are running into bankruptcies, and stock prices tend to be going down, people tend to move their funds to other asset classes such as silver and gold. When this happens, you need to analyze the market and then adjust your options trading plan to profit from the market changes.

D. Economic Data Releases

There is an impact of economic data on the market. And this is very important for options traders to know whether cash is flowing one asset class to another to increase prices on the economic data. The following are typical levels for which economic data are being released for trading activities:

1. Gross Domestic Product (GDP)
2. Retail Prices of Commodities
3. Consumer Inflation
4. Manufacturing Productivity
5. Unemployment Rate
6. Currencies

The news and information from these economic indicators have a way of affecting stock price movements. Companies are affected and influenced by the economic environment that they operate in. For example, an increase in prices of commodities like oil can cause some companies to increase the price of their goods and services. This will impact the stock price, trends and moods of the market.

Always be on the lookout for economic data and trend information. This information is very critical in determining stock trends. When things are tough, and the market gets hard, many people end up engaging in profit first decisions that ruin their lives. Thus, to understand success factors that lead to stock price movements and changes turns necessary.

E. Central Bank Meetings

Sometimes there can be an effect in stock prices with a change in interest rates. This can be influenced by the meeting of stockholders of central banks. Decisions of central banks affect interest rates, import/export rates. Setting stock volume/benchmarks and market volatility.

Key central banks whose decisions play a big impact on the global market include the following: US Federal Reserve, the European Central Bank, the Bank of England, the People's Bank of China, the Bank of Japan, the Swiss National Bank and the Bank of Australia.

Generally, an increase in interest rates will create a bearish effect on the market, which will decrease stock prices. In this case, the associated bearish strategies have to be adopted to ensure that the best trading results have been obtained.

The Bottom Line

From a fundamental analysis perspective arising through global economic uncertainty, options traders will begin to notice that the price of commodities like gold and silver will move upward. Option traders dealing in gold and silver can then feel bullish about the market and then adopt advanced bullish trading strategies to profit from the dynamic change in the market.

Many traders in the market use technical trading to realize profits in the market. But there are limitations to these approaches just as there are limitations to the fundamental approach. While there is no definitive answer as to where technical analysis should be done instead of fundamental analysis, the key is to make sure that you leverage both approaches to complement each other and make better trading decisions.

Advanced Trading Indicators

Once you develop your technical, analytical skills and find ways to predict the movement in the market accurately, you have to use a set of strategies to capitalize on that prediction. As you get into the advanced levels of your options trading, these trading methods will become familiar to you and enable you to make better profits with the trading capital at disposal. Advanced technical indicators help you to know which of the trades meets your analysis and outlook on the market so that you can be able to generate profits.

The following are the top advanced technical indicators for options trading:

1. Relative Strength Index
2. Commodity Channel Index
3. Stochastics
4. Fibonacci retracements
5. Debit Spreads
6. Credit Spreads
7. Butterfly Spreads
8. Iron Condors

Chapter 21

Selling Options

Selling options is a strategy that is used to generate regular income. In a sense, advanced techniques. Selling options is a little simpler but carries a higher risk. We have talked about selling options a little bit already, but we will look at the most basic ways to do it here first, before talking about selling naked options.

Review of Selling Covered Calls

If you have 100 or more shares of a particular stock, you can sell covered calls against your shares. This is a common strategy used by people to earn money off their shares, but you always face the risk that your shares will be called away if the option is exercised. One strategy that can be used is to sell out of the money calls when you don't expect the share price to rise to the strike price of the call option over the lifetime of the contract.

For example, Facebook is trading at $190.25 a share. You can sell a $210 call for $0.64, so for all 100 shares, one option contract would net you $64. This is for an expiration date in 30 days. Or you could take a higher level of risk and sell a $195 call for $4.05, which would give you a premium of $405 per option contract. If you had 500 shares, then you'd receive $2,025 in premiums. Not a bad passive income, and all you have to do is hope that the share price stays below the strike price.

If the share price closes in on the strike price, then you will be faced with a dilemma—risk having the option exercised if the share price rises above the strike price or you can buy back the option and cut into your profits. With a few days left to expiration, the option you sold may be worth $2.05, so you could buy back the five options you sold, and you'd reduce your net profit to $1,000.

You could go further out, even selling LEAPS. In that case, the premium paid is much larger. A Facebook LEAP with a $195 call that expires in 18 months has a premium of $30.58, so selling five contracts for your 500 shares could bring in an income of $15,290. Of course, there is a higher risk that the share price will rise above the strike price over 18 months than there is over the short term.

The one principle to keep in mind selling covered calls is that you could lose your shares if the option is exercised. With that in mind, you should only select a strike price that is of a higher amount than what you had paid for the shares. That way, if you are forced to sell the shares, then you are not taking a loss doing so. That can make losing the shares easier to deal with. So if we had purchased our shares at $200 a share, we would not select a $195 strike price because that represents a potential loss, which would be given by the price we paid for the shares minus the strike price and then less the premium aid, in this case, $200 - $195 - $4.05 so we'd end up losing $0.95 on the trade. If you had purchased the shares at a lower price, say $190 a share, then the $195 strike would make sense since if the stock price rose and the shares were called away, we'd still profit by selling the shares.

Protected puts are the put version of a covered call. The risk with a protected put is that the shares will be "put to you," and you will have to buy the shares, so you will be required to have enough capital in your account to cover the purchase.

Of course, the trick to selling options is to pick a strike price where you think the option will expire worthlessly. There is always the risk that you are wrong, but if you think the share price is going to rise for Facebook, to use an example, you could sell a protected $190 put for $4.95, earning $495 per contract. If the share price rises, the options will expire worthlessly, and you would keep the premium and profit from the deal.

Selling Naked Puts

Selling naked puts is a popular strategy for traders that are given level 4 status. If you can get this level from your broker, you can consider this possibly profitable strategy. Of course, the key is choosing the right strike price.

When a put is "naked," that means it isn't backed by anything. However, you are still required by law to meet your obligations if the option is exercised, but one way that traders avoid this problem is by buying the options back if there is a chance they would be exercised. The time value may work in your favor, which will make the options cheaper and so you can buy them back and still profit.

Another consideration is to choose a relatively low implied volatility, which reduces the chances that the stock will move much over the lifetime of the option. But that is a trade-off as well, as implied volatility that is a few points higher can result in a large increase in the premium received for selling the option.

Consider IBM. The stock price is at $139.20, but you could sell a 30 day $135 put for $2.44, or $244. You could even sell in the money puts. A $145 put would sell for $748 if you sold five contracts that would be a 30-day income of $3,640.

Selling in the money puts could be risky, but beneficial if it was believed that IBM shares were set to rise in price. If the price rises above the strike price, then the options will expire worthlessly.

Selling LEAPS, while it carries a higher risk for a long time to expiration, gives a higher probability that the option will move in the amount and also allows you to sell at high premiums. A $130 put for IBM expiring in 18 months would sell for $13.20, so selling five contracts would give you a premium of $6,600. Bid-Ask spreads can be large for LEAPS and the volume is probably small. For this particular option, we find that the bid-ask spread is about 80 cents, which isn't too bad, meaning selling it might not be that difficult. Daily volume is small at 10, but the open interest is 1,282. Experienced traders often recommend an open interest of 500 or higher since that indicates enough people are buying the contracts.

The risk with naked puts is that you will be forced to buy the shares. Again, if it looks like that might turn out to be the case, you can buy the contracts back. Selling out of the money options that expire in the near term can leave you in a better position since the options will probably expire worthlessly, and you will be able to keep the premium without having to buy back the options. If you have to buy the shares, the loss would be the share price minus the market price. But of course, you'd have to get the capital to buy the shares as well.

So if you sold a put option on IBM with a strike price of $138 expiring in 6 weeks, it would sell for $3.70. If the share price dropped to $136, you'd have to use cash to buy the shares at $138, and possibly lose $2 a share by selling them—or you could simply keep them and wait for the price to go back up. Plus, your loss would be offset by the premium, so your break-even point is the amount of the strike price minus the premium paid.

Selling Naked Calls

You can also sell naked calls. This means that you sell call options without owning the shares of stock. The risk that the option will be exercised means that you would have to buy the shares at a higher market price and then sell them at the lower strike price. So the key here would be to sell out of the money calls at strike prices that you doubt the stock will reach over the lifetime of the option. The same strategies can be used and if it looks like the share price is rising, you can buy the options back to avoid being assigned.

Looking at IBM, some modest out of the money call options 30 days to expiration have good prices. A $141 call, which is almost $2 out of the money, is $3.55, so selling one contract would give you $355.

Suppose that stock was trading at $195 a share. You could sell a call with a 45-day expiration with a strike price of $200 for $4.46, or $446. If we find that the share price has risen to $197 with ten days to expiration, the calls would now be priced at $1.88, or $188. So you could buy them back and still have a profit of $258 per contract, avoiding the risk that you would be assigned if the share price kept rising. Of course, at $3 out of the money, you might wait. When the price of the share rises to $199 with seven days left, the calls would be $218, so you'd be cutting a little more into your profits. But if it dropped $1 the next day, then the call option would only be worth $1.58.

Remember, when you sell options, you make money on the time premium; or put another way, time decay is your friend. Out of the money, options lose value rapidly as the expiration date approaches.

The biggest risk with selling naked call options if you can't buy them back is having to buy the shares at a high price and then selling them at a loss to honor your obligations. Supposed that a stock is trading at $95 a share, and you sell a call option that has a $100 strike price. If the stock breaks out and, say, rises to $130 a share, someone might exercise the option. Since you sold the call naked, you'd be forced to buy the shares at $130 and sell them at the $100 strike price, losing $30 a share, which would be partially offset by the premium, which might be around $1 per share.

So selling naked calls can be profitable, but carries a lot of risks as well. The key to selling naked calls successfully is picking the right strike price and choosing a stock that you don't believe is going to be having price movements that are large enough to cause the option to be in the money.

Broker May Force Sale

Note that options that expire in the money may be automatically exercised by most brokerages, so you will not want to let an option expire in the money unless you are prepared to buy or sell the shares as required.

Chapter 22
Tips for Success

Know when to go off-book: While sticking to your plan, even when your emotions are telling you to ignore it, is the mark of a successful trader; however, this in no way means that you must blindly follow your plan 100 percent of the time. You will, without a doubt, find yourself in a situation from time to time where your plan is going to be rendered completely useless by something outside of your control. You need to be aware enough of your plan's weaknesses, as well as changing market conditions, to know when following your predetermined course of action is going to lead to failure instead of success. Knowing when the situation is changing versus when your emotions are trying to hold sway is something that will come with practice, but even being aware of the disparity, it is a huge step in the right direction.

Avoid trades that are out of the money. While there are a few strategies out there that make it a point of picking up options that are currently out of the money, you can rest assured that they are most certainly the exception, not the rule. Remember, the options market is not like the traditional stock market, which means that even if you are trading options based on underlying stocks buying low and selling high is just not a viable strategy. If a call has dropped out of the money, there is generally less than a 10 percent chance that it will return to acceptable levels before it expires, which means that if you purchase these types of options, what you are doing is a little better than gambling. You can find ways to gamble with odds in your favor of much higher than 10 percent.

Avoid clinging too tightly to your initial strategy. Your primary business strategy is one that must always constantly evolve as the circumstances surrounding your business habits change and evolve as well. Also, outside of your main strategy, you will eventually want to create additional plans that are more specifically tailored to various market states or specific strategies that are only useful in a narrow band of situations. Remember, the more prepared you are before starting a trading day, the higher your overall profit level; It's as simple as that.

Use the extension. If you are not completely risk averse, when it comes to taking advantage of volatile trading, the best thing to do is to use margin as a way to safeguard your existing investments while also making a profit. To use a long margin, you'll want to generate a call and put option, both with the same underlying asset, expiration details, and share amounts, but with two very different strike prices. The call option should have a higher strike price and will mark the upper limit of your profits, and the put option will have a lower strike price that will mark the lower limit of your losses. When creating a margin, it is important that you buy both halves at the same time, as doing it in intervals and streaks can add strange variables to the formula that are difficult to adjust correctly.

Never proceed without knowing the market’s mood. While using a personalized trading plan is always the right choice, having one doesn’t change the fact that it is extremely important to consider the market's mood before moving forward with the day’s trades. First of all, it is important to note that the collective will of all traders currently participating in the market is as strong as anything else more concrete, including market news. Even if companies release good news to various outlets and the news is not quite as good as everyone was anticipating it to be, then related prices can still decrease.

To get a good idea of what the current market's mood is like, you are going to want to know the average daily numbers that are common for your market and be on the lookout for them to start dropping sharply. While a day or two of major fluctuation can be completely normal, anything longer than that is a sure sign that something is up. Additionally, you will always want to be aware of what the major players in your market are up to.

Never get started without a clear plan for entry and exit. While finding your first set of entry/exit points can be difficult without experience to guide you, you must have them locked down before starting trading, even if the stakes are relatively low. Unless you are extremely lucky, starting without a clear idea of the playing field is going to do little but lose your money. If you are not sure about what limits you should set, start with a generalized pair of points and work on fine-tuning it from there.

More important than setting entry and exit points, however, is using them, even when there is still the appearance of money on the table. One of the biggest hurdles that new options traders need to get over is the idea that you need to wring every last cent out of every successful trade. The fact of the matter is that, as long as you have a profitable trading plan, then there will always be more profitable trades in the future which means that instead of worrying about a small extra profit you should be more concerned with protecting the profit that the trade has already netted you. While you can occasionally make some extra profit by ignoring this tip, you are likely to lose much more than you make as profits hit an unexpected peak and begin to fall again before you can effectively pull the trigger. If you are still having a hard time with this concept, consider this: options trading is a marathon, not a sprint, slow and steady will always win the race.

Never double down. When they are caught up in the heat of the moment, many new options traders will find themselves in a scenario where the best way to recoup a serious loss is to double down on the underlying stock in question at its newest, significantly lowered, price to make a profit under the assumption that things are going to turn around and then continue to do so to the point that everything is completely profitable once again. While it can be difficult to get rid of an underlying stock that was once extremely profitable, doubling it is rarely the right decision. If you are at a point where you do not know if the trade you are about to make will be a good choice, all you need to do is ask yourself if you would do the same if you were in the blind situation, the answer should tell you everything. you need to know.

If you are in a time when doubling seems like the right choice, you will need to have the strength to convince yourself to withdraw from that investment platform and cut your losses as thoroughly as possible, given the current situation. The sooner you cut your losses and exit the trade that ended badly, the sooner you can start investing energy and investments in a trade that still has the potential to make a profit.

Never take anything personally. It is human nature to build stories around and, therefore, form relationships with all manner of inanimate objects, including individual stocks or currency pairs. This is why it is perfectly natural to feel a closer connection to particular trades, and possibly even consider throwing out your plan when one of them takes an unexpected dive. However, thinking and acting are two very different things, which is why being aware of these trends is so important to avoid them at all costs.

This scenario occurs as often with trades moving in positive as well as negative directions, but the results will always be the same. Specifically, it can be tempting to hang on to a given trade much longer than you might decide simply because you're on a hot streak that shows no signs of stopping. In these cases, the best option is to sell half of your shares and then set a new goal based on the updated information to ensure that you are fit to have your cake and eat it too.

Not taking your choice of broker seriously. With so many things to consider, it is easy to understand why many new option traders simply settle on the first broker that they find and go about their business from there. However, the fact of the matter is that the broker you choose is going to be a huge part of your overall trading experience, which means that the importance of choosing the right one should not be discounted if you are hoping for the best experience possible. This means that the first thing you are going to want to do is dig past the friendly exterior of their website and get to the meat and potatoes of what it is they truly offer. Remember, creating an eye-catching website is easy, filling it will legitimate information when you have ill intent is much more difficult.

First things first. This means looking into their history of customer service as a way of not only ensuring that they treat their customers in the right way, but also of checking to see that quality of service is where it needs to be as well. Remember, when you make a trade every second count, which means that if you need to contact your broker for help with a trade, you need to know that you are going to be speaking with a person who can solve your problem as quickly as possible. The best way to ensure the customer service is up to snuff is to give them a call and see how long it takes for them to get back to you. If you wait more than a single business day, take your business elsewhere as if they are this disinterested in a new client, consider what the service is going to be like when they already have you right where they want you.

With that out the way, the next thing you will need to consider is the fees that the broker is going to charge in exchange for their services. There is very little regulation when it comes to these fees, which means it is going to pay to shop around. In addition to fees, it is important to consider any account minimums that are required as well as any fees having to do with withdrawing funds from the account.

Chapter 23
How to Become a Millionaire with Options Trading

Most investors and traders at the securities markets often aim to buy low then sell high and make a profit. However, options traders are the key layers in any market. This is because they can earn large amounts of money, regardless of market conditions.

The options traders can make money in any market environment, even where there are no trades up or down. The reason is that options contracts are flexible in different ways. This versatility is what makes them such powerful market tools for continued profitability. Here are some profitable approaches that you can adopt.

Writing options

One of the best ways of winning at options is to write options. You can write some pretty sophisticated strategies which are capable of earning your top dollars. Take speculators, for instance. Now, any time they write a contract, they get paid for it. It is investors who pay for the options contracts.

As a writer, you get to earn what is known as a premium. This is money that you earn even if the investor doesn't eventually use it. It is possible to write profitable commodities-based options regularly. Speculators can come up with profitable options that they believe will fare well in the options markets. All you need to do is be on the lookout because writing an options contract without a suitable position on the underlying security can be rather risky.

The Straddle Strategy

This is another approach that can help you get rich with options trading. Options mostly involve the buying of security that then turns profitable when the underlying commodity moves in a particular direction. It could be up or down, but all that is necessary is a movement. A straddle is a great choice of options investment vehicle because it doesn't desire a specific outcome, as is the case in other situations.

With a straddle, you can purchase both calls and put options with the same expiry dates and at similar strike times. The combination strategy can be successful if and only if the underlying security of the option sees a movement in either direction, as long as the movement is large enough to cover the cost of premiums in both directions. Speculators can write straddle options if they believe that it is going to do well in the market.

The Collar Strategy

We also have a strategy known as the collar strategy. It is considered a pretty challenging options strategy to understand. However, a seasoned speculator can write one for you, but only if he/she owns the underlying asset. By owning the asset, he can take the risk.

In this instance, the best option is an out-of-the-money put option. This is beneficial because if the price of the raw material falls, the losses will only be minimal, since it is a put option. However, if the product moves up, the trader will make a considerable profit.

The Strangle Strategy

The strangle strategy is, in some ways, similar to the straddle. The only difference is that they have different strike prices. For speculators, it is possible to use the information available to enter a low-cost position.

When a trader or speculator opts for this strategy, they choose a low-cost entry because either or both of the options contracts may be bought out-of-the-money. As such, it may not be worthwhile exercising the right afforded by the shares. Both the straddle and strangle can be written by a speculator or even the trader.

So, what is the Most Profitable Options Strategy?

We have now looked at quite several options trading strategies, all of which are profitable and easy to execute. There are more than 40 different variations of options trading techniques. This makes it a pretty difficult job to determine the most profitable options trading strategy.

A lot of the time, traders try to find trades that will not lose their money. Also, there is a lot of varied opinions out there about the best and most profitable strategies. Fortunately, most options trading strategies offer very attractive returns with huge margins being quite common. However, it can be a risky venture, so it is advisable to proceed with caution even as you seek to become a wealthy millionaire.

A lot of people have made their wealth trading stock options. Many of them use different winning techniques and strategies. There is not one single strategy that works for everyone. What is important is having a great trading plan. First, get the education that you need and learn all about options trading. Next, you should put what you have learned into practice and continue practicing until you become an excellent options trader. You will then only need to identify your analysis tools and software before eventually starting to trade.

Options trading Is Quite Profitable

Some express concern about profitability as well as risks posed by options trading. Fortunately, it has been proven, over the years, to be quite profitable.

- Trade-in options provide you with leverage, which offers you the inherent right to control a huge number of shares. This kind of leverage offers returns far greater than what selling stocks only can offer.
- If you can make use of the leverage afforded by stock options, then you stand a great chance of making huge profits. These are profits made from just minuscule movements of the underlying stocks. By identifying the right strategies, then you will be able to make money regardless of the prevailing market conditions.

- This means making profits even when there is no movement in the market. However, with some strategies, you may lose money if you make a wrong move. Therefore, sufficient care needs to be taken to mitigate against any such losses as they can be significant.

The Most Profitable Options Trading Strategy

It is advisable, to begin with, the most basic options trading strategies first. This is the way most options traders start. By using these simple options trading strategies, you stand to make huge returns on your investments and trading skills. It is possible to enjoy a 100% return on investment within a couple of days and sometimes even in just a couple of hours.

You can also find plenty of websites and advisory services that provide advisory services and trading assistance to traders. Some trades may fail. But it is also likely that most of your trades will be successful. Therefore, a good strategy or approach for this challenge would be to make sure to do multiple trades each time. Ensure that your strategy will win you money even though one or two trades may lose some money.

What you need to do to achieve this level of success is to work hard on your technical analysis skills. With excellent analysis skills, you will be able to analyze trades and be able to accurately determine which ones are winners and which ones you should possibly avoid. Therefore, learn to use your technical analysis tools and skills and then put them to practice often. It is only with deep knowledge of technical analysis and lots of practice that you will then be able to hone your skills and become and wealthy and successful options trader.

Consistently Profitable Strategies - Selling Puts & Credit Spreads

There are some studies conducted by reputable institutions that indicate that the two most profitable options trading strategies are selling credit spreads and selling put options. The study found that the profits from such trades are consistent and regular over a long period. However, the study found something else. The study reveals that buying call and put options is more profitable in the long run, although it is not as consistent. You can earn between 7% and 12% per month on the total portfolio, which is approximately 84% to more than 144% per year. Considering that the techniques used are elementary, easy to apply and require the most basic technical analysis, then your chances of making money without stress are very high. You can expect to earn more than 80% from your trades if you create the right trading plan.

Overall Best Options Trading Strategy

According to findings, it is widely accepted that you will make the most profits selling puts. If you invested many of your trading resources into selling put options, then you stand to make a lot of money consistently and with very little risk of loss.

The only challenge with the selling option is that it has certain limitations. This is because selling put options works best in a market that trends upwards or is on the rise. You can complement selling puts with selling ITM puts for long term contracts. These are contracts that last six months or longer. They will make you tons of money simply because of the effect of time decay.

Also, when you sell, as a trader on the options market, credit spreads, you will be able to take advantage of the market in both directions. This means you will profit from an upward as well as downward market trend. This is great as even smaller traders can make some money regardless of experience. Therefore, always remember not to search for the size of the profits. When searching for the most profitable and successful options strategy, focus on factors like:

- Ability to come up with a reliable and safe plan
- Have a plan that generates regular income
- Associated risks are low
- Technical requirements are manageable

Sell Naked Puts is one of the most lucrative ways of making money trading options. The return on margin is almost as lucrative as selling credit spreads. However, it doesn't carry a similar level of risk. In short, anytime that you sell a put option, then you make it possible to purchase a stock at a price of your choosing.

A Closer Look at Naked Puts

It is the end of June, and XYZ stock is at $50. However, the market is fluctuating, and you prefer to buy this stock for $45. What you need to do at this stage is to sell a $45 put option for $2. You can put the expiration date on this option as the third week of July. Once you post the option, you will immediately receive $200 into your trading account. Now should the XYZ stock price fall below $45, you will be required to purchase 100 units. This will cost you $4,500.

Chapter 24
Predicting Directions

The world is full of uncertainty, and the stock market responds accordingly. Sure, financial instruments are based on the so-called fundamentals like monetary policy, interest rates and equity essentials like sales and taxes. We have a stereotype of market makers as being steely-eyed, cold and calculating automatons. They are not. They are human beings and are as emotionally involved in the market as an investor, 'man-on-the-street,' or anyone else. Emotions often affect the market based on the sometimes-irrational response to this uncertainty. Recent events like the BREXIT outcome are examples of that emotional reaction.

Basic academic economic theory assumes that investors act rationally, i.e., a manner that best satisfies their economic interests. In the real world, markets don't always act rationally because human beings don't always act rationally.

Certain internal events will affect market performance like the end of quarter movements by fund managers to establish positions to make their quarterly reports look better. You can also observe drops in stock prices and indexes on Fridays, as holders get ready for the weekend by taking profits. Predicting market moves is sometimes like reading tea leaves, with a similar amount of hocus-pocus and mystery. However, successful investors learn or develop a sense of where the market is going and when.

There are five things an investor must do to succeed. They are pretty obvious, but we need to keep them in mind. The first is the Fundamental Analysis, the second is the Technical Analysis, and they are sort of the 'meat and potatoes' of trading. Perhaps more important are the next three, Intuition, Patience, and Attention.

Intuition

Intuition can lead to many really good investments. Some years ago, a family was making regular vacation trips from Michigan to Florida. They soon noticed a new restaurant chain along the interstate highway called Cracker Barrel. Whenever they stopped at one, they had to stand in line, and the food was very good and at good prices. As they made more trips, they noticed that more and more Cracker Barrel restaurants were opening, all with the same waiting line. They invested in CRBL and watched the stock rise, from their entry price of about $5.00 to today's trading range of $150 to $175. That decision was an excellent example of intuition in trading. CBRL had identified a niche and filled it with good service and products.

L'eggs is a similar story. Consumers quickly reacted positively to the quality of the product and the catchy advertising, introduced in 1969. Those L'eggs plastic egg-like containers were a hit with crafts workers and carried the stock of Hanes to new highs. Many investors noticed that L'eggs was the right product at the time, was good quality and had an exciting marketing promotion. This is the essence of the Intuition component of successful investing. Look for products that are satisfying a market niche, have good quality and are well received by consumers.

Patience

Investing in the market, whether by buying and selling stocks themselves or by trading in options, requires patience. Sometimes an investor gets nervous and makes an irrational move just out of uncertainty. Traders must learn to be patient. No market moves so fast that the trader cannot make the proper trade in response to some change. Remember, trading options is not for the faint of heart. Nervous responses to extraneous conditions can wreck a well-planned strategy.

Attention

There is also no substitute for paying attention to the market and your positions. No, you don't have to spend every hour of every day watching the big boards. Remember that trading options are not a 'set it and forget it' activity. Traders can build very solid portfolios and make a handsome profit, but like any other job, the trader has to be current, not just in the market moves but also in global news and reports. Some resources have delightful features like daily free videos on changes in the market and outlooks from their experts. Keeping current is essential. Some traders will close out all positions while they are on vacation, and then resume trading when they return. And since most people use portable computer devices, laptops, tablets, smartphones, and so forth, they can spend time even on vacation, trading and investing. Either way, you choose to do it, remember that options trading requires the investor to pay attention. Make that commitment before you start.

There are many tools available to traders and analysts to predict what is going to happen, at least to some extent. There are two schools of thought on the subject of market predicting; technical and fundamental methods used by informed investors. Most traders use a mixture of the two.

Fundamental Analysis

Fundamental analysis looks at several indicators to determine, at least as an estimate, the direction of the economy, various industry groups and individual stocks.

It begins with the general trend of the entire economy, both national and global. That old saying about the flapping wings of a butterfly in Africa causing a hurricane in Florida suggests that no national economy exists in a vacuum. There is enormous interaction between them and among them. When the general economy rises, just like the tide, all individual boats rise, but not necessarily equally. Similarly, when the economy contracts, all sectors contract but not equally. Some sectors will contract more than others. In an expanding economy, sectors like technology, biotech, electronics manufacturing and cyclical industries like major appliances and automobiles tend to expand.

Here are some more cyclical industries:

- Heavy equipment
- Discretionary consumer goods
- Machines and tooling
- Restaurants and hotels
- Airlines

Typically, these stocks have a high Beta (β), meaning they respond quickly and strongly to fluctuations in the national and global economies.

Non-cyclical industries are those who are relatively safe during downturns, sectors like utilities, consumer staples, energy and retailers. Counter-cyclical are those that can even thrive in economic downturns, like discount retailers, auto parts retailers and big-box building suppliers.

Importantly, for option traders, option prices respond to the volatility and trend of the underlying stocks, so traders need to pay close attention to the business cycle and sectors of interest to them.When an investor or options trader has identified the economic trend, i.e., expanding or contracting, he/she will then focus on a sector of interest like durable goods, finance or hospitality, to name just a few. Within that sector or industry, they will then examine the individual companies, looking for those who will lead the way. They will do this by evaluating the company's business model, business plan, management quality and firm financials. Assessments of business models and business plans can be gained from resources like analyst's reports, annual reports and public commentary. They will examine management quality by looking at results, internal business indicators like return on investment, return on sales, and debt levels compared with market capitalization. They will read and understand the various documents like the balance sheet, the income or profit and loss statement, cash flow positions and debt positions for the firm they are interested in. Most of this information is available online and through public documents, including annual reports. Documents like annual reports, of course, are written by insiders and may not be completely objective. Various industry analysts and experts may offer more objective insights. These are available through brokers and online sites.

Technical Analysis

Many investors base their trading decisions on technical factors that look at past performance with knowledge of present and past economic conditions. This analysis is dominated by examining charts that reflect stock performance over some time. Using these charts, they can estimate upcoming stock moves and therefore act on those forecasts by buying and selling options. The following charts describe some important market moves that any options trader needs to know.

The Symmetrical Triangle in Chart 1 shows a stock that is trading within a diminishing range. The upper line represents a resistance line, and the lower is the support line. As the price varies between these converging lines, it is often an indication of a coming breakout. With a breakout to the upside, the options trader will buy calls to cover a long position in anticipation of the upside swing. On the other hand, if the pattern shows a likelihood of a breakout below the support line, the trader might choose to buy puts in anticipation of the drop in market price.

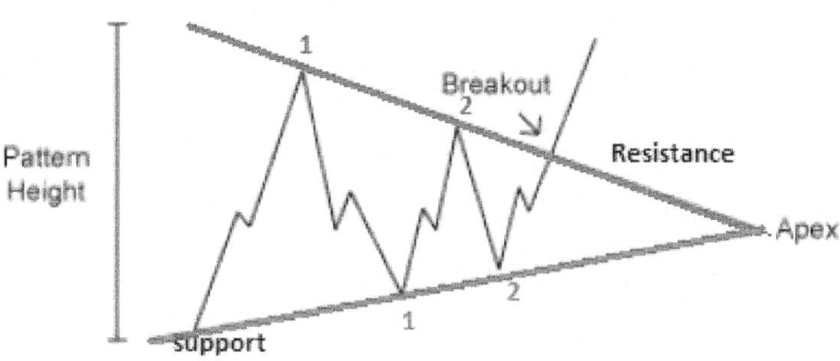

Chart 1 Symmetrical Triangle

The triangle pattern, in its three forms, is one of the common stock patterns for day trading that you should be aware of. Triangle patterns can also be pointed upward or downward, showing a general tendency for the stock to rise or fall.

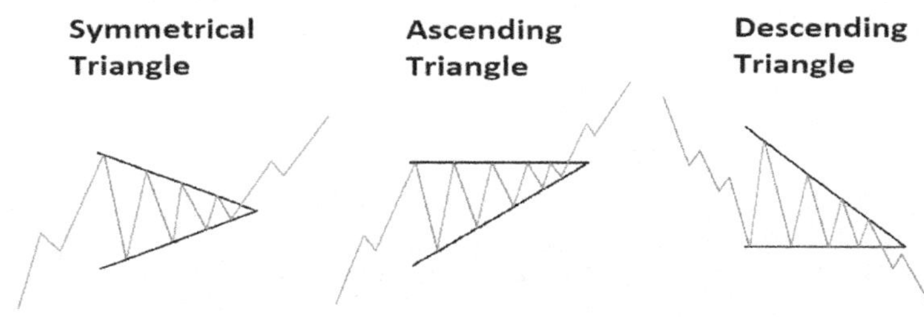

Chart 2 shows a condition called a triple top. The triple top is a type of chart pattern used in technical analysis to predict the reversal in the movement of an asset's price. Consisting of three peaks, a triple top signals that the asset may no longer be rallying, and that lower prices may be on the wayThe horizontal dotted line below the chart is the support line, and the upper dotted line is the resistance line. The chart shows the market price breaking out low. This is an occasion to sell puts. The pattern could have broken out upward, crossing the resistance line.

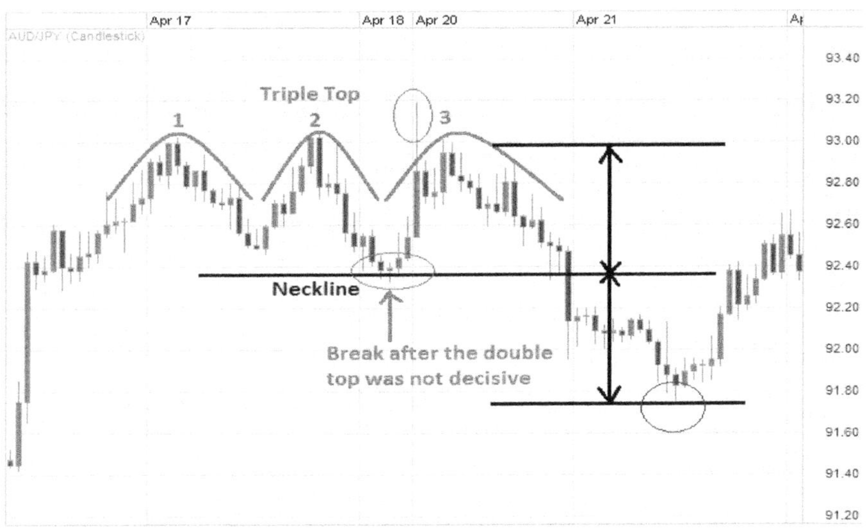

Chart 2 Triple Top

Notice that that chart can also be inverted, making a triple bottom. These charts indicate the direction of the stock and tips the options trader off to trade in either puts or calls.

Chart 3 shows a pattern called 'head and shoulders.' A head and shoulders pattern is a chart formation that appears as a baseline with three peaks, the outside two are close in height and the middle is highest. In technical analysis, a head and shoulders pattern describes a specific chart formation that predicts a bullish-to-bearish trend reversal. This is slightly different from a triple top pattern in that the middle peak tends to be higher. Head and shoulders patterns can breakout either up or down. Either way, it presents an opportunity for options traders. The dotted line shows the recent support line. This pattern happens to break out down, but it very well could have broken out upward.

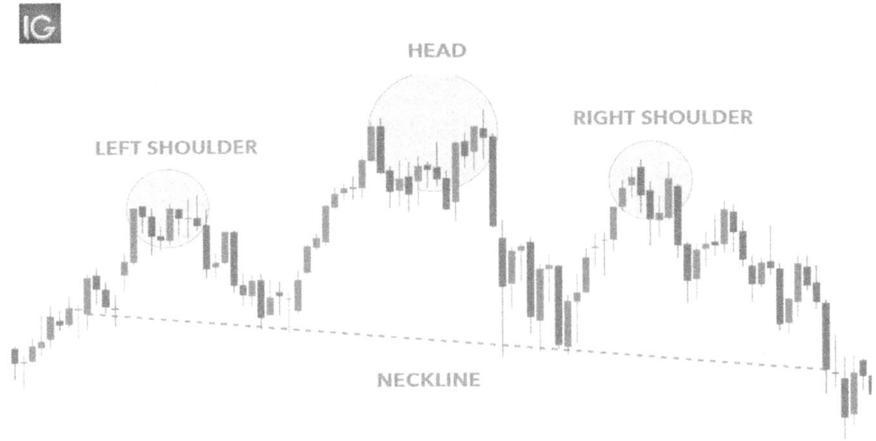

Chart 3 Head and Shoulders

Bollinger Bands

Bollinger bands are probability bands around a moving average line. These bands are usually set at either 1 or 2 standard deviations from the historical stock prices, the closing prices for each day. And the movement outside the Bollinger Bands indicates a change in the underlying stock reflecting market changes. So, breaking through the Bollinger Band acts as a signal to the options trader to take action.

Many other technical indicators are valuable to options traders. The various resources will provide excellent education and insights to both fundamental and technical analysis techniques. Most investors and traders use both fundamental and technical analysis, and the combination is a personal preference. Just make sure you are familiar with the various indicators and what they can tell you. Be careful to use the correct tools for each condition. There is no "one size fits all" tool; each trader has to develop her system of analysis. The key to success is Intuition, Patience, and Attention.

Conclusion

First of all, we would point out that the whole guide was written without relying on any kind of fee. As we already mentioned, fees vary, and every brokerage house has its own rules about it.

- Trading options have significant risks. If you are inexperienced with trading, we would recommend talking with a financial advisor before making any decision.
- Always keep in mind that every investment has its own risk and reward rating, which means that if the risk is high, the reward will be high too.
- Expiration date of American style options and European style options (the most commonly used ones) is always the third Saturday in the month for American and the last Friday before the third Saturday for European options.
- Phrase "in the money" describes that the option has a value higher than the strike price for call options and lower than the strike price for put options at the time of their expiration.

- The most common minimal bid for option sharing is one nickel or 5 dollars per contract. However, some more liquid contracts allow minimal bid to be one dollar per contract.
- 100 shares of the certain stock are one option contract
- If you pay 1 dollar for an option your premium for that option whether you buy or sell it is 1 dollar per share, which means that the option premium is 100 dollars per contract.
- All of the examples in this guide assume that every option order ever mentioned was filled successfully.
- Whenever you want to open a new position, you will have to sell or buy on the market to “open”. The same principle applies if you wish to close your position. You sell or buy to “close”.
- Phrase Open Interest represents the number of option contracts that are opened at the moment. Logically- more opened contracts mean a bigger number, and closed contracts mean a smaller number.
- Volume of the options is the number of contracts that are traded in one single day.

Be careful when signing the contracts; make sure you read all of the trading options.

They can be extremely profitable, but learning to trade them well takes time. You can choose to use indicators to determine your entry points, and I'm all for this approach at first, but remember that over the long term, you're better served learning the basics of order flow and using that.

There is no shortage of options strategies you can use to limit your risk dramatically, and depending on the volatility levels, you can deploy separate strategies to achieve the same ends. Contrast this with a directional trading strategy where you have just one method of entry, which is to either go short or go long, and only one way of managing risk, which is to use a stop loss.

Spread or market neutral trading puts you in the position of not having to care about what the market does. Besides, it brings another dimension of the market into focus, which is volatility. Volatility is the greatest thing for your gains, and options allow you to take full advantage of this, no matter what the volatility situation currently is.

Options can be a bit hard to get your head around at first since so many of us are used to looking at the market as a thing that goes up or down. Options bring a sideways and a different vertical element to it via spreads and volatility estimates. More advanced options strategies take full advantage of volatility and are more math-focused, so if this interests you, you should go for them.

That being said, don't assume the complexity means more gains. The strategies shown here are quite simple, and they will make you money thanks to the way options are structured. They bring you the advantage of leverage without having to borrow a single cent.

You can choose to borrow, of course, but you need to do this only if it is in line with your risk management math. Risk management is what will make or break your results, and at the center of quantitative risk management is your risk per trade. Keep this consistent and line up your success rate and reward to risk ratios, and you'll make money as a mathematical certainty.

Qualitative risk management requires you to adopt the right mindset with regards to trading, and you must adopt this as quickly as possible. Remember that the implications of your risk math mean that you need not be concerned with the outcome of a single trade. Instead, seek to maximize your gains over the long term.

The learning curve might get steep at times, but given the rewards on offer, this is a small price to pay. Keep hammering away at your skills, and soon you'll find yourself trading options profitably, and everything will be worth it. How much can you expect to make trading options?

Well, I said that I am not keen on putting numbers to this sort of thing. Generally, good options trade can expect around 50-80% returns on their capital. As you grow in size, this return amount will decrease naturally. However, to start with, these are beyond excellent returns.

Always make sure you're well-capitalized since this is the downfall of many traders. You need to be patient with the process. Many people rush headfirst into the market without adequate capitalization or learning and soon find that the markets are far tougher than they thought. So always ensure the mental stress you place yourself in is low and that you're never in a position where you 'have' to make money trading.

I wish you the best of luck in all of your trading efforts. The key to success is to simply never give up and to be resilient. Reduce the stress on yourself, and you'll be fine. Here is wishing you all the success in your options trading journey!

OPTIONS TRADING

The Best SWING and DAY Investing Strategies on How to Make Money and Maximize Your Profit in The Market, Becoming an intelligent and Profitable Investor. For Beginners

Ray Bears

Introduction

In the golden days, stock trading took place on the actual trading floor or over the phone. That might seem very rudimentary now. But, those were the roots of the financial markets we have come to know today.

With the advent of the digital age, it was only logical that stock trading would take place with the aid of computers. Computer-based trading now represents one of the biggest reasons why financial markets have become so volatile.

Computer-based trading represents a considerable amount of the trading volume that happens daily. While you are still able to call your broker up to place an order, the fact of the matter is that virtually every type of transaction is automated.

That is an important point to bear in mind since automated trading is what has enabled the emergence of the day trader. As such, day trading is a phenomenon which has enabled countless individuals to take control of their trading strategies and develop their investment strategy.

Consequently, we need to define what day trading is and how this might be a good option for you.

Definition of day trading

When you think of equities markets (stocks and bonds), I am sure you get images of Hollywood films in which bloodthirsty stockbrokers are engaging in high-risk, high-leverage deals in which they put their livelihood, and that of their investors, in harm's way.

Many of these films have glorified the irresponsible practices that stockbrokers have engaged in throughout the history of financial markets. Some have made it big, but countless others have been burned to the ground.

So, the role of a stockbroker is to take investors' money and put it to work in the stock market. Now, you generally hear the term "stock market" commonly used as an umbrella term to refer to financial markets in general. The more appropriate term to be used in this case should be "financial markets" as there are several different types of markets. In that regard, the stock market is where shares of a publicly-traded company are bought and sold on a daily basis. When I say "daily basis," I mean Monday through Friday as all markets break for the weekend. As a day trader, this is something that you need to keep in mind as Friday afternoon should be the time in which you are powering down.

Since the United States and virtually all nations that have mature stock markets have regulations in place which limit the amount of participation an average investor can have in the stock market, virtually all trading is done through brokerage firms.

I am sure that you have seen the ads on television for these firms (I will not name names to avoid it appearing that I am endorsing anyone). These firms offer a myriad of products and funds in which they can place their money. These funds are managed by individual stockbrokers, or money managers, who are duly licensed.

These brokers are the ones who place the trades and make the deals happen on a daily basis. It should be noted that a licensed broker has something which is known as a "fiduciary responsibility." This means that their responsibility is to make money for their clients and not for themselves.

Whether they do, that is up to the financial institution and the brokers themselves. However, if a rogue broker goes out and does their thing, the chances of this stockbroker landing in jail are almost assured.

Besides, financial institutions will not risk having their licenses revoked and even worse, having their customers bail on them because it has been proven that they are irresponsible in the management of their customer's money.

I would encourage you to watch the Hollywood film "Wall Street." This film depicts the irresponsible behavior that rogue traders engage in. One of the characters in the films ends up in jail while some of the other characters get away scot-free. If you believe that it is just a film and it is meant for entertainment purposes, I would like to tell you that similar events have happened in real life. So, you should not be surprised to learn that this film is not too distant from reality.

Now, you might be asking yourself what this has to do with day trading.

Well, it has everything to do with day trading.

You see, with the advent of computer-based trading and the internet, brokerage firms caught on to one of their customers' biggest requests: to be given access to trading stocks themselves.

This is an enormous shift in the traditional paradigm of stock trading. The almighty stockbroker, that often-glorified character, has now taken a secondary role as anyone can open their account and trade for themselves.

And while it is as simple as opening an account and getting started, being successful at it is not quite that simple. In fact, that is why we are here. We are here to learn about what day trading is that the tips and tricks that can help you become successful at it.

As such, day traders are individual investors, who play with their money (some of the more valiant day traders will take their friends' and family's money, too), will place their trades, and choose which companies they will invest in.

Thus, it is crucial to understand how markets work, how the pricing of stocks works, and how you can make money from these trades. These are the types of things that stockbrokers go to school to learn. However, you can learn them, too. It is not some occult science which only a privileged few had access to. In the past, it was like that, but not anymore. The internet has blocked the doors of this type of secrecy and hidden agenda.

Notwithstanding, an individual investor who opens his account and does his trading has total control of what is traded, when and at what price points. Now, the defining characteristic of day traders is that they open and close their positions within the same trading day. That means that they will not leave any open positions after the close of the trading day.

As such, if a day trader starts his trading day with $100, he will end his day with the same $100, plus some additional cash from the day's profits, hopefully. So that means that the day trader starts with cash and ends with cash.

Of course, you can keep open positions for far longer than that, but then having open positions for more extended periods refers to other types of trading. Consequently, day traders live from day to day. While they are keenly focused on what may or may not happen down the road, they are intent on making very short-time trades and profits.

You will learn why opening and closing positions within the same trading day is both crucial and useful as it reduces the overall risk of investors.

The difference between day trading vs. other types of trading

Since we have established that day traders, by definition, open and close their positions on the same trading day, it is important to note that there are other types of traders out there.

In the end, the type of trading strategy boils down to the underlying philosophy of that investor. As such, it is crucial for you to understand what you hope to get out of your investment strategy.

Thus, are you looking to make as much profit as you can, are you thinking about a long-term strategy, or are you simply content with getting a return without being actively involved in any of the transactions?

The answer to these questions will determine what approach you will take in your strategy and the type of transactions that you will conduct.

But first, a word of caution: I would highly advise you to avoid betting the farm on any deal. I know that it is tempting to try to hit a home run. Sure, there are cases where you have heard about folks who have smoked a grand slam to deep center. But those trades are few and far between. Day trading is not the sexiest approach, but it is certainly an approach that will help you win most of the time.

Consequently, betting the farm opens the door for an increased level of risk that I would never advise you to take. Even the safest trade has an inherent level of risk. What this implies is that if you are not careful and do your due diligence, you will be asking for trouble.

That being said, it is important to understand other types of traders out there. While you might not marry one type of trading, you could alter your overall trading strategy so that you can incorporate various approaches as per your circumstances.

Swing traders

Swing traders are folks who act pretty much the same way as day traders do, except that these folks will leave an open position overnight or even for a couple of days. However, they are sure to cash out before markets close on Friday evening as leaving open positions over the weekend can be a recipe for trouble.

In essence, the risk of leaving open positions overnight lies in the fact that financial markets are very psychological. What that means is that if something happens overnight, you could get hammered by the results of events in other parts of the world.

One case that rocked a major corporation was the unfortunate crash of Boeing aircraft in various parts of the world. These accidents happened overnight (for North America) in other parts of the world.

So, investors who held stock in Boeing woke up one day to the news of the unfortunate accidents. Besides the tragic loss of life, Boeing took a serious hit as the transportation agencies of just about every developed nation in the world ordered the grounding of their airplanes.

This did serious damage to the stock of this corporation. Its share price dropped from a high of $439 per share to a low of $362 per share. Unless you were somehow shorting the stock (betting that it would lose value), you most likely took a hit. Boeing's stock has rebounded somewhat, but the damage has already been done.

The damage main lies in the loss of investor confidence. This is the most critical point when looking into stock prices as a loss of investor confidence can tank a company's stock in a very short time. In some cases, stocks have tanked in a matter of hours.

The last example illustrates how dangerous it could be to leave open positions overnight. So, if you plan to hold on to stocks for extended periods, then you need to be sure that this stock is going to remain stable.

Chapter 1

Step Guide on How to Make Money with Options

Before reading this article, you should, from now on, have a comprehensive understanding of how the options work. On the off chance that this is not the situation, I exceptionally prescribe looking at my Beginner Options Trading Course. In this article, I will introduce a generally popular options trading style, to be specific high likelihood option selling. It is imperative to peruse the whole article cautiously, although it is long, so do not skip ahead. Instead of skipping portions of the material, enjoy a reprieve, and return later to complete it.

Note this is not the best way to profit with options. There are limitless different strategies out there. This is only one extremely well-known trading style.

Selling Options Premium

Selling options and gathering premium is the main thought of this trading style. The objective is to sell options that, in the long run, will terminate uselessly or, if nothing else, lose a portion of their worth. A high likelihood option seller works very like an insurance agency. Think about the option as a protection contract. How about if we accept house protection, for instance? Individuals purchase house protections to secure themselves against the impossible occasion that their home will burn to the ground. The protection profits because the biggest share of all protections is not 'essential.' The majority of the sold protection contracts will never be utilized as most houses will not burn to the ground.

High likelihood option sellers attempt to do likewise. They sell (OTM) options and anticipate that they should terminate uselessly. The purchaser of that option seeks after the impossible occasion that the basic resource's price moves more than expected, so his option does not lapse uselessly.

Be that as it may, sometimes, somebody's home burns. At that point, the insurance agency needs to pay out their protection money. The equivalent goes for the option sellers. Not every sold option will lapse uselessly. Now and again, an option will not expire uselessly, however. Ideally, the profits from a previous couple of trades will cover this misfortune.

In the accompanying article, I will display how you can trade options like an insurance agency sells protections.

An Introduction to Probabilities

You may (or may not) perceive the accompanying graph from the likelihood hypothesis. The figure is a typical conveyance/standard deviation chart. Ordinary conveyance outlines are utilized on a wide range of stuff. This is the situation because most things have a specific typical dispersion.

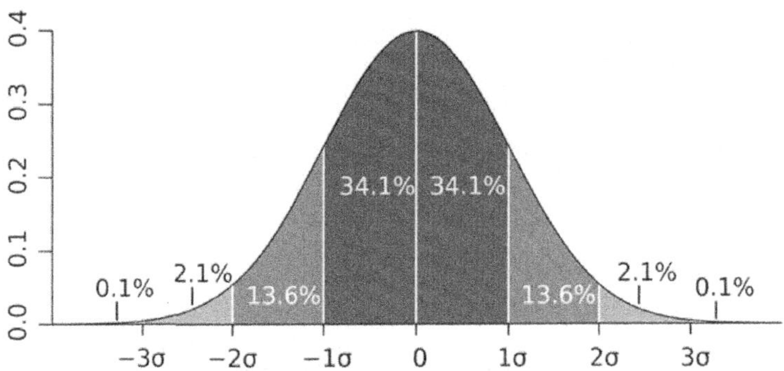

For instance, the vast majority have comparable body tallness. There are exemptions to both the up and drawback. Be that as it may, as a rule, the stature of by far most individuals is in a similar range. Along these lines, a typical dissemination graph can be utilized for sizes.

Around 68% surprisingly have body tallness in a specific range. The odds of having body tallness either under or over this range become littler the further you escape from the range. Somebody who is 2.10 meters (ca. 6,9 feet) could be viewed as an exception because truth be told, not very many individuals are this tall.

The equivalent can be applied to stocks and other trading resources. Stocks move in extents. As a general rule, stocks move maximal a couple of percent for every day (or even less). A $100 share, for the most part, does not run more than a couple of dollars all over consistently. Once in a while, a $100 stock goes up to $50 in one day. Hence, stock price development can be put into a standard deviation outline.

Variables to Consider

The significant principal factor that influences the likelihood of profit and the standard deviation is time left until lapse. If you give a stock's price ten days to move, it will, in all likelihood, move not exactly on the off chance that you would allow it 100 days.

A 10% move within one or a couple of days is substantially less likely than a 10% move in a year.

Along these lines, the typical conveyance outline of an advantage with heaps of time will be more extensive than an ordinary circulation chart with a brief period.

How about we return to the XYZ model one more time:

We said that a $10+ goes up or down within 40 days has a likelihood of profit of about 68%. On the off chance that we change the time allotment, this likelihood will change also. The possibility of profit for a $10+ climb/d will be a lot littler if the period varies to 10 days. As it were, a $10+ go up or down in XYZ will be significantly less likely happen inside 20 days than it would in 40 days.

On the off chance that we increment the period, the likelihood would increment also. A $10+ increment or lessening in XYZ's price will be almost guaranteed if we give the stock 200 days, then it would be if we would allow it 40 days.

The following central point to consider is Implied Volatility (IV). Inferred unpredictability is typical instability. On the off chance that advantage is relied upon to move a great deal, it has high suggested variability. Amid high inferred unpredictability, the ordinary appropriations graph is broadened out too. A more significant move within a moderately brief timeframe will turn out to be almost certain amid high IV.

The inverse is valid for times of low suggested unpredictability. When suggested instability is low, so when the benefit is not relied upon to move a ton, the ordinary dispersion outline will be fixed.

By and by, I will attempt to demonstrate this with our XYZ model. XYZ is as yet trading at $200, and the one standard deviation move would, in any case, be $10 up or down. Whenever suggested unpredictability would diminish, this one standard deviation range would likewise diminish. Presently there is a 68% likelihood that XYZ will not move more than $8 up or down rather than $10.

How and Where to Find the Probabilities

As you may have acknowledged at this point, probabilities assume a significant job in the realm of (options) trading. Realizing the probabilities is fundamental for your prosperity with options. Vast numbers of these probabilities depend on entangled numerical models or gigantic informational indexes.

Fortunately for us, we do not need to ascertain the probabilities ourselves. Each great specialist stage will do this for you! A few brokers demonstrate to you the probabilities straightforwardly on their option chain. Others have separate dissect tabs or different highlights.

Most dealer stages primarily show the likelihood of ITM for every option. This is the likelihood that an option will lapse In the Money (ITM). To discover the probability that an option will lapse OTM (Out of the Money), you need to subtract the likelihood of ITM from 100.

This Is Not Your Typical Strategy

Note that this trading style is very not quite the same as how most traders and investors make/envision profiting. As we mentioned earlier in this article, stocks and different resources don't move much without a delay of a moment. Clearly, there are exceptional cases, yet more often than not, most stocks will not increment or decline in an incentive by a generous sum in a brief timeframe.

At the end of the day, most of the time, stocks (and different resources) do not move more than one standard deviation up or down. Unfortunately, many people do not understand this. The vast majority try to anticipate these improbable huge up or down movements. This is a moderately low probability strategy in light of the fact that most resources do not move more than one standard deviation most of the time.

We, as high likelihood option sellers, attempt to do the accurate inverse. So, we take the opposite side of the trade. We are likely to sell an option with the expectation that the hidden resource will not have abnormally huge movement. High likelihood option sellers, in this way, frequently profit from range-bound/unbiased/sideways markets. Yet, regardless of whether the hidden resource moves up or down, we will not lose money right away. For whatever length of time that the fundamental resources do not move more than ordinarily, we ought to be fine.

For what reason Does it Work – Is it a Zero-Sum Game?

High likelihood option sellers will, for the most part, have a great deal of 'little' profits and a couple of 'greater' failures. In this manner, option selling may appear to be a lose-lose situation. If you win $300 70% of the time and lose $700 30% of the time, you will not profit in the long haul since every one of your increases will be cleared out by the infrequent massive failures (300 * 70 – 700 * 30 = 0). Fortunately, this is not the situation for high likelihood option selling and because of various reasons.

Chapter 2

The Risks of Not Investing

We have been reminded of one of the dangers of trading since the turn of the century – the threat of falling shares. Although it is not possible to prevent market crashes, buying value securities, or diversifying the portfolio will help you experience less uncertainty and show more stable performance over time.

Many people are thinking about investment "risk." But few take the risk of NOT spending. We need to understand both sides of the risk coin. Looking at the investment risk, we look at the potential price, and as people, we are scared of losing. If we look at an investment's "dropping out," we look at the cost of foregone profits, which is also called a loss. "I wish I traded in Bitcoin when it was..." is a lack in psychology. There is more to the threat of not engaging in blockchain, though, as it is not just a way to' make money,' it is a new technological step.

There have been many people back in the day who have decided not to participate in learning new technology, and there may always be. There were people in the 80s and 90s who decided not to get interested in learning about technology, people who were late on the internet because, as one of my brothers claimed, "It is a fad that will not last."

How Much Does It Cost, Not to Learn New Technology?

How many jobs can one do in this world without having any computer skill level? No, one does not have to be excellent in skill level, but usually, there has to be a skill level to at least enter some information, even if working in a supermarket register. I opted not to do a series in workplace training when I was 13 when we started to touch type in the first term. Okay, about 3 million words ago on the internet, maybe I would save some time and add 6 million if I did not just use three fingers and my nose to write.

The risk of not spending moves beyond its immediate economics and passes through most points into job opportunities, comfort, stress levels and overall quality of life as global adoption grows. Thanks to the social acceptance of technological advances, most people have been forced to learn how to do things like bank and pay electronic payments, how to use money, how to write, how to use a computer, how to set up a firewall, how to use cloud services and how to do other things that are of a technical nature – and they have PAID for it without any hope of ROI like that.

In the not-so-distant future, the planet will be forced to learn and use the same things we are doing here because they need to be interested in changing the economy. Of course, you can argue that, but if you discuss it here on my blog, it means you have studied technology that did not exist a decade or two ago. You probably didn't see most of it at the time as an acquisition phase; it was a natural progression of your existence.

Whether its ten years or 40 years away, retirement is sure to be one of your long-term financial goals. And if a job is no longer done, the savings will have to provide revenue. So how much money are you going to need? The rule of 25 is a strict thumb rule. Take from your investments each year the amount of money you need and divide the figure by 25. It is about the quality of your portfolio after your age.

Difficult to Meet Long-Term Goals with Short-Term Investments

Taking a sufficient amount of market risk may be appropriate because, with only short-term investments, it is difficult to achieve long-term goals. This argument is demonstrated by the most cited “law” for investment: the “Law of 72.” Take 72 and divide it by your expected return, which is how long it will take to double your capital. Consequently, achieving a gain of 7 percent will take just under ten years to double, while a gain of 3 percent will take almost 24 years, and a return of 1 percent will take nearly 70 years to double.

Rule of 72

Average Annual Return	Years to Double Investment
7%	~11
3%	~24
1%	~70

So, what can investors do?

They concentrate on the long-term. Market losses are not usually what detract from our investment strategy, they are our responses to those declines. Although stocks may be unpredictable in the short term, there has been a reliable long-term trend in stocks. And to increase your portfolio's diversification, we recommend holding some of your portfolio inequity with fixed income. Your precise stock and bond balance will be driven primarily by your individual financial goals, risk-based security and timetable for retirement.

Be careful. It is essential to stay focused and stick to your long-term strategy when moving towards your goals.

Consider systemic investing, which spends a fixed amount each month regardless of what the economy is doing, helping to remove emotions from the equation. This approach could help turn the downturn of the economy into opportunities. As we work through these losses, cautious buyers have the ability through market declines to redeem some of their holdings.

Remember why you are investing

Whenever you go through cycles of volatility in the economy, it is important to remember why you are saving to meet your financial goals. Although investment poses threats, such as declines in the economy, not investing can also pose a risk to your financial future. The key is finding equilibrium – taking an acceptable amount of risk to ensure that you have enough growth potential to achieve your long-term goals. To help keep your investment strategy on the right track, speak to your financial advisor today.

Stocks & Bonds

Without stocks and bonds, much of the economic activity in the world would be unlikely. Stocks and bonds are shares issued to raise money to start a new business or to extend an existing business. Sometimes called shares or stocks and bonds, and those who purchase them, are considered investors.

It is time for your capital to be spent. So, where are you going to do that exactly? It is time to buy some shares after you get your money together and agree on an investment strategy. These are tradable commodities like shares, bonds and options — all of which have a monetary value. With these bonds, investors are building a portfolio of diversified investments.

Stocks and bonds are two of the most commonly traded items — each available for sale on a variety of platforms and markets. Stocks are used in a publicly-traded company, known as stock market. Bonds are simply a fixed-income debt to a government or corporate agency that the lender makes.

Bond Market

The bond market is where creditors exchange (buy and sell) debt instruments that can be sold by companies or states, especially bonds. It is also referred to as the borrowing and credit market. On the bond market, bonds issued are all different forms of borrowing. When buying a mortgage, loan or collateral insurance, you are lending money over a set period and charging interest — just as a lender does to its debtors.

The bond market offers a stable, although marginal, source of regular income for the creditors. In some situations, creditors receive two-year interest payments, such as Treasury bonds sold by the federal government. Most investors choose to keep bonds in their portfolios as a means of saving for retirement, education for their kids, or other long-term needs.

Where Bonds are sold

The bond market has no single venue for trading, which means securities are mainly priced over the counter (OTC). Usually, individual investors are not interested in the bond market as such. But those that are includes large institutional investors, such as pension and grant fund families, as well as investment banks, hedge funds, and asset management companies. Through a bond fund operated by an asset manager, private investors who wish to invest in bonds do so.

In the primary market, new shares are put up for sale, and any resulting trade takes place on the secondary market, where investors buy and sell stocks that they already own. Such instruments with fixed income vary from shares to bills to notes. Through selling these bonds on the bond market, issuers may receive the requisite funding for projects or other expenditures.

Who Takes Part in the Bond Market?

The three main groups involved in the bond market include:

Single issuers: these are the companies that create, sign or distribute bond market instruments, be they corporations or different levels of government. For starters, the United States Treasury offers Treasury bonds, long-term investments that provide creditors with two-year interest payments that mature after ten years.

Underwriters: Underwriters typically determine the financial world's threats. An underwriter buys bonds from the issuers on the bond market and resells them for a fee.

Participants: Purchase and sell bonds and other associated assets by these bodies. The applicant issues a mortgage for the lifetime of the protection by selling bonds and collects interest in return. Once it matures, the bond's face value is returned to the borrower.

Bond Ratings

A bond rating firm such as Standard & Poor's and Moody's usually gives debt an investment grade. This score conveyed through a letter grade, shows investors how much of the defaulting risk a bond has: the high-quality securities with an "AAA" or "A" rating, whereas medium-risk bonds with an "A" or "BBB" rating. Bonds with or below a BB rating are considered high-risk.

Stock Market

A stock market is a venue where traders go to purchase investment instruments, including options and futures, such as common shares and derivatives. In stock exchanges, shares are exchanged. Buying capital shares or bonds means buying a very small share of a company's ownership. Although bondholders are borrowing money with interest, equity holders are buying small stakes in companies with the expectation that the company is doing well and that the price of the acquired shares will rise.

The stock market's primary function is to put buyers and sellers together in an equal, managed and controlled environment where they can carry out their trade. This gives those concerned the confidence that there is consistency in trade, fair and honest pricing. Such legislation is benefiting not only investors but also businesses whose shares are being exchanged. When the stock market preserves its robustness and overall health, the economy thrives.

Like the bond market, the stock market has two parts. The secondary market is reserved for first-run equities to release initial public offerings (IPOs) on this segment. Underwriters, who set the initial price of shares, promote this business. In the secondary market, which is where the most economic activity takes place, equities are then opened up.

Chapter 3
How to Maximize Profits

You Can Profit from Any Market Situation

Most options strategies are carried out by combining different option positions and sometimes even the underlying stock's position. A trading strategy can be used singly or in combination with others to profit from market situations.

You can make big profits with options trading, but your risk and exposure are limited. Ordinary stock trading does not afford you such opportunities. The most crucial aspects of options trading know when to exit a trade and how to exit. Knowing how and when to exit is vital for successful trading.

Options strategies are the most versatile strategies in the financial markets. They provide traders and investors with numerous profit-making opportunities with limited exposure and risk. These strategies can be favorable whether the stock price of the underlying security rises, remains the same or falls.

Taking Profits with Options Trading

One of the best-known ways of profiting from options is through the purchase of undervalued options. You can even buy options at the right price and still benefit from them. The most crucial part is knowing when to take profit and exactly how to go about it.

Options prices usually are extremely volatile. This provides an excellent chance to benefit from profit-taking. However, when you miss the right moment to take profits, you will have lost out on an amazing opportunity.

Take Advantage of Volatility and Collect Profits

Options are unlike stocks because they have a time limit. Stocks can be held indefinitely, but options can expire. This means that the time for trades is limited. As a trader, you cannot afford to miss this window. Should such a chance be missed, then it might not be seen again in a long while.

You should avoid long-term strategies when trading options. Strategies such as the averaged are unsuitable for options trading because of the limited time that options have. Also, watch out for margin requirements. Such requirements have the capacity to severely impact your trading funds requirements.

Watch out for multiple factors that may affect a favorable price. For instance, the price of the underlying stock may go up, which is a good thing. However, any accruing benefit may be eroded by other factors such as dividend payment, time decay or volatility. Such constraints make it imperative that you learn to follow profit-taking strategies. Here are some of these crucial profit-taking strategies that you can use as a trader.

Trailing Stop Strategy

One of the most popular options trading strategies for profit taking is the trailing stop. When using this strategy, you will set a pre-determined percentage for a particular target. For instance, you can buy options contracts with each costing $80 with a profit target at $100 and a $70 stop-loss.

Set a Profit-Taking Stop-Loss

We can set a stop-loss at 5%, which means if our target price of $100 is attained, then our trailing target will be $95. If the upward trend continues and our price gets to $120, then the trailing target of 5% becomes $114. If the price movement continues, say $150, then the end goal this time becomes $142.5.

Should the price now start falling, you will exit and collect profits at this level of $142.5. The trailing stop enables you to enjoy protection as the price increases and then exit a trade once the price turns around. The most crucial point to note here is that the stop-loss levels should neither be too small nor too large. If they are too small, they will cause frequent triggers, whereas too large will make profit-taking unachievable.

Partial Profit Booking

Seasoned traders have a routine that they follow to book partial profits. First, they set a target and to take profits when it is attained. There are good reasons why this is done.

First of all, partial profit booking helps to protect the trader's capital to a large extent. This essentially has the effect of preventing capital losses in the event of a sudden price change. Such price reversals are commonly observed in options trading. For instance, we can declare to take partial profits with some of the options and then wait to collect additional profits at a later stage.

Book Partial Profits at Regular Time Intervals

Also, as a trader, you can book partial profits at regular time intervals. However, you will need to pay close attention to the time limit. A massive portion of your options premium is made of its time value. As time runs out, then its value also goes down. As a trader, you should keep a keen eye on the time value of your options as this erodes its value. Buyers should be careful about the time limit.

Sell Covered Call Options against Long Positions

Selling options is a lucrative income-generating process. It is not uncommon for traders to make 2%—2.5% returns each month. However, this is not the only pathway to riches in the markets. You can also sell naked puts. This is similar in a way to selling shares or stocks that you do not.

When you sell naked put options, you will free up your time so that you can do a lot more. Stock trading allows you an opportunity to sell stocks of shares that you do not have for a profit. This tends to free up your capital so you can invest it or trade with it indefinitely. It is advisable to stick to stocks that you understand very well and those that you would not mind. There is still hedging that is associated with options trading, so always be careful and watch about that. Most large investors who deal in options are often hedging.

Options Trading and Leverage

One of the other larger applications of options trading is leveraging. Leverage allows you to manipulate situations in your favor. Let us use an example to illustrate this. Let us assume that an investor has about $1000 to trade.

The investor desired to purchase options that will provide him with the best profit margin. He chooses to buy bullish ABC, Inc. shares.

ABC shares cost $100 a piece so he can afford to purchase only ten shares. Now, ABC also has several call options. These have a price of $105 and 3 months. Each option costs $3. Now instead of opting for the shares, our investor decides to purchase three call option contracts. They cost him $300. Shortly after that, the stock price moves to $113.

Now, if he had invested the money in the shares, he would have made a profit.

$100 * 10 = $1000

$113 * 10 = $1,300

Difference is $1,300—$1,000 = $130

Buying the shares outright brings in $130 only.

Now, what if he had opted for options?

3 options at $3 per each is = $9

Profit for this trade is $9 * 100 * 3 = $2,700

$2,700—$900 (premium) = $1,600

It is evident to note that options trading is much more lucrative compared to a direct stock purchase. There is some risk associated with buying the options. Some of these include insufficient price movement and so on. There is also the risk of time decay where an option's time runs out.

Always consider all the Options Available to You

A lot of the time, we make assumptions that traders will hold their positions till the end. However, this is not always the case, especially if you are trading American options. In this instance, you can choose from several options to ensure that you can leverage any time you want if you see the need for it. In our situation above, our trader could have done any of the following.

- Sold off the option to lock in some profits
- Sold off the option before time ran out to just recoup losses
- Exercised the right to buy shares and then simply bought the shares

Learn to Select the Right Options to Trade

There are some guidelines that you need to learn and follow every time you want to acquire options. This way, you will be able to identify options that will see you earn a profit. Here is a look at the guidelines.

- Determine whether you are bullish or bearish on the market, sector or just the stock. Also, make sure you determine whether you are strongly bullish or just a tiny bit bullish. When you make these decisions, then you will be able to identify the kind of options that you wish to buy.

- Consider volatility and think about how it would affect your options trading strategy. Also, think about the status of the market. Is it calm or is it volatile? If it is not very high, then you should be able to buy call options based on the underlying stock. These are normally quite cheap.

You may also want to consider the expiration date and strike price. If you only have a couple of shares, then this would be a great time and opportunity to purchase more stock.

Here are Some Options Trading Tips

- If you are purchasing options, you will aim to acquire those with the longest expiration dates. This way, you would be giving your trades the sufficient time to work out. However, if you are considering options, then please try and opt for the options offering the shortest time possible. This way, you will limit your liability.

- Also, when you buy your options as in the case above, remember to go for the cheapest of them all. Cheap options will likely help to improve your chances of making a profit. Such trades also have minimal volatility and also tend to perform well at the markets. When this trade works out, then the rewards will be huge. It is better to buy options with low volatility than those with high. This will minimize the risk of losses if the trade doesn't work out.

- Always ensure that you understand as much as you can about the specific sector you will be trading. Take the biotech sector, for example. Trade-in these stocks often end up with binary outcomes. This tends to happen mostly during announcements of clinical trials of an important type of medication. You can then find or choose out-of-the-money put options and call options.

- If you are to buy a deeply out-of-the-money call option, then it is much better to purchase stocks in the telecoms and energy firms. Such firms showcase very little volatility and are considered a safe bet. On the other hand, you can buy out-of-the-money options just before an earnings report is considered a profitable venture, especially if that stock had been down for a while.

In short, if you are a trader who prefers lower-risk options, then you should focus your energy on buying low volatility options. Options are generally profitable because there are many different paths you can follow to attain maximum profitability at low risk.

Chapter 4
Investors Do's and Do not's

What Every Investor Should Do

Understand Market Basics

In the modern world, investment has been made accessible to the average person. Most employers, who offer retirement savings plans, often sponsor a day of education so that employees can become familiar with the types of retirement plans and the options available to them. Also, with the proliferation of cable news networks, specialized programming, the internet and social media, there is no shortage of information widely available to virtually anyone, anywhere.

Especially in the information age, knowledge is power. Before you jump right into trading on the options market, take some time to familiarize yourself with the basics of market dynamics. Options traders use a language that is unique to their niche in the investment world, and many outsiders may be completely perplexed and unable to understand much of what they say. Besides, the ability to tolerate a certain amount of financial risk is an integral component of successful investing. Thus, by understanding not only the terminology of the options market but also the fundamental dynamics of the stock market in general, investors can exponentially increase their chances of assembling a profitable career in options trading.

Play by the Rules

As an options trader, you will compete with other traders and investors. Much of your success in investing – including making valuable connections in the investment world – will result from your ability to play by the rules. The stock market is a living thing, and the activity of traders has a huge impact on its health and volatility. We are all tempted to be maverick investors who leave a legacy of innovation, but understanding the fundamentals will work in your favor.

Specifically, option prices increase or decrease as a result of changes in share prices and volatility.

So, when share prices increase, call options make money and put options lose money; when share prices decrease, put options make money and call options lose money. Options also move about volatility; when share prices are stable, greater volatility can increase the options pricing. So, when volatility increases, buying options make money; when volatility decreases, selling options make money.

Understanding These Two Basic Rules Can Help You Become a Better Trader

Adapt Your Strategy to Market Conditions

Once you are up and running in the world of professional options trading, you will gain confidence as you see your efforts pay off in returns to your options account. As you move from a Level 1 trading account to a Level 2 trading account, you will likely develop a preference for a certain type of options trades—may be covered calls or married puts. Familiarity with the language and mechanics of the options trading profession is something that will work in your favor. However, it is important to remember that as you move up the ladder, you will gain access to a wider array of trading tools and strategies. As you gain knowledge and experience, remember that no matter how comfortable you have become with a select number of options trading strategies, there will always be additional aspects of nuance that can enhance your skill as a trader and increase the profitability of your efforts. The key to ensuring success is not just in choosing the best strategy with the performance of the underlying asset. You must also consider the overall market conditions and whether those conditions may affect the future performance of that asset. Although one strategy may have worked in the past under similar conditions, considering changes in current conditions will help you adjust your strategy to ensure you continue to build on your past success.

Always Have an Exit Plan

Picking a stock, formulating an options strategy to generate income from the stock's performance and then contacting your broker to initiate an opening transaction is a good beginning. But this plan is not a complete strategy. The most important part of any options strategy is not how to get in—it is how to get out.

The payoff of an options strategy can result from buying the underlying stock below market value, accepting a cash settlement deposit for a put option on a declining stock, or even benefiting from a rise in the cost of the option premium for selling the contract before it expires.

You believe the asset you have identified may provide you with an opportunity to construct a profitable options trading strategy, but conjecture and hope should not be part of that strategy. Before you complete an opening transaction, make sure you are very clear about your specific goal for entering the contract. After you complete the opening transaction, you will be faced with one of three possible outcomes:

1. The market and the target stocks moved in the direction you predicted.
2. The market or the target stocks move in a direction you did not predict, resulting in unexpected losses.
3. The market or the target stocks move in a direction you did not predict, resulting in unexpected gains.

Similarly, you should have three responses ready for each of these developments:

1. If you are faced with the first result, you should have an exit strategy already prepared. Whatever else is happening around you, as long as your assets are on the right track, do not deviate from your plan.
2. If there are unexpected changes that are not favorable to your position on the underlying asset, what plan did you formulate to exit the contract so you can minimize your losses?
3. If there are unexpected changes that are favorable to your position on the underlying asset, what plan did you formulate to exit the contract so you can capitalize on these gains?

No matter what happens, make sure you can answer all three questions before you enter an options contract. Then, once you have laid the groundwork for a successful options trade, stick with your plan, even if you think you could make a few more dollars by improvising.

What Every Investor Should Avoid

Doubling up to Cover Losses

"Doubling up" is a prime example of how an options trader may ignore his original exit strategy if the market or the underlying stocks fail to perform the way he had expected when he originally constructed his strategy.

For example, let us say a trader buys a call option for 100 shares of Company B, with a strike price of $45. At the time he purchased the call option, Company B was trading at $44. The trader expects the share price to rise to $47 before the contract expires. Immediately after the opening transaction, though, the stock price slips to $43.

The premium for a call option with a strike price of $45 is further out-of-the-money now than at opening; besides, there is still plenty of time before expiration. As a result, to compensate for any potential losses if the stock rises to only $46, the trader may be tempted to "double-up" by buying another $45 call option at the reduced premium price.

If this trader were only purchasing stocks, he might have celebrated the unexpected drop in share value and immediately purchased as many additional shares as possible, with a goal of greater long-term return, but options trading works differently. The options trader is focused on short-term profits, and if the stock price fails to put the contract in-the-money by the expiration date, the trader loses on not only one contract, but two.

The smart trader will remember that he created an exit plan for this scenario and will stick with it. Though it may be tempting to purchase an additional call option, he should judge the wisdom of such a purchase by asking himself if he would buy the second call option in case he was not already in the middle of a trade. If this is not ordinarily a contract he will enter into – and it is not, because that was not his strategy in his opening transaction – then market conditions and stock performance that defy expectations are probably the worst reasons for him to change that view.

Instead, he should either stay in his contract to see if the stock eventually rebounds and makes the contract profitable, or sell the contract immediately, cut his losses and look for another opportunity that makes more sense.

Trying to Hit a "Home Run" Every Time

Popular culture portrays Wall Street as a sort of heaven for adrenaline junkies, in which highly skilled traders spend their days chasing down successively bigger, sexier and more lucrative deals. The only barriers for these imaginary gods of the stock market appear to be failing to out-trade and outperform all their friends and colleagues, and thereby missing out on bragging rights at the local pub at the end of the trading day.

A skilled options trader can make huge gains using well-planned strategies. Indeed, this should be a goal for every options trader, but it is a challenging goal to achieve for many reasons. First, the perfect storm of daily skyrocketing corporate share prices hardly ever occurs. Most stocks maintain stability and change very little from day to day, so the textbook conditions for a highly profitable options contract are hard to come by. As a result, if your approach to options trading strategies consists of trying to arrange contracts that guarantee payouts that are not likely to occur, or to approach market analysis from a perspective that a lesser degree of volatility is the exception rather than the rule, you will be missing the considerable opportunities the options trading market presents for disciplined investors.

Markets and indexes may not make dramatic swings very often, and that is probably a good thing. However, markets do consistently move by several points in both directions each day. By studying market behavior, you will have a better grasp of what types of changes are likely to occur and when. Using this knowledge to buy and sell options contracts that conform to sound market fundamentals can help you earn steady weekly returns. Practiced correctly, a well-disciplined approach to options trading can provide any skilled investor with the opportunity to create a source of steady residual income to enhance an existing portfolio.

Buying Cheap Options

An options contract that is very far out-of-the-money will likely have a comparatively low premium. For example, let us say Company ABC is trading at $30.00 per share. Your broker tells you the share price is likely to increase and that there is a call option on this company with a strike price of $32.00 for a premium of $3.25. You find another call option for the same company with a strike price of $35.00 and a premium of only $1.10. You know the share price is going to increase and the call option with the lower premium would result in a larger profit, but there is a reason for that; the lower premium results from the fact that the share price is not likely to reach $35.00 by the expiration date. These types of options are traps for beginning traders, so avoid them whenever you can.

Chapter 5

How Day Trading Works?

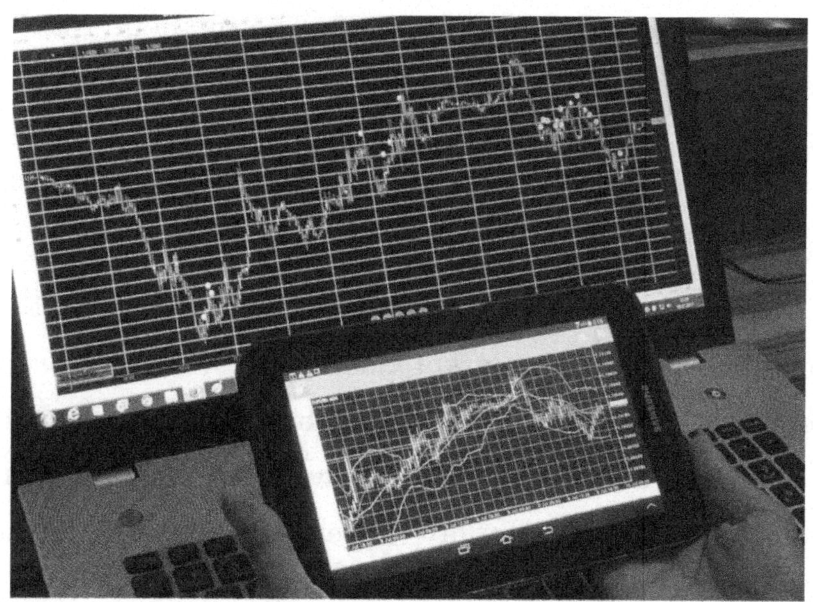

There are two trading categories of trading in the current global market. They are known as day trading and swing trading. An individual who has an in-depth desire to venture into trading is supposed to know them. However, day trading has been a focal point for several traders. For an individual to understand what it entails, he or she is supposed to know its definition. It can be described as the speculation of securities by specifically selling and buying financial instruments on the same trading day.

During this period, market positions are always closed before the market closing for the trading day.

Traders who engage in this type of trade intending to get profits are known as speculators. The methods that are used for day trading are very different from those used in long term trade. Long term trade deals with trade strategies of underlying buying, holding of the financial instruments and investing in value. Day trading is regularly associated with its traders exiting their positions before the market closes. The main aim of this act is to avoid risks that cannot be managed and price gaps that are negative. The negative price gaps can result from the closing one-day prices and opening of the following day prices at the open.

Day trading often involves the use of margin leverage. An excellent depiction of this phenomenon can be used in the United States of America. Regulation has the potential to permit initial maximum leverage of up to 2:1. However, many brokers go to levels of promoting up to 4:1 leverage during the moments the leverages are reduced to 2:1 or even less. This is mostly done near the end of the trading day. The market of United States terms traders who trade for more than four days as pattern day traders. These forms of traders must maintain a minimum of twenty-five thousand dollars in their accounts as equity.

Traders in the day can end up not fees for interests that are charged for margin benefit. It is because margin interest is a typical charge for the balances that are accrued at midnight. However, this does not brush away the risks of a margin call that are experienced sometimes. A broker is a person who is the determinant of the margin interests because of his or her call. Several financial instruments are commonly traded in the modern era day trading. These financial instruments include currencies, stocks, contracts for difference, hosts for future contracts and options. The common future contracts that are traded include interest rates futures, commodity futures, and equity index futures.

There was a day when trading was an exclusive activity. It was a form of trade that was associated with professional speculators and financial firms. A large portion of day trading individuals is the employees of banks and other financial institutions. This group of employees tasked with such roles is always competent specialists in managing funds and equity investment. The year 1975 saw the popularization of day trading with several parties joining the trade. It was because the commissions in the United States were deregulated. The rise of electronic platforms for trading was witnessed in the years of 1990s. The volatility of stock prices was also seen during the periods of the dot-com bubble, as represented in figure 1 below. Scalping is a new intraday trading technique that is used by traders in the day trading. It involves holding the trading position for a couple of minutes or seconds.

Profit and Risks of Day Trading

The process of day trading involves sloppy financial leverage, and speedy returns are probable. This

phenomenon makes the trade to be either extremely profitable or extremely unprofitable. Those people who are described as high-risk profile traders are also significantly impacted by such an event. These groups of traders have the probability of making enormous percentages of profit or, on the other hand, undergo massive amounts of parentage loss. Day trading trader's individuals are sometimes referred to as bandits or gamblers by other traders or investors. It is because these traders can either make vast amounts of profits or losses during the trade.

Several factors can make this form of trade to be very risky while an individual is trading. They include individual trading on a deal with low odds instead of trading on one that has high odds of winning; the presence of risk capital that is inadequate, which is tied together with overload stress of surviving and presence of poor management of funds, which entails poor execution of the trade.

Gains and losses are mostly amplified by the widespread usage of buying on margin. The process of buying on margin can be described as the use of borrowed funds. This action usually results in a trader experiencing a substantial loss or gain in a short span during the day. Brokers have the common tendency of allowing more significant trade margins for day traders.

Difference between Day Trading and Swing Trading

The main aim of traders in business is to be able to generate profit. Several forms of trading can be used. For an individual to understand what day trading is about, he or she is supposed to also have insight about swing trading. Having this knowledge and knowing the difference between swing trade and day trade will help them have a clear line of how to perform the trade to impeccable standards.

The first step to understanding swing trading is by getting what its definition is. This is the form of trade that involves a trader to buy or sell financial instruments and hold them for a varied time of a few days. The holding on time of financial instruments can go on to an extended period of several weeks. Several factors can make a trader practicing swing trade to be in a sell or buy position. These circumstances are based on technical, quantitative, or fundamental valuations by the trader. Such occurrence may mean that a swing trader may take longer working periods than the day trader.

Most people who practice swing trade have a standard set of beliefs amongst themselves. They mostly go for the thought of accumulating gains or losses. This process is done in a swift manner that is very slow and smooth compared to day trading. However, there are certain instances where a trader practicing swing trading can experience swings in his or her trades. The results of these swings are always too extreme in two ways. He or she can either gain large percentages of profits or experience huge rates of loss in a very short time. Individual trading as a swing trader usually does not take part as a full-time trader in the market.

There are four critical differences between swing trading and day trading. They include:

- An individual practicing day trading sells or buys financial instruments and liquidates his or her position on the same day. On the other hand, a swing trader upholds his or her position for a variation of days or even weeks.

- A person in day trading is meant to invest a huge number of hours in a day to be able to monitor the flow of prices in their portfolios. However, a swing trader is estimated to use few hours in trading as he or she can maintain his or her position for days or weeks.
- Day trading is involved with several sessions of being fast-paced and having adrenaline rushes. It is because there are quick decisions to be made, and the trade is fast-paced. This is the exact opposite of people who practice swing trading. They need to be calm when making decisions to focus more on long-term profitability.
- Day trading involves the usage of an advanced system of charting. The charting system is designed to accommodate short intervals of trade. These intervals can be programmed to track one to up to thirty minutes. However, swing traders are prone to using a less complex charting system. These charting systems can be programmed to monitor the market for a varied time of about one to four or five hours.

Short Trades and Long Trades

The terms regarding short trades are common terms to an individual who is participating in stock trading. These terms are majorly used in situations where a trader is either buying or selling first. There are several expectations that a trader always has in mind if he or she is either doing short trade or long trade. When a trader is participating in a short trade, he or she purchases the financial instruments intending to sell them at a higher price in the future to make profits. On the other hand, short trade involves a trader selling financial instruments with the intent of later buying them at a lower price to make his or her profits.

Long Trade

Various day traders are participants that are common in the long trade. They are purchase financial instruments with hopes that they will increase in value. This makes their prices rise in turn. The term that is mostly used by day traders always buys and long, which are interchangeable. Software developed to help long trade, with buttons that are either marked long or buy. These buttons are used to represent an open position entered by a trader. This position simply means an individual has shares in a certain firm or trade.

When a trader decides to go long, he or she is always interested in purchasing a specific financial instrument. If the decision for such is perused, the potential for profit levels is always unlimited. It is because the prices of the purchased financial instruments can get higher indefinitely. This is despite a day trader participating in small moves. The risks in this form of trade have a lower risk potential of the purchased instruments to fall to zero. It is because profits and risks are always controlled by the multiple small moves that are made.

Short Trade

Day traders in short trades always sell their financial instruments before purchasing them. During moments they buy the financial instrument, they hope the prices will have gone. This is the moment they can realize their profits because they will be buying the financial instruments at a lower price from that which they had sold. Short trading is one of the most confusing forms of trade because people across the globe are used to buying first before selling. However, one can be able to sell and buy in the financial markets.

There are common terms that are used by traders participating in short trades. These terms include short and sell, which are used interchangeably. Software developed to aid short trade also has buttons marked short or sell. The term short usually means a trader has an open position to shorting some financial instruments. Profit levels are always limited in this situation when compared to the initial amount that was used to purchase the financial instruments. Various traders are used to taking short positions to reduce or minimize risks.

Chapter 6
Different Day Trading Strategies

Trading Strategies

Quite a few people are trying to make money with day trading strategies, but these are highly risky practices. Long-term investment by buying and holding investment instruments can make a great deal of sense, particularly after studying the history of a particular company or industry sector and the market potential of its related services and products. Still, day traders tend to look only briefly at a company or investment before deciding to buy or sell it.

Some industry experts think this is not any different than traditional gambling, which is why the Securities and Exchange Commission tried to protect small-fund investors by putting several restrictions on how they can play the stock market in this way.

The following trading strategies illustrate how to reduce your risks and increase your chances of making money with day trading.

Selecting the instruments

You will start by choosing your preferred investment instruments. You can choose stock indexes ETFs commodities futures options. Each instrument has its characteristics and level of risk. If you decide to focus on an entire economic field, such as commercial real estate, then your best bet is to choose sector-related ETFs. Note that most ETFs show low beta, meaning that significant stock market shifts would result in smaller changes in those ETFs. High-beta ETFs, which change considerably when the stock market rises or falls, are ideal for day trading. When choosing your trading strategy, you need to be careful.

In any case, you will determine beforehand which instruments work best for your desired risk levels.

Knowledge is power

Including knowledge of basic trading techniques, daily traders must keep up with the latest news and events from the stock market affecting stocks — the Fed's interest rate plans, the economic outlook, etc. So do the homework. Make a wish list of stocks you want to trade and keep you up to date on selected companies and general markets. Check news about the company and visit reputable financial websites.

Set Aside Funds

Evaluate how much capital you are willing to risk for every trade. Many successful day traders lose their account per trade from less than 1 percent to 2 percent. If you have a trading account of $40,000 and are willing to risk 0.5 percent of your capital on each transaction, the maximum loss is $200 (0.005 x $40,000) per contract. Set aside a surplus amount of funds with which you can exchange, and you are ready to lose. Note, it can happen or it may not.

Set aside days

It takes time to trade on the same day. That is why it is called day trading. You will need to give up most of your day. If you have little time to spare, do not do it. The process requires a trader to track the markets and spot opportunities that may arise during hours of trading at any time. Rapid movement is essential.

Start small

Throughout a session, emphasize on a maximum of one to two stocks. With only a few inventories, monitoring and seeking opportunities becomes simpler.

Time those trades

Many investors and traders place orders that start executing as soon as the morning markets open, which contributes to price volatility. A seasoned player can recognize trends and select suitably to make profits. But for newbies, it may be easier to just read the market for the first 15 to 20 minutes without making any moves. Even though the rush hours offer opportunities, at first, it is safer for beginners to avoid them.

Be Realistic

About Profits, a strategy needs not win for profit all the time. Many traders win just 50 to 60 percent of their companies. They do make more on their winners, however, than they lose on their losers. Make sure that the risk for each exchange is limited to a particular percentage of the account and those methods of entry and exit are clearly defined and written.

Stick to the Plan

Successful traders need to move quickly, but they do not have to think quickly. Why? For what? Because in advance, they developed a trading strategy, along with the discipline to stick to that strategy, so it is important to be closely following your formula rather than trying to chase profits. Do not let your emotions get the best out of you and give up the strategy. Among day traders, there is a mantra: “Planning your trade and trading your plan.”

You may use a basic peak and trough chart or a technical metric like the ADX (Average Directional Index) to define the current trend. The uptrend market forms consecutively higher highs and higher lows, while a downtrend market forms regularly lower and lower peaks. Sometimes you will find that securities are over-sold during an uptrend exactly at the point of a fresh higher low, which is the price level you would consider purchasing the security or currency pair at.

Likewise, securities are generally overbought during downtrend right at the point where a fresh lower high is emerging, which suggests a possible selling opportunity.

If you want to define and trade patterns using the ADX predictor, then follow the direction of the ADX rows. A value below 25 shows that the market is not a trend, a value between 25 and 50 indicates a non-run, whereas values above 50 suggest a very strong trend. Using the lines –DI and +DI to define the direction of the trend – if the line –DI is above the line +DI, you are dealing with a downtrend and if the line +DI is above the line –DI, you are dealing with an uptrend.

Countertrend

The opposite approach to trend-following, counter-pattern trading refers to trading in the opposite direction of an existing pattern.

Breakout

Breakout strategies are based around when the price reaches a defined point on your map, with increased volume. After the asset or security breaks over resistance, the breakout trader enters a long position. Instead, once the stock falls below support, you will reach a short position.

Following an asset or commodity trades beyond the defined price limit, volatility usually increases, and prices frequently trend towards a breakout.

You need to find the right tool for the trade. Bear in mind the level of support and resistance of the asset when doing so. The more often those points have been hit by the market, the more they are validated and significant.

Entry Points

This part is nice and simple. Prices set to close and higher levels of resistance warrant a bearish role. Prices set to close and need a bullish place below the support level.

Plan your exits

Make use of the recent performance of the asset to set a reasonable price target. Using chart patterns will exacerbate this process even more. To create a target, you can compute the average recent price swings. If the average price change over the last several price fluctuations has been 3 points, this would be a reasonable target. Once that goal is reached, you can exit the trade and enjoy it.

Stop-Loss Orders Day trading

Without stop-loss orders, it is like walking on a tight wire with no safety net. A bad fall will seriously hurt you. Set up a stop-loss order before you accept an investment to avoid the possibility of losing all your money before you realize what is going on. Great measures for stop-loss orders are moving averages and pivot points. That is a very popular strategy for trade.

Time over Sales

Close monitoring of real-time sales data is of critical importance. If unusually large orders occur at or above the current asking price for an instrument, then you can take advantage of this by taking long positions. Waiting for the strong demand behind this action will result in a heavy profit to further increase the selling price of the instrument. Likewise, seeing unusually big orders at the current bid price or lower quite likely means it is time for that instrument to enter short positions and abandon longer positions.

This kind of potentially profitable occurrence does not happen frequently, but the most likely path to success with trading strategies is to wait patiently for such opportunities.

No matter what daytime trading tactics you follow, the secret is consistency. Make a plan and stick to it. Also, trading on penny-stock falls within the same rules. Traders still keeping their hearts and their eyes open will always do well than wild traders who do not think first. Stay calm and remain focused, and you will find your way to wealth.

Planning and Executing Day Trading Strategies

One of the major problems facing a trader is bridging the gap between planning and execution of the trade.

How many times will we hear a trader ask if they have done what they have said they will do? How many times does "No" respond?

Moving from a strategy that looks good on paper to success in real-world trading is what it is all about.

No doubt, if you cannot execute and reap the benefits of your success, all the preparation in the world will do you no better.

Many feelings are rational. The first thing that many people would suggest is that this must be a psychological problem because business psychology is often spoken of as a cog in the wheel of business success.

But there is a big difference between psychological issues that arise during trading and normal emotional responses that have triggered certain forms of situation.

Yeah, different individuals may have varying degrees of tolerance, but anger following, for example, a series of losses is a natural emotion to feel.

Because wins and losses come in a random distribution, sitting through a series of losing trades is not unfair, even if you have done everything according to schedule.

So, if it is not about some sort of psychological disorder needing some re-wiring, what is it?

Chapter 7
Differences and Similarities between Day Trading and Swing Trading

Which one is easier, day trading or swing trading? What are the benefits of day trading and swing trading? What are the benefits of being a Day Trader or a Swing Trader? Within this article, I will clarify the distinction between day trading and swing trading, and I will also show you the advantages and drawbacks of both.

What Is Day Trading?

This is the concept of day trading in the form of forex markets: purchasing and selling of currency pairs over one day to profit from market fluctuations made on that day. Day trading is also known as 'Intraday trading,' where day traders typically enter and leave markets on the same business day. It means that no trade is going on overnight. And is forex scalping traded on a day? The answer is yes ... forex scalping is an intra-day trading strategy that falls into the day trading group. Therefore, day traders, they are far more involved in quicker and lower money. Day traders do all their deals throughout the day because once the day is over, they will down (stop selling).

Benefits of Day Trading

What are the benefits of day trading? Okay, here is a list of 6 I can think of:

- Day trading is about taking lower profit targets, and if you choose smaller profit targets, then the cost of the transaction you take is also low.
- Efficient day traders may use the influence of compounding to maximize net earnings due to the multiple transactions they position regularly.
- Day traders can make profits a lot quicker than someday traders simply because of the rush.
- At the same time, a day trader is still aggressively investing in the market.
- When traders close their trades at the end of the day, they are then able to take advantage of interest gained on their portfolio.
- They reduce the risk of keeping their trades going overnight because something unforeseen can happen in the market or negative economic news, etc. that can cause the price to fluctuate

dramatically and wipe out their earnings or even their forex trading accounts.

Drawbacks of Day Trading

- Day Traders trade a lot, so their exchange costs are even higher because of the spread and, as day trader, you will risk your money quicker.
- Attractive Day trading can be quite challenging to understand and practice, and it can be very difficult for anyone to achieve.
- As a day trader, you tend to spend a lot of time in front of your computer waiting for orders and it is very time-intensive, so if you have a full-time career, day trading will not work for you.
- Day trading is a high moving operation, and day traders require a lot of focus, and it can be tough.
- As a day trader, you will put your trading portfolio at a significantly greater risk as you are doing a lot of business in a day, and you can lose a lot of money in a short period.
- During day-to-day trade, a small error will result in a big loss. For example, if you have lost 20 consecutive trades in a row during the day, on the 21st trade, you will be trading a big contract to reclaim your 20 losses. Yet the trade is turning into

a significant loss. You know, day trading requires a lot of planning, sound money management, and good risk: rewarding a successful trading program.

- Because day traders rely on a very short time, they neglect the broader patterns that trigger major price fluctuations, and thus it can be a little difficult to forecast the price.
- Day trading can become addictive, and if a day trader is not patient, it will almost make day trading like gambling.

What Is Swing Trading?

Swing trading is different from day trading, as when swing traders sell, they abandon their exchange for more than one day or perhaps one month or more. As a consequence, swing trading is a short to medium-term phenomenon pursuing the trading strategy. Generally, swing traders are searching for small market reversals to enter trades in the course of the dominant market.

For example, in the main uptrend phase, swing traders will reach a minor side in the expectation that the market will move back to an uptrend. As a result, pattern reversals, retracements, Fibonacci rates, support turned opposition and opposition turned support levels, trader's activity zone thresholds are critical levels where swing traders aim to join trading.

Swing trading is usually a short to medium-term phenomenon following a method that lasts anywhere from 1 to 30 days. Traders who swing trading continue to search for pattern reversals & retracements for their entry/exit points.

Benefits of Swing Trading

The costs of business transactions due to the spread are much lower than those of daily transactions because there are fewer transactions.

You have a lot of time to evaluate trades and then take trades. Therefore, swing trading will be suitable for anyone who has a day job.

Swing trading does not take a lot of your time ... you can put your trade and walk away instead of sitting on a day of trading.

Swing trading is much less competitive than day trading.

Gains made are a lot better than in day trading if you let the trades run longer than one day, and the risk of increased income is much higher than in day trading.

Swing trading helps swing traders to conquer the pattern for full benefit productivity by using this best trailing stop strategy.

Swing Trading Drawbacks

Many forex traders may find swing trading challenging to understand and may not match the trader's trading style.

Swing trading can be time-consuming, particularly when you are evaluating your trading setups, so you have got to wait a long time before your trading setups happen, and you can do your business.

Swing trading is not a ‘set and forget system.’ You have to track your trades every day to move the stop loss to break even, transfer trailing stops, etc.

A swing trader can get so attached to a trade because he may be in that trade for a while, and instead of withdrawing and taking profits, his attachment will confuse his judgment.

As in day trading, trading discipline, and risk management as well as holding them. It is not uncommon for momentum traders to step out of the way or shift the pattern just to have the market immediately switch back and head in the original direction, and to be quite frank, this is sometimes quite frustrating.

So, Which Is Better Between Day Trading or Swing Trading?

I have shown you the pros and cons of day trading as well as swing trading. You should make your decision based on the details provided above.

But, what is the safest trading strategy? Day trading or swing trading?

For me, I like swing trading because I like looking at the big picture, so for me, swing trading is perfect.

You will decide how involved you want to be before you start trading. It is one of the main problems that will help clear the way for the future. What are your main duties, and how much time do you have at your disposal?

Only after you have traded regularly or buy-and-hold for a few days or weeks you will be able to truly work out the type of trading that suits you.

Traders are usually split into two camps — day and swing — and there are important distinctions that you will consider when you map your course. In the end, it is all about timeframes, level of technological competence, and your personal preference, of course.

In this post, we would like to explain the key distinctions between the two and see which one is better suited for you. I am trying to do my best to help you see which way you could be better served based on your particular situation.

Day Trading vs. Swing Trading

The ultimate aim for day traders and swing traders is the same, namely, to produce income. The retention period — and hence the technological methods to be used — is what the various components are.

Day trading means making several trades regularly, as the name implies. Day traders are seeking to take advantage of demand differentials. We can be put in positions depending on technological, basic or quantitative purposes. Day traders seek to earn a profit by selling shares and typically do not keep positions overnight.

This law labels anyone making more than four trades in the same protection over five business days as a "template day trader." This is given that the trades account for more than 6% of the trader's activity in this field. Template Day traders must have a minimum balance of $25,000 in their account every day they intend to sell (and must exceed the cap before they start trading for the day).

So, which style of trading should you adopt?

Day Trading or Swing Trade? That depends entirely on how you plan to move forward. There is no perfect answer that will apply to everyone. It is just a moral preference if you ask me about it. All the swing trader and the day trader are here to make money, but their methods, ways of working, and anticipated standards of competence differ.

If you can invest thoroughly in learning the methods of technical analysis and making the most of them for a big gain, you may call yourself a swing trader. But, in the end, you would have to be very good at using these devices. Day traders would still need to be extremely successful at charting programs and applications. In reality, you are going to see them even more frequently.

Day trading offers more gains in general. It is especially true of small accounts. Nevertheless, analysts have split in their view that others agree that swing trading, with its broader timing range, has greater scope for gain.

Chapter 8
How Swing Trading Works

Swing trading is the demonstration of bringing in money from protections that have transient value developments in a couple of days, to half a month long. Sometimes this can affect a month or two, but generally, it's within a couple of days' time frame. For the most part, they do not have positions 100% of the time; instead, they hang tight for the correct opportunities to bounce in. Their goal is to exploit information exchange or downtrend in evaluating. At the point when the securities exchange is gaining and progressing admirably, they purchase all the more then they sell. At the point when the market is feeble, they are short increasingly then they are buying. In the end, when the market is not getting along admirably by any stretch of the imagination, they sit as an afterthought and sit tight for another opportunity.

Are far as taxes go with Swing Trading, there are a couple of important things to know. How much tax you pay on your earnings relies upon a couple of different variables. First is to what extent you are holding your positions. On the off chance that you hold a position 366 days, only one day longer than a year, at that point you sell it, you will pay a lower tax rate than ordinary on your profit. This income rate is ordinarily at about 15% for a great many people; however, it can be as low as 5% for people with lower income. The current tax law that sets the 15% tax rate is set to lapse toward the finish of 2010, so it could change after that date.

Swing traders will, for the most part, not meet all requirements for this rate as they do not hold onto positions for exceptionally long. Momentary profits are generally taxed at a person's ordinary taxation rate. There are exemptions to this standard. On the off chance that you are delegated an example informal investor, and you trade at least four full circle day trades every five business days, at that point, you can regard your profits and losses at the expense of working together. You likewise need to keep up a record with $25,000 or more in it. This can be extremely helpful as you can group capital increases and losses as ordinary income and misfortune. On the off chance that you are doing high volumes of trading, you can set aside a good deal of cash along these lines. This is not for everybody, as you must have a decent measure of money to trade with.

There contrast between a swing trader and a purchase and hold financial specialist is that the purchase and hold speculators could not care less about value swings. They are just keen on the long-term growth of their money, so they accept that their positions will go up in cost over a more extended measure of time. As a rule, this is quite a long while not far off, so they are not taking a gander at the daily value swings, only the master plan. Purchase and hold investing are not very time-concentrated and can bring a great deal of profit if you do not need cash flow.

Swing trading is not for everybody, except for somebody that has a ton of restraint and a decent, hard-working attitude, there is a great deal of profit to be made. Being taught, experienced and committed is a huge piece of being a successful swing trader.

How You Can Get Rich Swing Trading

A celebrated burglar once said that he burglarizes a bank since that is the place the money is. So also, if you need to make money and make it quickly, you have to go where the money is: Wall Street. One of the best ways to make money off Wall Street is through swing trading. You can get rich through this type of momentary trading.

Fortunately, it does not require extravagant software or broad fund and values trading foundations to pull off. You simply have the correct plan and mindset. Here is a general conversation on how you can make the most of the opportunities in the stock market through swing trading.

What is Swing Trading?

Much the same as day trading, swing trading is tied in with buying dependent on the momentum or trend of stocks. The most widely recognized way to make money is to purchase low and sell high. You can short stock and sell high and buy low, yet this is harder to accomplish for apprentice swing traders. Notwithstanding, swing trading is tied in with making momentary gains by wagering on the momentum or trend of stocks. Not at all like day trading where you wager on exceptionally brief timeframe frames like 3-moment or 5-minute time frames, swing trading can include more extended time frames like single days or a few days.

Rather than being stuck to your PC screen attempting to cash in on a couple of divisions of a percent moves, you can pull down some conventional money holding up somewhat longer. The tight hang time for swing trading is all family members. The measure of time you pause while swing trading is still a lot shorter than the average trading strategy of a principal or value investor. Here are some tips.

1. This is day trading. Swing trading should not be this intensive

Consider swing trading as wagering on ships on a sea. While the measure of money you make will be determined by the specific movements and actions of the particular boats you are wagering on, the general state of the sea despite everything assumes a job in how your boats do. While this may be a little factor during most days, in specific days, similar to when there is a storm that is moving towards the sea your boat is working in, by and large, market sentiment can significantly affect your specific swing trade positions. Pay thoughtfulness regarding geopolitical occasions or national bank activities along with expansive market news trends.

2. Determine different segments' sentiments

Your particular stocks' movements are additionally influenced by the more extensive industry the organization you are wagering on operates in. Think extensively, take a gander at related areas. These might affect your stock's industry, and this can drive the stock up or down. Likewise, pay consideration regarding long term trends inside parts. Negative division sentiment allows you to get ready for a quick exit once your stocks' numbers begin trending toward a specific level.

3. The intensity of the correct news

The stock market is about psychology and seen value. Without a doubt, strong earnings proclamation from the organizations you are covering has an incredible effect; however, in general, stocks are impacted by momentum and trends. Pay consideration regarding the news flow and volume concerning your secured stocks. Prepare to swoop in when certain conditions show up. Then again, prepare to sell when certain news trends show up.

4. Riding the market's crowd mindset

As much as Wall Street administrators like to think they are unique or creative scholars, there is a ton of crowd mindset or gathering thinking going on with regards to stock trends. This is the reason you need to thrash the market and scoop stocks before positive trends knock those stocks' prices up because of Wall Street firms heaping on an area or a gathering of specific stocks. Ride the group mindset and set your price targets. When the market's group movement hits your target price, leave the stock and sit tight for an opportunity to enter the stock again after a fall or price union.

5. You will appear as though this after a successful swing trade

As indicated above, you need to pay thoughtfulness regarding industry trends and news to see which stocks are potential breakout stocks. These are stocks that are ready for a decent knock up in value. As a rule, these are simpler to spot than you might suspect. You just need to take a gander at the industry heads in a given space, industry trends and hot players. Investigate the news and stock price trend of these different stocks and you can see which players are approaching breakout status. Enter these stocks and give yourself a couple of days or even a long time for the breakout. However, if the stocks do not arrive at the start stage, do not stop for a second to drop them. Why? Opportunity costs. The additional time you spend trusting that a stock will increment is time, and you could have gone through creation money off an all the more encouraging stock.

6. Create watch records

Create a watch run of trending stocks. This is easy to do with trading software. Keep track of their daily volumes and their daily high and low prices. Check whether there is a trend relationship between their volume and their movement. Connect this with the news with the stocks. Some news is quite predictable-earnings reports, for example. Keep an eye on your watch run and perceive how the stocks react to certain news.

7. Setting limit orders to purchase/to sell

When you have set up your watch records and associated their movements with trends and news factors, you have to set up modified orders on your trading software. Set up the price points where you will purchase the stock. When you have entered a position in the stock, swing trading allows you to set a present moment (inside seven days) price where you can set up a customized deal. Along these lines, you are not ripping your hair out as the stock you are tracking vacillates. When it arrives at your target price, your software can dump the stock, and you can move on. This additionally works for robotized selling once your watched stocks hit the floor price you set for them.

What Is Swing Trading and How It Can Help You?

Swing trading happens when the trader is in the position to realize that the type of stock or commodity that he has bought is dependent upon extraordinary price unpredictability. This implies, all the time, the price of the unit will be dependent upon a few changes in a single cycle, and that is truly down to the nature of the financial instrument. They are nothing like trend-following trades, which can typically be in the long-term cycle and can continue for a long time. Swing trades occur constantly because they take a gander at the temporary positions of the financial instrument.

An excellent example of this is items like currency exchange, which tend to have little pip (focuses in percentage) developments up or down inside a single trading day. What we are examining is a position that occurs or is open longer than a typical trading day; however, it is far shorter than ordinary trend following techniques. What you have to comprehend is that as a swing trader, you are trading on the knowledge that the stock price will have imminent, various changes not too far off, and you will enter a trade not long before the price swings to another course.

Chapter 9

How to Start Swing Trading?

To see success with swing trading, you need to make sure that you are working on the right strategy. There are a lot of different strategies that you can work with when you are ready to join the market, and each of them has potential to earn you a profit if you properly use them. But you have to know how each of them will work and you need to stick with that strategy throughout your whole time trading.

Learn from Your Mistakes Instead of Being Discouraged by Them

If everyone makes mistakes, why should you think it's an exemption and punish yourself for them? Successful swing traders remain unfazed by losing trades, but instead persist wisely learning from their mistakes.

Find and Stick to Trading Strategies That Work for You

While starting with the most popular trading strategies is a good place to start swing trading, you should come to evaluate the results you are getting from your chosen strategy to see if it is worth continuing, modifying or replacing. What do you need to consider when evaluating whether a trading strategy is something that you should stick to, tweak or ditch? One is risk appetite. If your risk appetite is on the low side, maybe you shouldn't even be trading at all. If it's moderate, your trading strategy must be one that carries a moderate amount of risk, too.

Plan Your Swing Trades

Many traders make the mistake of just following the herd with nary a clue of why they're adopting the strategies of the trading herd and what the risk-reward tradeoffs of such strategies.

Looking at good patterns

One thing that you can look at is the charts for a particular stock you would like to look through. There are a lot of different patterns that can come up all the time and the way that they look will determine whether they are a good one to use for your trade or if you should go with another option. When you notice these patterns, you will be better able to predict how the stocks that you want to work with will behave in the future and use this to make a profit.

Ditch the Micro Time Frames

With swing trading, you must focus more on the longer time frames because they're less volatile and by doing so, you minimize your risks for "false triggers" or whiplashes that can make you take positions on securities whose prices are still on a decline. The shortest time frame you should consider is daily, nothing less. The longer your time frame, the lesser the false triggers and noise you'll encounter, and the more you can maintain your winning swing trading streak.

Trend Following

No matter what strategy you decide to use, you will need to make sure that you understand how to read charts and trend lines.

Even though the current price is the most important price, you will want to pay attention to all of the prices that you see for every day that you take into your analysis.

Managing Your Money

One of the biggest tips to help you figure out how much money to put towards a stock is by evaluating the risks associated with the stock. You will be able to do this through any strategy that you will use and various other factors that are part of your trading plan.

Follow the Rules and Guidelines

One of the biggest reasons you need to make sure that you are following your guidelines is because the more consistent you are with your trading, the more likely you are to become successful. Furthermore, you will want to make sure that you follow the guidelines as they will help you to think systematically when it comes to making decisions.

Diversity

Diversity is one of the more popular controversies when it comes to trading. While some traders feel you need to have great diversity, which is a variety of stocks, in your portfolio others feel that this isn't as important. In reality, the more serious you want to be with your trading, the more you will focus on diversity. However, this isn't always true when it comes to investors. But, as stated before, investing and trading are two different career paths in the stock market.

Always Note the Risk

Another important factor to pay attention to when you are looking into trend following is how much risk is involved if you decide to take on the financial instrument you are looking at. When you are looking at the risk, you always have to pay attention to your guidelines and your trading plan.

Using Options as a Strategy

Options are known to be a great strategy if you are looking for leverage, which is when you increase a return on a trade through borrowed money. It is important that you need to make sure you will only use this strategy if it will help you to receive more of a profit. In fact, this is one of the most important factors of choosing a strategy. You have to make sure that it is going to help you gain a profit and decrease your risks.

Short Interest

This is a great strategy to learn as a swing trader because it can show when the stock market is about to go into bearish conditions, which means that the stock prices will start to go down. Furthermore, short interest can also warn you about short squeezing.

Pay Attention to the Float

However, this is also the trick when it comes to the float strategy. There is usually a fine line between having a massive float and having a float that will give you the best returns. The reason why a massive float, which would be too many shares, can cause you to lose capital instead of increasing your profits is because if you have a huge float, the price won't move as quickly. However, if you have a smaller amount of shares in your float, then you will find that the price moves a bit higher, of course this gives you a larger profit. With this said, you also don't want to have too little shares in your float. If this happens, then you won't be able to make much of a profit either as this can stop your float from increasing in price.

Breakout and Breakdown Strategies

When you focus on the breakout strategy, you are looking at the history of your stock's trend line in a microscopic fashion. When you are looking at the trend line, you will see every time the price has gone up and down. Stock prices are almost constantly changing throughout the day, which is what the trend line shows. Every now and then, you will notice in the trend line that you have a several high points and several low points. These high points indicated the highest prices of the stock and the lowest points show the lowest prices.

The biggest difference between the breakout strategies compared to the breakdown strategy is the condition of the market. If you notice that the stock has been going on an upward trend for a while, you will use the breakout strategy. However, if you notice that the trend shows the price has been decreasing over time, you will use the breakdown strategy.

News Playing

As you know by now, one of the most important parts of your day is your pre-trading portion. This is one of the first things you will do once you start your day. You will want to do this before you start trading; however, you will probably be checking out the stock market so you can see the changes in your stocks and any target stocks that you are watching.

However, one of the most important parts of this part of the day is reading the news that happened over night. This is important because you need to know what news is going to affect what stock, especially if you own the stock. You should always make note that any type of news can affect the pricing of financial instruments. For example, if you read that a company donated a large amount of money towards a nonprofit organization, people might be more likely to invest in that stock. However, if you read any negative news about a company, you will find the stock price going down because people are selling their shares.

Be Flexible

While you want to follow the rules and guidelines, you should also remain flexible. First, you want to remember that life happens. Sometimes we plan to sit down to work but we have to go pick up a sick child from school or have a family emergency. When this happens, we might not be able to complete the financial instruments that we took on. This means that you will either keep them in your portfolio and take any loss or hope for a gain or you can trade them and close out for the day. When you are flexible, you will realize that this situation will be fine, and you won't dwell on the fact that you couldn't complete the job as you should have.

Remaining flexible will also help when you find yourself with unrealistic expectations, which is a common mistake among traders. On top of this, it will help you realize that mistakes happen and you shouldn't put too much emphasis on them.

Remember the Research

Learning is a common theme as a trader. It doesn't matter what type of trading you find yourself taking on, you will always want to make sure that you learn as much as you can before you start your career and continue to learn. There are a variety of ways that you can focus on research and learning with swing trading.

Join an Online Community

Another great way to learn about swing trading and meet other traders is to join an online community. There are several websites that are comprised of forums run by some of the most experienced swing traders today. These forums are extremely beneficial to any trader for a variety of reasons. First, beginners can go join the community and receive more tips, trading lessons, and other information that will help them become successful. Second, this is often a location where beginners meet their trading mentor. Third, this is a place where traders can go to not only get the most up-to-date information on the profession but also get to know people who are like them. It is always important to feel that you are not alone, especially when find yourself struggling with a part of trading. There will be hundreds, if not thousands, of people who will be interested in helping you.

Pick a strategy that is easy

Some beginners think that complex strategies are the best to increase their profits. But these complex strategies can be really confusing and overwhelming for someone who is just beginning. Go with a simple strategy, at least until you learn more about the market.

Start in one place

Many beginner traders will start out by trying out too many markets at once. This can make it hard to know what you are doing. Stick with one market and one pattern and concentrate on that for now.

Chapter 10

What are Financial Leverages?

Leverage is a concept that is used by both companies and investors. For investors, the notion of leverage is used to try and increase returns that come on investment. To use leverage, you have to make use of various instruments, including future, options, and margin accounts.

The use of leverage options trading helps boost your profits. Trading in options can give you huge leverage and allow you to generate huge profits from a small investment.

Definition

Leverage is the ability to trade a large number of options using just a small amount of capital. Many traders feel that leverage is, but studies have found that the risk in leveraged options is nearly the same as non-leveraged securities.

Why Is Leverage Riskier?

Trading options using leverage is usually considered riskier because it exaggerates the potential of the business. For instance, you can use $500 to enter a trade that has a potential of $7000. Remember the first rule of trading – do not trade what you cannot lose.

This is not as true as it seems, which is why you must know what you are doing at all times.

Leverage makes you utilize capital more efficiently. For this reason, many traders love the trade because it allows them to go for larger positions with limited capital.

When you use leverage, you do not reduce the potential profit that you will gain; rather, you reduce the risk in specific trades. For instance, if you want to put your money in 10,000 options at $8 per share, you will need to risk $80,000 worth of investment. This means that the whole amount of $80,000 would be at risk. However, you can use leverage to place a smaller amount of money, thus reducing the risk of loss.

This is the way you need to look at leverage, which is the right way.

Before you can trade leverage, you need to find a way to maximize the gains in each trade. Here are a few tips that you can explore:

Know When to Run

You need to cut losses early enough and then let your winning trades run to completion. Just the way you run other trades, you need to know when to cut your losses so that you do not end up bankrupt. You need to make use of stop losses when running leverage in trades.

Have a Stop Loss Set

As a trader, you need to determine your stop-loss set so that you do not lose more than you can afford. The set that you come up with will depend upon the situation of the market at any time. Whatever the case, always make sure you have a set to guide you.

Do not go with the Trade

Many traders try to chase a trade to the finish, something that ends up discouraging them and making them lose money. Once a move happens, you need to accept and wait for the next opening. Always be patient because, just like the other opportunity came along, another one will come by.

Have Limit Orders

Instead of placing market limits, opt for limit orders instead so that you can save on fees. The limit orders also help you reign in your emotions when you trade.

Learn About Technical Analysis

Make sure you learn about technical analysis before you jump into trading. Technical analysis will make sure you have the information that you need to make decisions fast.

The Advantages of Leverage in Options Trading

When you use leverage, you increase your financial capability as a trader and enjoy better trading results. You can change the amount of leverage at your discretion. This is because when you open a trading account, you have all the power of managing the amount of capital that you place on a trade. The good news is that you can use leverage free of charge, but you need to make sure you know how it works and whether it will work for you or not.

The level of leverage varies. Some trading platforms offer leverage from as low as 1:1 up to and beyond 1:1000. As a trader, you should go for the largest leverage possible so that you can make the biggest returns.

Another advantage is that low leverage allows you as a new trader to survive. When starting in options trading, you can make small trades with little to show for your efforts. With leverage, you can make use of leverage to place trades that run into thousands of dollars without risking the same amount in terms of investment. As long as you know what you are doing, you can enjoy massive profits.

Disadvantages of Leverage in Options Trading

As much as it is a good way to make huge profits, you also need to understand that leverage comes with many demerits. These include:

Magnifies the Losses

With leverage, you will be faced with huge losses if the trader decides to go the other way. And since the original outlay is way smaller than what you end up losing, many traders forget that they are placing their capital at risk. Make sure you come up with a ratio that will help protect your interests and then know how to manage trade risk.

No Privileges

When you use leverage to trade, you sacrifice full ownership of the asset. For instance, when you use leverage, you give up the opportunity of enjoying dividends. This is because the amount on the dividend is deducted from the account regardless of the position of the trade.

Margin Calls

A margin call is when the lender asks you to add funds so that you keep the trade open. You have to decide whether you wish to add funds or exit a position to reduce the exposure.

Incur Expenses

When you use leverage to trade options, you will receive the money from the lender so that you can use the full position. Most traders opt to keep their positions open overnight, which attracts a fee to cover the costs.

How Much Leverage Do You Need in Options Trading

Knowing how to trade options needs detailed knowledge about the various aspects of economics. For many people, the lack of knowledge to use leverage is the primary cause of losses.

Studies show that many traders who opt for options lose money in the process. This happens whether for smaller or high leverage.

Risks of High Leverage

In options trading, the capital for placing a trade is usually sourced from a broker. While you can borrow huge amounts to place on a trade, you can gain more if the trade is successful.

A few years ago, traders were able to offer leverage of up to 400 times the initial capital. However, the rules and regulations have changed, and at the moment you can only access 50 times more than you have. For example, if you have $1000, you can control up to $50,000.

Choosing the Right Leverage

You need to look at different factors when choosing the kind of leverage that will work for you.

First, you need to start with low levels of leverage, because the more you borrow, the more you will need to pay back. Second, you need to use stops to make sure you protect the amount you have borrowed. Remember, losses will not go well with you.

All in all, you need to choose leverage which you find is comfortable for you. If you are a beginner, go for low leverage so that you minimize risks. If you know what you are doing, then go for maximum leverage to build your returns.

Using stops on order allows you to reduce losses when the trade changes direction. As a newbie, this is the only protection you need to make it in the market. This is because you will learn about the trades and how to place them while limiting any losses that might arise.

How to Manage Risk in Options Trading

Options trading comes with several risks that you need to manage so that you can enjoy the profits and minimize losses.

Here are a few risks and how to deal with them.

Losing More than What You Have

This risk is inherent in options trading, especially if you are using leverage to make a trade. It means that you put up a small fraction of the initial deposit to open the trade. This means that your fate is in the hands of the direction of the market. If it goes along with your prediction, you will gain more than they deposit. On the other hand, if the direction changes and you lose the position, you might end up losing more than your initial deposit.

When this happens, you need to have a strategy in place to help mitigate the risk. What you need to do in this case is to set a limit so that you define the exact level at which the trade should stop so that you do not lose more than you can handle.

Positions Closing Unexpectedly

When positions close unexpectedly, they lead to loss of money. To keep the trades open, you need to have some money in the account. This aspect is called the margin, and if you do not have enough funds to cover the margin, then the position might close.

To mitigate this, you need to keep an eye on the running balances and always add funds as needed.

Sudden Huge Losses or Gains

The market can turn out to be volatile, and when it does, you need to move fast. Markets change depending on the news or something else in the market, which can be an announcement, event, or changes in trader behavior.

Apart from having stopped, you also need to get notifications regarding any upcoming movement, which tells you whether to react or not,

Orders Filled in Erroneously

When you give instructions to a broker to place a trade for you, and the broker instead does the opposite, this is termed slippage. When this happens, use guaranteed stops to make sure you protect yourself against any slippage that might occur.

How to Trade Smarter Using Leverage

Even with leverage in tow, you need to have a way to trade better. With many mistakes occurring during a trade, you stand to lose more than gain if you do not have the right tips to excel. Let us look at the top mistakes that you go through to get to the top.

Misunderstanding Leverage

Many beginners do not understand leverage and go ahead to misuse this feature, barely realizing the risk they are exposing themselves to.

To make this work for you, learn about leverage, and master it. Understand what it is and what it is not and then find out the best ways to make use of it. You also need to understand how much you can put in without running huge losses.

Having No Exit Plan

Just like socks, you need to control your emotions when trading options. It does not mean that you have to swallow your greed and fear; rather, you need to have a plan that you can go with. Once you have a plan, you need to stick to it so that even when things are not going your way, you have something to guide you to make a recovery.

You need to have an exit plan, which means you know when to drop a trade.

Failure to Try New Strategies

You need to make sure you try out a few new strategies depending on the level of trading you want to achieve. Most traders get a single strategy and then stick to it even when it is not working out for them. When this happens, you are often tempted to go against the rules that you set down.

Maintain an open mind so that you can learn new option trading strategies to help you get more out of your trades.

Chapter 11
Technical Analysis

To put with technical analysis, it is a way Option Traders finds a framework to study the price movement. The simple theory behind this method is that a person will look at the previous prices and the changes, hence determine the current trading conditions and the potential price movement. The only problem with this method would be that it is philosophical, meaning that all technical analysis is that it is reflected in the price. The price reflects the information, which is out there, and the price action is all you would need to make a trade. The technical analysis banks on history and the trends and the Traders will keep an eye on the past, and they will keep an eye on the future as well, and based on that, they will decide if they want to trade or not. More importantly, the people who are going to be trading using the technical analysis will use history to determine whether they are going to make the trade or not. Essentially the way to check out technical analysis would be to look up the trading price of a particular stock in five years. This is what many Option Traders used to determine the history and the future of the capital, and whether or not they should trade using technical analysis. There are many charts you can look up online to figure out how technical analysis takes place. However, we have given you a brief explanation of what technical analysis is.

Using technical analysis, they also look at trends that took place in the past. Most of the time, the stock fluctuates simply due to the trends that took place at the time, with that in mind, Traders will look to the future and see if the trends will retake the position. If so, they will definitely trade or not trade depending on whether that will benefit them or not. Although many people would consider technical analysis a "textbook", it is still very subjective. The reason it's very personal is that people interpret things differently. Some might think that the past will help action, while others might think that it won't, which is why technical analysis is textbook and subjective at the same time. The reason it is a textbook is that you have to do a lot of research before pulling the trigger, and it is subjective because the final decision will be based on how you feel about the operation. Many people say that technical analysis is something more short-term; however, some still believe that the technical report can be used in the long term. In our opinion, we think the technical analysis is short. The reason we believe that technical analysis is short-term is that we primarily base our assumptions on the past and the trends that took place.

Keeping that in mind, the capital gains you might see from technical analysis might be short-term, which means that the tray that you will make will not keep going in the long-term and will be a quick gain for you. Keeping that in mind, technical analysis is a great tool to use for people who are looking to make more money from Options Trading rather quickly. However, make sure that you do research properly on the stock before you make a trade on it. Many people make a trade on it by looking at the 5-year chart. However, it is much deeper than you need to make sure that the trends that took place during those five years are going to retake the position. If not, then it will be entirely subjective for you to make a trade or not. The great thing about technical analysis would be that if you do it correctly, you will have a better chance of seeing success from it, and it can build a ton of confidence in new traders. This will be a significant thing for newbies or could be a bad thing for them since you will become extremely confident and make a blunder.

Technical analysis believes that the current price of the underlying asset in question is the only metric that matters when it comes to looking into the current state of things outside of the market, specifically because everything else is already automatically factored in when the current price is set as it is. As such, to accurately use this type of analysis, all you need to know is the current price of the potential trade-in question as well as the greater economic climate as a whole.

Those who practice technical analysis are then able to interpret what the price is suggesting about market sentiment to make predictions about where the price of a given cryptocurrency is going to go in the future. This is possible since pricing movements are not random. Instead, they follow trends that appear in both the short and the long-term. Determining these trends in advance is key to using technical analysis successfully because all trends are likely to repeat themselves over time.

When it comes to technical analysis, what will always be more important than why? The fact that the price moved in a specific way is far more important to a technical analyst than why it made that particular move. Supply and demand should always be looked at, but beyond that, there are likely too many variables to be worth considering all of them rather than their results.

Technical indicators are used in options trading as a way to determine trends as well as potential turning points in the price of underlying stocks. When used correctly, they can accurately predict movement cycles as well as determine when the most profitable time to buy or sell is going to be.

Technical indicators are typically calculated based on the price pattern of a derivative or stock. Relevant data includes closing price, opening price, lows, highs, and volume. Indicators typically take the data regarding a stock's price from the past few periods depending on the charts the analyst favors and use it to generate a trend that will show what has been happening with a specific stock as well as what is likely to happen next.

There are two primary types of technical indicators, leading and lagging. Lagging indicators are used to determine if a new trend is forming or if the underlying stock is currently moving within an expected range through the use of existing data. If the lagging indicator points to a strong trend, then there is a better than 50 percent chance the trend will continue moving forward. Unfortunately, they are not especially useful when it comes to determining pullbacks or rally points that may appear in the future.

Alternately, leading indicators tend to come into play when traders need to predict a likely future price point when it is currently unclear if the current price is going to crash or rally. They tend to manifest as momentum indicators, which help to determine the strength of the movement of the current trend, which will help to determine if the trend is going to continue or reverse. As no trend will continue forever, the momentum indicator will allow you to determine how long of a timeframe your options should be in to ensure that you get out before the disruption begins.

Leading indicators are also useful if you find yourself needing to determine if the price of a specific stock has reached a point where it is unsustainable as this means a slow in the price is forthcoming. As overbought or oversold stocks experience a pullback when a slow occurs, knowing when this type of movement is coming can thus be supremely useful for several different trading strategies.

Fundamental Analysis

Fundamental analysis is more realistic and feasible in the long term. The whole premise behind the theoretical analysis is that you look at the economy of the country and the trading system that is going on to determine whether it is a good trade or not. More focusing on economics, that is why it helps you to figure out which dollar is going up or down and what is causing it.

One of the greatest things you can do when it comes to Options Trading is to understand why a dollar is dropping or going up. Once you can understand that, you will be in a much better position for gaining profits in your Option Trading endeavors. When using the fundamental analysis, you will be looking at the country's employment and unemployment rate, also see how the training with different countries overall sing the country's economy before you decide on whether you should try it or not. Many successful Option Traders solely believe in fundamental analysis, as it is factual, unlike technical analysis. Even though technical analysis is accurate, it is not guaranteed like the theoretical analysis. Instead of looking at the trends, you will be looking at what is causing the highs and the lows. Not only that, based on the highs and lows, but you will also be able to determine the country's current and future economic outlook, whether it is good or not. One rule of thumb to look into with be how good the state is doing, the better the state is doing, the more foreign investors are going to take part in it. Once starting the piece in it, the dollar or the stock in that country will go up tremendously.

The idea behind fundamental analysis is that you need to look at the economies of the country. For you to understand, fundamental analysis is mainly when you invest in a country that is doing well in the economy and you don't invest in a company when it does poorly in the market, which makes sense since the economy dictates how high and low the prices will be per dollar. Most of the time, investors will invest the money as soon as they see the dollar going up. The reason why they will do that is that they know the dollar will keep climbing up since the economy is getting better. One of the great examples would be when the US dollar fell in 2007-2008, and the Canadian dollar rose, at that time, many investors were investing in Canadian dollars rather than US dollars. After a very long time, the US dollar was dropping tremendously, whereas the Canadian dollar was more expensive than the US dollar. This was one of the anomalies which took place back in the day. If you were to use technical analysis in this instance, then you will not get a lot of success out of this economy drop. This is the reason why fundamental analysis could work a lot better for most people in the long-term and in the short-term, and why many top traders recommend you follow fundamental analysis instead of technical analysis to find out which dollar you are going to be investing in.

Chapter 12
Sector Analysis – Technical and Fundamental

Principles of Technical Analysis

To better understand the technical analysis, we will summarize its fundamental principles; we will show the importance of the psychological dimension of technical analysis.

Fundamental Principles

Based on the work of renowned technical analyst John Murphy, we will present the main properties of technical analysis:

Technical analysis focuses on what is, rather than what should be. It is interested in the market itself and not the external factors that it reflects or that may have influenced it. It describes market movements, not the reasons behind them.

This method focuses on the psychology of the operators and not on the fundamentals. Indeed, what matters is not the news, but the way operators react to it. This is a strategic approach to the stock market and not a fundamental approach, whose main purpose is the search for the intrinsic value of the asset. The technical analysis does not question the concept of fundamental value but argues that there may be lasting divergences between the stock price and the latter.

The market value is entirely and solely determined by the game of supply and demand. Supply and demand depend on many factors, some of which are rational and some not. The market results from the permanent interaction of all these behaviors and the differences in interpretation of the speakers. Fundamentals are just one price determinant, among many others.

The courses evolve according to trends that can last a certain time. The trend changes are due to a change in the dominant consensus that will change the balance of power between suppliers and applicants. The graphs consider all the information available at a given moment. History repeats itself, and markets are governed by the psychology of crowds. The phenomena of euphoria and panic are very often found on the markets and this cyclically. The following sentence, attributed to the famous speculator Jesse Livermore, sums up perfectly these words:

"I learned early on that there was nothing new on Wall Street. Indeed, speculation is as old as the hills. What is happening today in the markets has happened in the past and will happen again in the future."

These basic principles are favored by many leading operators (analysts, traders ...)

Consideration of the Psychological Dimension

Fundamental analysis focuses on the real value of a financial asset but neglected psychological components, determining for the proponents of the behavioral approach. This approach has shown that psychological biases explain price shifts with the fundamental value. Technical analysis, therefore, takes into account this psychological dimension and focuses on the emotions of operators.

The fundamentals are supposed to be known to all, and the technical analyst's main task is to determine how the operators react to economic news. Basic information (growth rate, inflation rate, unemployment rate, contracts signed by a company, etc.) has a significant impact on stock prices, but most professional traders attach importance even greater at the behavioral reaction of traders.

Finally, as we have seen above, history repeats itself. In financial markets governed by crowd psychology, it is common to note that the phenomena of euphoria are followed by panic movements.

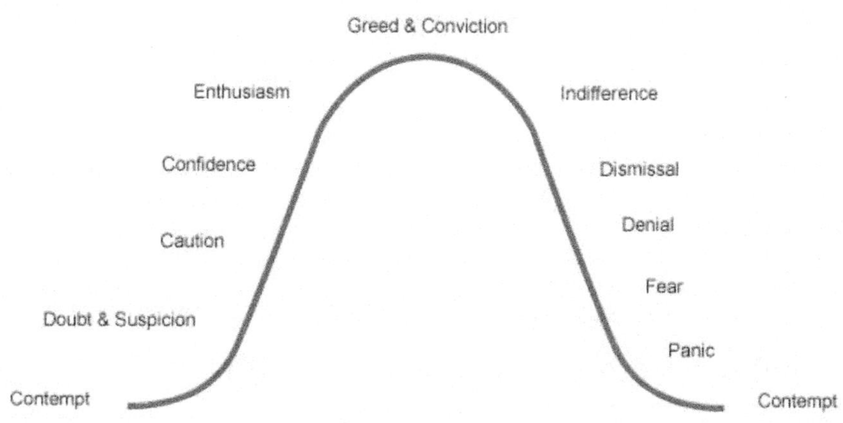

In a reference book, Gerald Loeb explains that a stock market price is only partly determined by a balance sheet and an income statement:

"It is much more by the hopes and fears of humanity, by greed, ambition, events beyond the reach of humanity such as natural disasters, inventions, stress, and tensions in the financial world. Time, discoveries, fashion and innumerable causes that it is impossible to enumerate."

The famous American financier Bernard Baruch going in the same direction as he explains:

"Fluctuations in the stock market do not correspond to the recording of events as such, but to human reactions to these events or how millions of men and women feel the potential impact of these events on the future. In other words, the stock market is a reflection of individuals."

Technical analysis also helps to take a strategic approach capitalizing on the emotions of other traders. The great economist Keynes was also a great speculator. In his financial operations, he relied heavily on crowd psychology and put aside basic analysis, which may seem surprising to a person who has had such a strong impact on economic theory. We owe him the following sentence: "There is nothing more irrational than investing rationally in the markets. This sentence does not mean that the investor must be irrational, but rather that the use of analytical tools considered rational must be used vigilantly. In his General Theory of Employment, Interest, and Money, published in 1936, John Maynard Keynes describes the markets as follows:

"Most professional investors and speculators are less concerned with making accurate forecasts in the long run than with predicting the future changes to the conventional valuation base shortly before the general public. The unacknowledged object of enlightened investment is to steal the departure, as Americans say so well, to be smarter than the public and to pass the wrong or belittled piece to the neighbor."

The Law of Supply and Demand

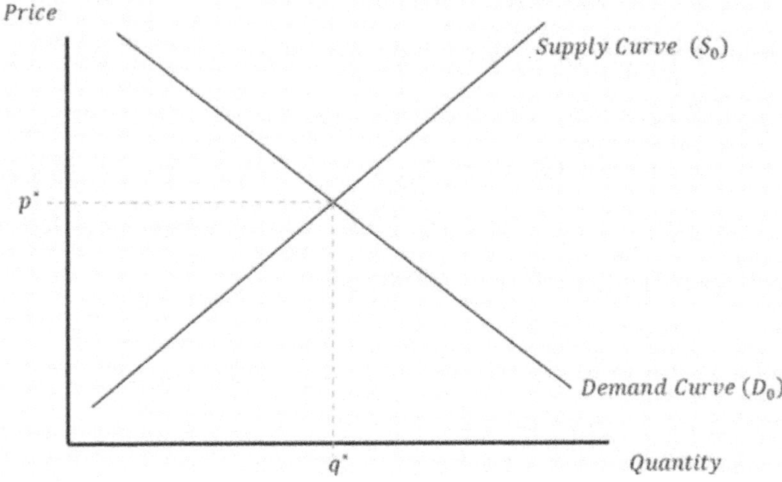

Technical analysis assumes that all the necessary information to the decision is contained in stock prices. The graphs represent a good barometer of investor psychology. Indeed, the technical analysis considers that it is the operators who are at the origin of the stock market fluctuations and not the economic and financial news. If a stock goes up, it is that there are simply more buyers than sellers; conversely, if a stock is down, it means that the sellers are in surplus and plummet the stock prices. If this view of market fluctuations is also shared by fundamental analysis, the two methods diverge on the determinants of stock prices:

For the fundamental analysis, the officers and the plaintiffs focus essentially on the real value of the security. Security will be asked if it is undervalued (price below its fundamental value), and conversely, it will be offered when the stock price is higher than its intrinsic value. Investors are rational and position themselves solely based on the fundamental importance of the security.

For technical analysis, the concept of fundamental value is not necessarily called into question. However, the security can fluctuate quite a bit before returning to its underlying value. Besides, technical analysts consider it difficult to gather all the information needed to perform a fundamental analysis worthy of the name. It is for this reason that technical analysts seek, first of all, to identify the forces involved to determine the probable evolution of prices. The technical analysis simply aims to answer the following question: "Which bull or bear will win the fight?"

The reality is that behind every offer or each application, there are many explanatory factors of fundamental and psychological reasons. The theory of conventions explains that it may be rational to include in its analysis factors that have no connection with fundamentals, such as fashion phenomena, for example. The stock price results from the permanent interaction of all these behaviors and the fundamentals are only one price determinant among all the others. The prices evolve according to "tendencies," which can last a certain time, because of the existence of a dominant convention. A change of trend can be explained in different ways: the fragility of the convention is updated by the financial community which turns away quickly from the financial asset (example of the technological values); the players have positioned themselves massively for the purchase and cannot, therefore, more support the market. Any bad news will have a massive effect and will cause massive sales related to the panic of operators.

Some technical analysts consider that there is no contradiction with the assumption of market efficiency since the graphs take into account all the information available at a given moment. Nevertheless, they forget that fundamental analysis considers operators to be rational, which is not the case for technical analysis. Market movements are predictable because the stakeholders regularly make the same mistakes and systematically deviate from this state of rationality.

Technical Analysis Is Not a Crystal Ball

Technical analysis is a method that can predict the evolution of prices with some reliability, even if it is not an exact science. This pragmatic method focuses primarily on the psychology of operators. It was developed by people operating in the financial markets (Charles Dow, GANN, Homma, Schabacker, and others). The technical analysis serves mainly as a market barometer and can detect excessive movements of crowds. Some of its detractors equate it with a crystal ball, whereas it is simply an effective tool for analyzing market movements.

There is no such thing as a martingale on the financial markets, that is, an infallible system that makes it possible to win every time. First of all, the only "martingale" is the result of hard work, iron discipline, and the courage to stand up even when events are unfavorable.

Operators generally have imperfect knowledge of technical analysis. Besides, it should be noted that the mastery of this approach is insufficient to succeed in the markets. Indeed, it is not enough to correctly predict the evolution of stock prices to beat the markets. The trader must also develop certain qualities that have nothing to do with his analytical know-how (independence of mind, absence of ego, self-control, acceptance of uncertainty, and risk).

The Limits of Fundamental Analysis

First of all, part of the success of technical analysis can be explained by the somewhat dull assessment of the fundamental analysis. This approach has been strongly criticized in recent years due not only to the bad, or even "misleading," recommendations of financial analysts but also because of the numerous financial scandals.

Laura Unger (president of the SEC13 in 2000), in a report, showed that 99% of the recommendations of the 28,000 US financial analysts were to "buy" or "keep" securities in March 2000. Besides, some stars of financial analysis did not stop their buying recommendations despite the market turn. This has been very misinterpreted by individual investors and has given rise to numerous lawsuits.

Henry Blodget, an analyst at Merrill Lynch, waited until August of 2000 to lower his rating (which he recommended for buying when they had already lost more than 75% of their value.)

Mary Meeker, a senior analyst at Morgan Stanley, gained tremendous notoriety by issuing a very positive report on Internet values in 1995. After March 2000, she remained on the purchase and the titles she advised collapsed.

Even after assuming that fundamental analysis has a predictive quality, the many financial scandals have shown that it is very difficult for an investor, whether individual or professional, to obtain complete and reliable information on the fundamental value of a security. They are operated by insider operators taking advantage of their privileged position.

Chapter 13
Choosing the Right Strategy

Before you can start trading, you must understand your reasons for trading, find the right broker, discover the opportunities to trade, and come up with a trading plan. One of the most important steps while making a trade is to decide when to enter and the position to assume. You might probably have all the information you need about options, but it will not do you much good unless you start using that information to make the right decisions to improve your overall finances. Perhaps the most challenging part of planning every trade you make is to select a strategy you use. This stands true, especially if you are just getting started with options trading. At times, even experienced traders tend to struggle with all this. So, do not worry if you are a little confused right now. You will be in a better position to make smart financial decisions.

Important Aspects

When it comes to the perfect strategy for trading in options, there are five various aspects you must consider, and they are as follows.

Your outlook

Your outlook about an option primarily refers to what you expect from the underlying security. Your perspective is about whether you expect a rise or fall in the price of the underlying security in the future. In various forms of investing, these are the only two outlooks that are profitable. For instance, a stock trader can purchase talks that he expects will increase in value or short sell such stocks, which he thinks will decrease in value. These are the only ways in which he can on a profit. However, when it comes to trading in options, there are four potential outlooks, and they are an expectation that the market will be bullish, bearish, neutral, or volatile. This certainly means there is a lot to think about, but it also increases the chances of your profitability. The four market conditions to be mindful of are.

Bullish- expecting the price to increase

Bearish- expecting the price the decrease

Neutral- price will stay relatively stable

Volatile- price can significantly sway either way.

Your outlook can be made more specific. For instance, your outlook can be significantly bullish or even moderately bullish. By making this outlook as precise as possible, you are making it easier to select the right strategy for investing. For instance, if you are expecting that the price of the underlying security will experience a significant increase in its price, you will not opt for a strategy, which generates profits based on small movements in the price. Given the various plans available, you are also free to combine your outlook. For instance, you might expect the price of an underlying security to stay neutral in the short-term and increase significantly in the long run. Some strategies can be used to help you earn a profit by combining these outlooks. This just goes on to prove the flexibility offered by options.

The Risk Involved

When it comes to investing, there is always a certain degree of risk involved. There are some strategies, which have to reduce your risk, whereas others are quite risky. According to your risk profile, and you must opt for a specific approach. Apart from this, you must also consider the risk to reward ratio. It is a general belief that the higher the risk involved, the greater the reward you can receive. So, take some time and calculate the total risk you can easily sustain without denting your finances. Once you have this number, it becomes easier to select a strategy. Also, never invest more than you can stand to lose. This is a cardinal rule of investing you must never overlook.

Single Position versus Options Spread

Options trading usually works on the creation of various spreads. It essentially means the combination of multiple positions you must assume to enter an overall position. By using spreads, you can effectively reduce the risk associated with investing in options along with the cost of investment. It is always better to use sprites instead of a single position. By entering a single position, you are essentially buying a writing only one specific type of options contract. The advantages of this technique are that the number of transactions involved and less; therefore, the commission payable on each trade will certainly be less when compared to options spread. If you are interested in only making small trades initially, then a single position is quite profitable. Therefore, whether you opt for a single position or options spread will depend on the occasion and the market conditions.

Amount of Trading Involves

For becoming an options trader, you must create a trading account with a broker. Usually, these accounts are assigned a specific trading limit. These limits help protect their customers from assuming risks higher than what they can stand and also for certain regulatory purposes. If the trading level is quite low, then there are only a few trading strategies you can use. So, the trading level helps to determine your overall investment and trading strategies you use.

The Complexity of the Strategy

Certain trading strategies are quite simple, and then some are a little complex. Some strategies only involve dealing in one or two transactions, whereas others combine several transactions. So, the complexity involved also influences the strategy you opt for. An important aspect of determining the potential profit or loss you incur depends on your entry and exit points. If there are multiple transactions and assets involved, it becomes slightly complex. You will realize certain strategies are quite easy to understand others, which will take some practice. If you do not understand a strategy initially, do not attempt it. Once you gain the required confidence and have been trading for some time, you can attempt any of the complex strategies. After all, the idea is to maximize your earnings.

Types of Strategies

The various strategies you can choose from can be classified as follows.

Bullish trading outlook

Strategies you can use when you expect a positive movement in the price of an underlying security or asset is referred to as a bullish options trading strategy. Perhaps the most obvious way to benefit from an increase in the price of the underlying security is by investing in calls. However, this is not the best strategy to use to honor return when the movement of price is only moderate. It does not offer any security if there is a decrease in the price of the underlying asset.

Buying calls is a strategy itself, to begin with, and there are several circumstances where an emir purchase of calls can be profitable. There are a couple of disadvantages to buying calls as well. For instance, you stand the risk of the contract you invest in expiring worthless and providing nonprofit at all – it essentially means losing out on your entire investment. The negative effects of time decay are something you must watch out for, and you stand to gain only if there is a significant increase in the price of the underlying security to on a profit. This does not mean buying calls is a bad idea. However, to avoid these risks, you can opt for a bullish trading strategy.

For instance, you can use a strategy that reduces the cost of purchasing calls by simultaneously writing calls that have a higher strike price. This can help in reducing the negative impact of time decay on the position you hold. Another advantage of using bullish strategies as it allows you to create credit spreads that provide an upfront returned instead of an upfront cost, which is associated with a debit spread. The main reason to use bullish trading strategies is it allows you to enter opposition, which profits from an increase in the price of the underlying asset and also helps control other factors that are important you like the associated level of risk and the capital required.

Long call and a short put, bull call spread, bull put spread, bull ratio spread, short bull ratio spread, will butterfly spread, bull condor spread and bullish call ladder spread are various examples of bullish options trading strategies.

Bearish Trading Strategies

When you have a bearish outlook toward the market, it essentially means you are expecting the price of the underlying assets to decrease. Perhaps the most straightforward way to go about earning a profit while the price of an underlying security decreases is by buying put options. If there is no change in the price of the underlying security, then the option will expire worthlessly; if you are expecting a small drop in the price of the underlying asset, then buying or investing in a put option is not a good idea. It is if you are willing to take a position on an underlying asset whose prices are decreasing but are not interested in risking a lot of capital, then the good idea is to invest in options. Writing puts reduce any upfront cost payable. You can also include the writing of calls to minimize the effect of time decay on your investment.

Long put, short call, bear put spread, bear call spread, bear ratio spread, short bear ratio spread, bear butterfly spread, and bear put ladder spread are various types of bearish trading strategies.

Strategies in a Neutral Market

The term neutral is used for describing all such financial instruments that do not exhibit any change in price. When it comes to options, the term neutral has a broader meaning. Neutral trading strategies are such strategies that help the investor earn a profit when the price of the underlying security stays unchanged or when the price moves within a fixed range. An instrument is believed to be moving sideways when it exhibits slight up and down movements in its price. When the price moves sideways, then the underlying security is showing a neutral trend.

The apparent advantage of this strategy is its mere existence. The ability to profit from instruments that show relatively stable prices gives investors plenty of investing options. There are three ways in which a trader can benefit from this trend – the cost of the security does not move, there is a slight increase in the price or there is a slight decrease in the price.

Chapter 14
Buying Calls

Assuming a Long Position

When you buy stock, you get what is known as a long position. When you buy a call option, you get into a potential long position based on the underlying stock. On the other hand, when you sell a stock short, then you are short selling.

This essentially gives you a short position. Short selling means that you sell at a loss, while long selling implies a profit. When you sell a naked call or an uncovered call, you will enter a potentially short position based on the underlying stock.

Assuming a Short Position

You enter a potential short position based on the underlying stock when you purchase a put option. Should you sell a naked put, you will enter a potential long position relative to the underlying stock.

If you can understand these four positions and keep them in mind, then you will easily understand the intricacies of selling and buying options. Ideally, you can buy call options and put options as well as sell call options and put options.

Holders: Anyone who buys options is generally referred to as the holder of an option.

Writers: A person who sells an option is generally referred to as an options writer.

Call and put holders are also known as buyers. They have the right to buy options but are not obligated to do so. They can exercise this right but only within the stipulated time and under the agreed conditions. This way, call and put holders only suffer losses equivalent to the premium charged for the options contract.

Call and put writers are sellers. They should sell options or buy if the option expire, and the contract makes money. Therefore, sellers are always expected to oblige to the buyer's wishes. This exposes them to more risks. Therefore, writers stand to lose a lot more than just the cost of writing the options contract.

Example

Think about this company that you like, such that you would like to become a shareholder. According to your predictions, the stock price is going to rise. For instance, the current stock price of this company is $25, but you believe the price will be $35 in a year. You can buy a call option that will grant you the right to purchase the stock.

On the contract, you can agree to a price of approximately $27 within the succeeding year. This contract will most likely cost you close to $1 per 100 shares. Now, if the price does get to $35 as predicted, then you can exercise your right to buy the shares at $27. However, if the price remains constant or falls, you will not be obliged to buy, and the only loss you will incur is the options fee.

Basic Put and Call Options Chain

This is a specific chain that is among the most popular options chains used by investors and traders, especially beginners. It is an excellent choice for those seeking to learn more about options.

This chain presents a splittable with put options to the right and calls options to the left. The different strike prices relevant to the options run to fight down the center of the table. This way, investors and traders can easily track put and call options of various strike prices. This is demonstrated via the image presented below.

If we closely examine the options chain above, we note that the strike prices run through the middle from top to bottom. We also note that the put options are located on the right side while the call options are on the left-hand side.

Other parameters such as bid price, last price, ask price, volumes, price change from the preceding trading day, and open interested are displayed for both putting and call options. When it comes to trading or investing, this chain is the most widely used. It is popular with traders basically because it presents a lot of the information they consider crucial.

Important information necessary to execute trades is presented in a simple manner that is easy to read and understand. Using this chain, a trader can easily trace and identify the available call and put options as well as other parameters affiliated to each option. However, this chain is most suitable for traders interested in simple options trading strategies. There are other ideal chains for more complex strategies.

The Call and Put Options Price

The put and call pricer is a chain that presents the necessary data relating to basic call and put options. It also projects each option with five option Greeks. This way, an investor or trader who needs to use delta neutral options trading strategies and arbitrage strategies, will be able to effectively make exact calculations regarding size and position to take.

Looking at a relevant chain, you will easily note that all the five Greek symbols that include Vega, Rho, Theta, Gamma and Delta are used. They are visible in the call and put options pricer. However, due to challenges in full-screen presentations, options pricers usually present as either put options or call options only.

Options Strategies Chains

Specific options strategies chains are ideal for options traders or investors who prefer standardized options strategies like the covered call or the long straddle. The reason is that these chains drastically reduce the amount of work necessary to work out and calculate the options outlay as well as other specifics that relate to the specific strategy.

Options chains like this one generally present only the essential aspects of an options trading strategy across the various expiration dates and strike prices. This way, it can easily calculate and work out the net effect of a position and plenty of other useful detail. This way, a trader can make quick decisions on the spread to choose fast without spending time doing calculations and working out arithmetic.

Call and Put Options Matrix

This chain is the least used by investors and traders, especially beginners and retail options traders. This chain aims to present information on many options, including their bid and ask prices over numerous expiration dates all on one page.

This options matrix generally presents only the ask and bid prices for all options listed on the chain but without additional information. This makes it a less useful table, especially for beginners, amateurs and retail traders who need a lot more information. However, it is considered by many traders to be the least useful chain out there.

Learn about Options Pricing

Another useful aspect of options trading that you need to be familiar with is the aspect of pricing options. The option price is also known as the option premium and consists of two distinct components. These are the intrinsic value and extrinsic value. Both are governed by the Put-Call Parity principle.

Tips for Buying Call Options

Do not buy a call option with a strike price that you do not think the stock can beat.

Always include the premium price in your analysis.

Look for calls that are just in the money. These are likely to bring a modest profit.

Call options that are out of the money might give you an option for a cheaper premium.

However, the premium should not be your primary consideration when looking to buy a call option. Compared to the money required to buy the shares and the potential profits if the stock goes past the strike price, the premium is going to be a trivial cost in most cases – provided, of course, the strike price is high enough to take the premium into account.

Look at the time value. If you are looking for larger profits, it is better to aim for longer contracts. Remember that with any call option, you have the option to buy the stock at the strike price at any time between today's date and the deadline when the stock market price exceeds the strike price. Longer time frames mean you increase the chances of that happening. Even if the price goes a little above the strike price and dips down, with a longer window of time before the deadline, you can wait and see if it rebounds. Remember, if it never does, you are only out the premium.

Start small. Beginning traders should not bet the farm on options. You will end up broke if you do that. The better approach is to start by investing in one contract at a time and gaining experience as you go.

The best-case scenario for you, as the buyer, is that the stock suddenly starts rising at high speed before the deadline arrives. You want it to go beyond the strike price so that, when it comes time to exercise your right, you are purchasing your stock at a lower rate than it is now worth. You then have the option to instantly list that stock as a covered sell, which would allow you to realize that profit in real money.

That final piece of the puzzle is the important one. As an options trader, you are not in the business of building a stock portfolio. You do not want those shares – you want to make a profit on them as they pass through your hands. You want to buy them for less than they are worth and then sell them on, perhaps even for more than they are worth if you are lucky. It is within that transaction your money will be made.

Buying calls has several advantages for you as an options trader:

It does not cost much to get involved in the movement of a stock. You only need to fork out the amount for the premium, after which you can sit back and wait to see what the stock does before making your purchase decision based on actual information rather than on speculating what the market will do.

It allows you to make use of the kinds of "tips" that market experts have a bad habit of swearing by. You read the news, you are watching the markets and you have information that makes you think a certain stock is about to rise fast and hard. You want to take advantage of that, and options trading allows you to do so much more safely than simply buying the stock. If you are wrong, you will only lose your premium and you may even make a small profit. If you were wrong and purchased the stock and then it plummeted rather than rose, you stand to lose a whole lot more cash.

Chapter 15
Covered Calls

Setting up covered calls is relatively low risk and will help you get familiar with many of the aspects of options trading. While it is probably not going to make you rich overnight, it is a good way to learn the tools of the trade.

Covered Calls Involve a Long Position

To create a covered call, you need to have at least 100 shares of stock in one underlying equity. When you create a call, you are going to be offering potential buyers a chance to buy these shares from you. Of course, the strategy is that you are only going to sell high, but your real goal is to get the income stream from the premium.

The premium is a one-time non-refundable fee. If a buyer purchases your call option and pays you the premium, that money is yours. No matter what happens after that, you have got that cash to keep. If the stock does not reach the strike price, the contract will expire, and you can create a new call option on the same underlying shares. Of course, if the stock price does pass the strike price, the buyer of the contract will probably exercise their right to buy the shares. You will still earn money on the trade, but the risk is you are giving up the potential to make as much money that could have been earned on the trade.

You write a covered call option that has a strike price of $67. Suppose that for some unforeseen reason, the shares skyrocket to $90 a share. The buyer of your call option will be able to purchase the shares from you at $67. So, you have gained $2 a share. However, you have missed out on the chance to sell the shares at a profit of $35 a share. Instead, the investor who purchased the call option from you will turn around and sell the shares on the markets for the actual spot price, and they will reap the benefits.

However, you have not lost anything. You have earned the premium plus sold your shares of stock for a modest profit.

That risk – that the stocks will rise to a price that is much higher than the strike price – always exists, but if you do your homework, you are going to be offering stocks that you do not expect to change much in price over the lifetime of your call. So, suppose instead that the price only rose to $68. The price exceeded the strike price, so the buyer may exercise their option. In that case, you are still missing out on some profit that you could have had otherwise, but it is a small amount, and we are not taking into account the premium.

If the stock price does not exceed the strike price over the length of the contract, then you get to keep the premium and you get to keep the shares. The premium is yours to keep no matter what.

In reality, in most situations, a covered call is going to be a win-win situation for you.

Covered Calls are a Neutral Strategy

A covered call is known as a "neutral" strategy. Investors create covered calls for stocks in their portfolio, where they only expect small moves over the lifetime of the contract. Moreover, investors will use covered calls on stocks that they expect to hold for the long term. It is a way to earn money on the stocks during a period in which the investor assumes that the stock will not move much at a price and so will have no earning potential from selling.

An Example of a Covered Call

Let us say that you buy 100 shares of Acme Communications. It is currently trading at $40 a share. Over the next several months, nobody is expecting the stock to move very much, but as an investor, you feel Acme Communications has solid long-term growth potential. To make a little bit of money, you sell a call option on Acme Communications with a strike price of $43. Suppose that the premium is $0.78 and that the call option lasts three months.

For 100 shares, you will earn a total premium payment of $0.78 x 100 = $78. No matter what happens, you pocket the $78.

Now let us say that over the next three months, the stock drops a bit in price so that it never comes close to the strike price, and at the end of the three months, it is trading at $39 a share.

The options contract will expire, and it is worthless. The buyer of the options contract ends up empty-handed. You have a win-win situation. You have earned the extra $78 per 100 shares, and you still have your shares at the end of the contract.

Now let us say that the stock does increase a bit in value. Over time, it jumps up to $42, and then to $42.75, but then drops down to $41.80 by the time the options contract expires. In this scenario, you are finding yourself in a much better position. In this case, the strike price of $43 was never reached, so the buyer of the call option is again left out in the cold. You, on the other hand, keep the premium of $78, and you still get to keep the shares of stock. This time since the shares have increased in value, you are a lot better off than you were before, so it is a win-win situation for you, even though it is a losing situation for the poor soul who purchased your call.

Sadly, there is another possibility that the stock price exceeds the strike price before the contract expires. In that case, you are required to sell the stock. You still end up in a position that is not all that bad, however. You did not lose any actual money, but you lost a potential profit. You still get the premium of $78, plus the earnings from the sale of the 100 shares at the strike price of $43.

A covered call is almost a zero-risk situation because you never lose money even though if the stock price soars, you missed out an opportunity. You can minimize that risk by choosing stocks you use for a covered call option carefully. For example, if you hold shares in a pharmaceutical company that is rumored to be announcing a cure for cancer in two months, you probably do not want to use those shares for a covered call. A company that has more long-term prospects but probably is not going anywhere in the next few months is a better bet.

How to go about creating a covered call

To create a covered call, you will need to 100 shares of stock. While you do not want to risk a stock that is likely to take off shortly, you do not want to pick a total dud either. There is always someone willing to buy something – at the right price. But you want to go with a decent stock so that you can earn a decent premium.

You start by getting online at your brokerage and looking up the stock online. When you look up stocks online, you will be able to look at their "option chain," which will give you information from a table on premiums that are available for calls on this stock. You can see these listed under bid price. The bid price is given on a per-share basis, but a call contract has 100 shares. If your bid price is $1.75, then the actual premium you are going to get is $1.75 x 100 = $175.

An important note is that the further out the expiration date, the higher the premium. A good rule of thumb is to pick an expiry that is between two and three months from the present date. Remember that the longer you go, the higher the risk because that increases the odds that the stock price will exceed the strike price, and you will end up having to sell the shares.

You have an option (no pun intended) with the premium you want to charge. Theoretically, you can set any price you want. Of course, that requires a buyer willing to pay that price for you to make money. A more reasonable strategy is to look at prices people are currently requesting for call options on this stock. You can do this by checking the asking price for the call options on the stock. You can also see prices that buyers are currently offering by looking at the bid prices. For an instant sale, you can simply set your price to a bid price that is already out there. If you want to go a little bit higher, you can submit the order and then wait until someone comes along to buy your call option at the bid price.

To sell a covered call, you select "sell to open."

Benefits of Covered Calls

- A covered call is a relatively low-risk option. The worst-case scenario is that you will be out of your shares but earn a small profit, a smaller profit than you could have made if you had not created the call contract and simply sold your shares. However, you also get the premium.
- A covered call allows you to generate income from your portfolio in the form of premiums.
- If you do not expect any price moves on the stock in the near term and you plan on holding it long term, it is a reasonable strategy to generate income without taking much risk.

Risks of Covered Calls

- Covered calls can be a risk if you are bullish on the stock and your expectations are realized, and there is a price spike. In that case, you have traded the small amount of income of the premium with a voluntary cap of the strike price for the potential upside you could have had if you had simply held the stock and sold it at the high price.

- If the stock price plummets, while you still get the premium, the stocks will be worthless unless they rebound over the long term. You should not use a call option on stocks that you expect to be on the path to a major drop in the coming months. In that case, rather than writing a covered call, you should simply sell the stocks and take your losses. Alternatively, you can continue holding the stocks to see if they rebound over the long term.

Chapter 16
Market Strategies

Why Use Stock Market Strategies?

Here is a good question. Why is it worth using stock market strategies? You need to know that the financial instruments you are trading on, such as CFDs (contracts for difference), are already designed to be simplified and accessible for investment.

Even the platforms where you will find yourself performing from a practical point of view, your trading operations are very intuitive. They can, therefore, be exploited both by industry experts who demand the possibility of trading professionally, via beginners who may never have put to this kind of tools but still want to create a monthly income by investing in the stock market.

One of the right reasons why it is worth learning the stock market strategies lies in the fact that we are sure that you also have always dreamed of finding a job that would not force you to move for long stretches, perhaps remaining stuck in traffic and city chaos. This job does not oblige you to say yes to the boss on duty who may not even deserve to occupy that place, a job where you should not be forced to work overtime to be able to reach the end of the month charging you with stress and fatigue.

This is why we believe that trading with stock market strategies is the best possible alternative, not only offline but also online. Being independent in this promising world guarantees you the possibility to shake off the problems linked to the crisis to earn your freedom, even before the money, to become the master of your life.

A thousand good reasons to trade with the right strategy

If you find yourself somehow, you have heard about the possibility of trading on the stock exchange, and maybe you know there is no way to do it online. If you want to take this path, we ask you not to feel intimidated or frightened by your possible future as a financial operator.

The stock exchange trading online has become a beginner's measure. If, until today, you have only played lowly professions and do not have a higher degree, perhaps you think that you are not up to this kind of activity.

Perhaps you believe that the Stock Exchange and Markets, as well as the strategies to earn money, are beyond your means. Enough of this loser mentality!

The truth is that you are second to none, and you have the potential to be on a par with others and, why not, also to excel, especially in a world where meritocracy reigns like that of the stock market and financial markets on the internet.

Millions of people around the world have chosen the path of investment of their online capital, although very small. Now you can do it yourself by putting into practice the stock market strategies that we will propose to you during this guide.

Apply the right bag techniques

Do you think that all these people know every single nation and all the secrets of the financial markets to be able to earn a salary at the end of the month in this kind of activity?

This is not the case. Anyone who makes money from online trading does so from little to useful knowledge. It is, therefore, not a question of quantity; it is only a question of quality.

Few but good stock market strategies will allow you to become an established and successful trader who can afford to buy whatever he wants, in total independence, and without having to ask anyone for anything.

It is necessary to know as well as to apply the right bag technique. Learn it first through theory, then put it into practice in the field of trading, testing it continuously and optimizing it based on your trading methodology.

Do not miss the topics to come and immediately discover the best stock exchange strategies, the path that will lead you to become a real trader may be extended and tortuous. Still, in the end, it will be worth it, and you will finally feel satisfied in an occupation free from conditioning and the harassment of the world of work as it has always known it.

If you start trading today, your old life will already be in the past, because you are about to be immersed in a virtuous circle of real opportunities to become an ace of stock trading. Cheers!

Difference between Tactics and Stock Market Strategies

Modern stock exchange strategies have been devised to permanently change the old canons of traditional investment that made everything too slow and stiff, too challenging to apply, and this caused traders many problems and dissatisfactions, so much that many were eventually led to abandon this promising activity.

With the new strategies, the goal has been to make trading affordable and feasible for everyone, the doors are wide open, and anyone who wants it today can enter without suffering the typical problems of the past.

What it takes to make the most of the strategies that we propose to you in all respects is the only basic knowledge of the subject of trading. Consequently, you are not called to know everything to start earning.

Therefore, trading does not mean having a degree in economics. After all, those who would be prepared today to face five years of studies to earn money, it is too much time and too much sacrifice to put in place, so the techniques that you have to use to earn are simple but effective strategies that guarantee the success of the trades in most cases.

But because in stock trading, we talk about strategies and not tactics and because the former is much more successful and secure than the latter. The speech is very simple, and we want to clarify it with the following short definitions.

Investment Strategies

The strategy is the description of a long-term action plan used to set and subsequently coordinate all the actions that serve to achieve a particular, specific purpose. Strategies can be applied in all fields to reach the goal.

They, therefore, carry out the task of obtaining greater security by making a series of separate operations that help to reach an end goal. In the case of trading, we are talking about profit, which is undoubtedly the only primary aim that drives people to enter this business.

The simple tactic, on the other hand, is a course of action adopted according to the achievement of specific objectives, but in this case, we speak of small achievements in the short-term.

Adopting tactics would not be effective or satisfactory in the field of trading because it is not a structured plan, but simple plans to achieve small temporary objectives.

In short, with a tactic, you can also win a battle, but not war; winning a war requires a broader STRATEGY.

What all traders aim to achieve is a constant and lasting success over time that gives total security of a monthly income and specific collections on an annual basis. In stock exchange trading, it is possible to achieve all this by using strategies. Without strategies, you might perish as a trader very soon.

Applying stock exchange strategies requires attention and many precautions, especially at the beginning, when you are not much of an expert. In certain situations, when the markets become uncertain or careless, you do not know how to act, and you risk making mistakes.

At specific errors, however, the strategies cannot be remedied; in those cases, it will be the experience to act as a master and to suggest the right moves to make.

How much do you earn if you use the best strategy to invest?

With financial instruments available today, profit margins are simply impressive; operating in the right way, you can earn a lot of money even daily, but at that point, you have to take into account other factors such as the skill of the trader, the ability to avoid the losses, the amount of capital you have available, but also the small strokes of luck that from time to time can help to increase profits.

The amount of money that can be earned then also depends, above all, on the financial product you intend to use. There are not very marked differences but still tangible, depending on whether you prefer to trade forex, CFD, or investing in social trading.

Stock Market Strategies and Money Management

If you intend to trade on the stock exchange, there is no doubt that you will, sooner or later, have to come into contact with the rules of money management or all that concerns the management of money and your precious investment capital.

Money Management shows you the way to correct money management, so it is fundamental in trading. Still, its rules are also applied in other fields that are as varied as in the domestic or business economy. Ultimately, the rules it dictates are quite simple and due to pure and simple common sense. Still, in any case, it will be necessary to observe them religiously to avoid running into severe problems in your career as a trader.

The creators of the first money management techniques had a clear idea that it was necessary to produce a new awareness of the use of money in their investments, for the first time imposing the concept of diversification and differentiation of the investment portfolio to reduce the risks of trading and losses on investment capital drastically.

A strategic approach to stock exchange trading cannot, therefore, ignore the knowledge of the fundamental precepts of money management that require you to always establish the spending limit and the budget available at the beginning.

In the field of trading, this will mean establishing the risks that you are willing to run within certain limits that not even an "Indiana Jones" of trading could ever think of crossing; otherwise, it would face economic suicide at the speed of light! The principles of money management help you put both the risks and the potential profits on the scales to understand if a particular movement on the markets should be exploited or not; in other words, it helps you to know if the game is worth the candle.

If you learn to put the rules of money management into practice, your long-term success can be practically assured. Still, even the short and medium-term will be more probable and easily accessible. In short, all this talk turns to a need for investment efficiency.

The best traders are those who can minimize losses, which not even the guru of the economy could ever avoid and increase profits more and more.

The key to all this is precisely the fact that before learning to earn aspiring traders, the importance of learning to lose should be taught! Suffering losses and spilling money is a natural thing in trading, and you have to try to understand it and not give too much weight when a loss occurs.

Chapter 17
Advanced Strategies

Starter Strategies

To ensure a level of maximum profit with this strategy, you are going to need to set your stop losses at such a point that they are just underneath the last high that the currency experienced. If you are investing in short positions, then you will want to set your stop losses, so they are just above the current low price point instead. This will ensure that you do not lose out if the trend loses momentum before it reaches the price you are hoping for. By doing so, you ensure that the short-term strategy remains as versatile as possible.

This strategy is not without risks; however, as the short-term charts are prone to changing dramatically with little or no advanced notice. This means that if you hope to profit when using this strategy, you are going to need to make sure that you can react quickly to unexpected changes. The best reaction most of the time is going to be waiting for the currency to settle down before setting a new stop loss based on the new landscape that is slightly in the money without getting greedy.

Fibonacci retracement. To use a Fibonacci retracement, the first thing you are going to want to look for in a market is trending. The general idea here is to go long on a retracement, a temporary reversal of direction in the price of the currency, at a specific level when the market is positively trending and to go short on retracements when the market is trending in the other direction. To find a retracement level, you are going to want to find moments when pricing indicators you are looking for reach high or low, points that are higher or lower, than the average high or low point.

Strategies in the Nest and the Bad Situation

To understand the Fibonacci ratios that are useful in forex, it is important to understand the basics behind the Fibonacci numbers, which were discovered by the man whose name they bear; they start as 0, 1, 2, 3, 5, 7, 13, 21, etc. Essentially, to find the next number in the sequence, you simply add the previous two numbers in the sequence together. Now, if you measure the ratio of each number to the following number in the sequence, you get the Fibonacci ratios that are used in the forex. These start off as .236, .382, .5, .618 etc. While the exact reason that Fibonacci ratios apply to the forex market is not completely clear, it is clear that they resonate throughout the world at large from the smallest instance in individual molecules of DNA to the grandest in the organization of the planets in the sky.

Luckily, when it comes to utilizing the Fibonacci ratio in your trades, you do not need to memorize these numbers as all forex trading platforms will have a tool that will do the calculations for you. This means that all you need to do is to learn how, when and why to use them in a technical analysis sense. It is essential to keep in mind that Fibonacci levels are going to act as resistance as well as support for the price in question. As the price increases, the Fibonacci levels will act as resistance, and as the price decreases, they will act as support. Additionally, much like with regular support or resistance, they can be broken.

Trades that are based around the Fibonacci retracement can be on the charts for timeframes less than 10 minutes. Fibonacci retracements can be used to determine reasonable reward/risk levels either by selling a credit spread to the level in question or through buying options that are already in the money that is likely to experience a bounce at these levels. It is generally going to be in your best interest to look for Fibonacci levels that are likely to overlap at multiple timeframes as well as corresponding to the most recent trend experienced by the underlying stock. If you are so inclined, you can also utilize candlestick price patterns as a means of confirming a buy at specific Fibonacci levels.

Alternately, you may find success with oversold or overbought indicators when it comes to range-bound or trendless stocks. You can then sell credit spreads or buy into options that are already in the money and near the current level of resistance and support with tight stops. It is important to keep in mind that a given stock might not move quickly enough to make these levels worthwhile, so it is crucial to do your research ahead of time to have a reasonable expectation about the future movement.

Indicators that are used to signal lower than average volatility such as Bollinger bands are especially useful when it comes to place trades that you anticipate big moves from. Breakout indicators time, especially for the shorter charts, are also especially useful.

Using the Fibonacci sequence to perform a retracement gives you the ability to determine how much an asset moved at a price initially. It uses multiple horizontal lines to point out resistance or support at 23.6, 38.2, 50, 61.8, or 100 percent. When used properly, they make it easier to identify the spots transactions should be started, what prices to target and what stop losses to set.

This does not mean that you should apply the Fibonacci retracements blindly as doing so can lead to failure as easily as it can succeed. It is important to avoid choosing inconsistent reference points, which can easily lead to mistakes as well as misanalysis, for example, mistaking the wick for the body of a candle. Retracements using the Fibonacci sequence should always be applied wick-to-wick, which in turn leads to a clearly defined and actionable resistance level.

Likewise, it is essential to always keep the big picture in mind and keep an eye on trends that are of the longer variety as well. Failing to keep a broad perspective in mind makes short-term trades more likely to fail as it makes it harder to project the correct momentum and direction, any potential opportunities might be moving in. Keeping the larger trends in mind will help you pick more reliable trades while also preventing you from accidentally trading against a specific trend.

Spread Strategies

Options trading attracts many advantages. You can make a lot of profit and even limit your losses if you know how to make the market work for you. The best thing that you can do is pick out the right strategy that is meant to help you, no matter how the market is moving.

First is the bull put spread. This is considered a directional and a credit spread. One advantage that you will find is that it can work against the time decay issue, so you will not lose money from that. You would choose to work with the bull put spread any time that you expect a stock to either fall, stay stagnant or fall just a little bit (if at all) during the near future. The risk on this one is pretty low, so it is often a good strategy for beginners to get started with.

You can also choose to work with the bear call spread. This is another directional strategy, a credit spread, and gives you the advantage of working against the issue of time decay. You would choose to go with the bear call spread any time that you expect a fall, stagnant, or rise just a bit over the short term. This one is another low-risk strategy that can help you to get used to the market and see some results.

The bull call spread is the next strategy for options trading on our list. It is different from the other two in that it is a debit spread, and you will have to still work against the issue of time decay with it. It is still a directional choice, though, which is something you may be familiar with if you have used some of the other strategies. You will want to work with the bull call spread any time that you expect your stock is going to rise moderately over the short term. The risk that you will face when working with the bull call spread is considered to be moderate.

The bear put spread is one that is similar to the bull call spread, but it works oppositely. This is another debit spread, and it will not help you to fight against the issue of time decay, so you will have to limit the amount of time that you are holding onto the option. It is still considered one of the directional strategies, though. This is the strategy that you will work with any time that you think your chosen stock is going to fall moderately within a short amount of time. The risk that comes with this strategy is considered moderate, so a bit riskier than the first two we talked about, but not too bad for a beginner to work with.

Next on the list is the iron condor strategy. This one is considered a credit spread. You will still get the advantage against the time decay issue, but it is considered a non-directional strategy because you are betting against both directions rather than just one. You might choose to work with this strategy when you have a stock that is either stable and not moving all that much or goes up and down, but those movements stay within a specified range, and you think the stock will stay there for the short term. The risk of the iron condor strategy is considered low.

Bollinger Band Strategies

The importance of volatility when it comes to correctly valuing an option is well known. This is why Bollinger bands are so useful than they make it easy to grasp this facet of a particular stock, in turn, making it easier to identify lower and upper ranges. They work by generating bands based on the way the stock price has recently been moving. Bollinger bands trend to provide two types of indications:

The bands tend to contract and expand, depending on how volatility decreases or increases based on the way the price has been moving recently. If the bands expand, then volatility is increasing if they contract, then volatility is decreasing. With this in mind, you can feel safer taking on reversal-based option positions.

The range of the current band can also be compared to the current market price as a means of determining any potential breakout patterns. If the breakout occurs at the top of the band, then you know the market has been overbought, which means it is time to buy puts or short existing calls. If the breakout occurs at the bottom of the lower band, then you know the market is oversold, which means it is time to buy short puts or calls that come with lower overall volatility.

Chapter 18
Trader Psychology

To be a successful trader, you need to have a trader mindset. It is important to be disciplined as a trader so that you can avoid the pitfalls that suck in novice traders and lead them to large losses.

Do not Let Emotion Rule Your Trades

One of the problems that happen with trading is that emotions can get intense when there are the possibilities of losing or earning a great deal of money over a short time. This problem also impacts long term investors, who may become fearful of losing their money when they see stock prices collapsing.

In either case, we are talking about people ruling their investments or trades using emotion instead of the logic that is needed to make good decisions. For traders, you can help get around this by automating your trades, at least to mitigate downside risk. That way, you decide ahead of time what the amount of loss you are willing to accept on the trade is, hopefully, by using the 2% rule. That rule has been arrived at by financial experts as a result of analyzing large numbers of trades and determining what a safe level of loss is that you can take on a single trade and largely keep your overall brokerage account relatively intact. That way, you are going to be able to live to trade another day.

Long term investors often do not have this kind of protection. The reason is that you do not want to be placing stop-loss orders on long term investments, you are hoping to stay in these investments for the long term, after all. And that means that you are going to need to ride out drops in the stock market without panic. But all too often, long term investors – or people that think of themselves as long term investors, give in to the panic and join the other lemmings running off the cliff and they sell their shares. As we have said repeatedly, this is not something that you want to let yourself do. But, since there is no stop-loss order, you can place to prevent it, you are going to have to seek out discipline and avoid doing it using your mental effort. This can be difficult during a major crash when you are going to see yourself losing a lot of money on paper. Remember that downtrends are buying opportunities, and so you should be buying up stocks instead of selling them. It is often best to go against the crowd in the stock market, especially when we are talking about small investors.

Traders also need to avoid getting sucked in by greed. In most cases, swing traders are looking at the possibility of making profits from relatively small price movements, and if the price moves to the point at which they need to take profits, but they do not, it can drop 50 cents a share or a dollar a share, and the trader might see the opportunity for profit evaporate. You do not want to hold on too long for profits in a trade, but many traders get overcome by greed and think if they just hold on a little bit longer, they can make big money.

Plan Ahead

This brings us to the next necessary trader mindset, which is planning. A trader, whether you are a long-term investor or some kind of trader like a swing trader, needs to have carefully thought out plans in place that they can use to direct their actions when they enter a position.

Before entering a trade, a swing trader needs to have the stop loss value for the shares and the take profit value already figured out before you buy your shares. A trader who is not planning, and executing specific plans are just groping around in the dark. Instead of doing that, you should know beforehand what your goals are and how you are going to reach your goals. You need to have specific ideas as to how much money you are going to make and how much you are hoping to make every week.

Have a Trading Routine

It is a good idea to have a trading routine. If you are trading full-time, then you want to have a morning routine that you use to start your trading day. This should include paying attention to financial news so that you can get wind of unexpected results that could impact your trades. Sometimes, there are going to be surprised, which means you might need to change your trading plans.

If you are only trading on a part-time basis, then you should still have a routine that you use daily to stay on top of your trades. Maybe you will do this in part on your lunch hour during workdays so that you can make sure that you are keeping up with the progress of your trades, and you can make some adjustments. Besides, you should also have some time either in the early morning hours or in the evening, or even both if you can, where you analyze your trades or study to find new trades to enter.

The specifics of your routine are less important than the fact that you either have one or you do not. Those who do not have a method are unlikely to be the ones that are successful as swing traders.

Keep Educating Yourself

As a swing trader, you need to recognize that this is a specialized skill. It is not a hobby; it is a professional activity. To succeed in any professional activity, you need to keep up with your education and keep honing and improving your skills. So, you should study swing trading and the financial markets at every opportunity so that over time you are going to become a better trader.

Maintain a Journal

Traders and investors should keep a trading journal. Enter all your activities related to your trading as if it was a diary. You should also keep a section where you keep a record of your trades, including how much you paid to enter the position and how much you got out of it, including losses if they occur. You should also keep a net running total for each month and for the year. It is essential to go on actual recorded information to know if you are succeeding or failing at trading, rather than going off the hope of a couple of recent wins and fooling yourself by neglecting to remember the losses that have also occurred.

Do not be impulsive

Next to panic, when you are facing losses on a trade or greed when you think you can get more and more money, the worst kind of emotion or action that you can take while trading is making impulsive moves. Unfortunately, being impulsive is very common among novice traders.

Impulsive decisions often result from hyper-excitement. A trader might see a trend or hear some news that in their mind makes a trade a "sure thing." Then without doing any kind of analysis, they enter the trade with no planning, and since there was no analysis done, they can quickly find out that the trade goes the wrong way and works against them instead.

Stick to One Trading Technique

Do not try to be a jack of all trades. So, if you want to be a day trader, you should become a day trader. If you want to become a swing trader, then become a swing trader. You should not try being all things at once, even if you hear that others are successful in doing so. Some people can do both styles of trading, while also maintaining long term investments. But most people are not going to find success trying to do everything. Pick one trading style and become an expert at it.

Become an expert on a small number of securities

The market, by its very nature, is volatile. This means that most, if not all, stocks provide plenty of opportunities to earn money by swing trading. It can help your swing trading if you primarily on a few different stocks. Pick 3-5 to use to do your swing trading. Learn the stocks inside and out, so that you know their 52-week highs and lows, and so that you have time to carefully study their charts and look for the right opportunities to enter trades. Having at most five means that you are going to be able to look at the stocks and find good opportunities for swing trading, while not getting overwhelmed. Having at least three ensures that at any given time, you are going to be able to find trades to enter.

Do not be afraid to wait on your trades

As a swing trader, you may be anxious to earn money from your trades, but there is not any rule that says you have to get out of a position before making the profits that you hope to earn. Unless the stock has crashed down and just is not going to rebound up to a level where you can earn profits, you should be patient and wait long enough for the price to rise to the appropriate pricing level for profits. Unlike day traders, which are high-pressure types that have to act fast, swing trading is a more relaxed and patient trading style. Have the patience to wait overnight, and even weeks if you have to realize your profits.

Do not be afraid to sit on the sidelines

Sometimes, the opportunities to swing trade and earn profits – while still doing the careful analysis – are not going to be there. As a swing trader being anxious is not going to be a helpful characteristic. You are going to want to be able to sit on the sidelines if necessary, waiting for the right trade before you jump into a position. Remember that at the end of the year, your total annual results of wins and losses are what is going to matter. Being constantly in trades is not what matters. So, if you have to wait a few days or even a week to find a solid trade that is likely to be a winner, then be prepared to wait. It is better to wait a few days to get into a winning trade than it is to be impulsive and then have your money tied up in less promising or even losing trades, while you see the good trades pass you by.

Chapter 19

Trading Flexible

There is high flexibility for the persons involved in the trade when it comes to trading goods as well as services. You are not restricted or limited to the amount of money to use while trading. There are no excess rules as well as regulations that have been put in place to be followed by the ones involved in trading. It is as well a market that operates for twenty-four hours and throughout the week. Hence, it is wise considering as a part-time engagement by anyone who does a regular job since it has no time restriction. You do not have to wait for the market to open, and as well the market does not sleep. You have the freedom to choose when and at what time you want to get into trading. You are no restrictions for you to waiting for a specific session to trade as it is the case with trading stock. You get into the trade when you have the time to do that. It is always in operation since it is not affected by any situation. You can get updates anytime you need and as well get to view the trend when you have time to see. The different trading styles will enable you to trade at your convenience. If you intend to take the position for a short duration, Forex trading is an excellent opportunity for you. It is the easily accessible market to any trader.

There is High Liquidity

There are high numbers of people involved in the foreign exchange market compared to any financial market. Despite its significant size, it is as well extremely liquid. Because of the high liquidity, big players get attracted to Forex trading. It, in turn, leads to filling the gap of the big orders of money trade with either small or no price deviation. Efficient pricing is promoted since there is no price manipulation, as well as no deviation, is experienced, from the actual price. Under the apparent market conditions, you can buy as well as sell any time since there are always people who are ready to trade. There are constant price patterns throughout the trade despite the level of volatility. The high liquidity makes the Forex market efficient, and the heat of competition not felt. It is so despite the high number of traders involved on either side. The significant number of persons engaged in the trade ensures there are always transactions going on in the market. You will be lucky to get an opportunity because the prices do not shift dramatically. Transactions are completed quickly as well as efficiently, and hence the spread, as well as the transaction costs accrued, are relatively low. You can make suppositions of the price movement in the market.

Central Exchange is not involved

The central exchange interferes with the market in rare cases or either in extreme conditions. It is a guarantee that there will be no cases of prices dropping or either price manipulation. That serves as an advantage to anyone who wants or has invested in Forex trading. The market does not experience changes as it is the case in the markets that trade in equity shares and many others. There are no regulators since trade is conducted over the counter in the entire globe. The central banks interfere in exceptional cases, and this rarely happens. Localizing, as well as deregulating the market aids in avoiding those interferences.

Volatility

You can easily change to a different currency if there are higher profits or either good investment associated with it. There are higher risks associated with investing in the money-driven market. But volatility provides significant benefits by changing from one currency to another, which yields a good return. It makes it an advantage to lower the risk factors involved as well as increase the profit. You can get some benefit once you speculate on the price changes, either rising or falling. The Forex trading gives maximum grasp compared to any other financial investing trade out there. It serves as an added advantage to level your investment. The exchange rates are very lively, and profit can be gained anytime when the prices shift anytime you are willing. You require a short duration for you to open as well as close positions. High volatility attracts opportunities to make huge profits.

Low barriers in case you want to enter the market

To invest in being a currency trader, you are not required to have a vast amount of money. You can quickly get into Forex trading even with little initial capital. To have a trading account, you are required to have a deposit of $25 as a minimum. Compared to the future, options as well as trading stock, which requires you to have the right amount of money. It is relatively cheap since a large amount of capital associated with opening an account does not apply in this case. Hence, it is more accessible to an average person who is interested and does not have much money for a start. The trading attracts traders with different experience levels, and hence, experience does not serve as a barrier to enter into currency trading. For a person entering the market for the first time, there are no many risks involved. They can test, improve as well as organize their new skills, which later turns to be a future benefit.

Different methods can be used to trade

The trading method that you will prefer, you will be provided with an opportunity by the Forex market. The advantage associated is you can buy as well as sell currencies according to specific responses. The world events taking place within a particular location or either change in the economy can be a determinant. You can as well base on the history of price patterns, and hence, you can identify the trends. Currency is linked to an economy known to sustain it. You can as well put several views together to come up with a trade-picking approach that is unique. Forex trading is put to use in several trading plan categories. Whether you have a short-term or a long-term goal, Forex trading will not disappoint you in any way. They have a lot to offer to you as a small beginner.

Leverage will make your finances go further

A contract for differences subjected under a force will make your money go for a long duration. You are then in a position to pay a small portion of the entire value. Profits, as well as losses, made the aggregate value at the time of closure. Doing trade on the margin will give you an opportunity to reaping a good profit even from your small investment. You will be equipped with tools to manage risks, including price alerts, as well as running balances. You are allowed to several strategic positions as a way to curb unwanted risks. Hedging serves as the right approach of mitigating as well as limiting losses to a considerable and known amount. You can choose Forex pairs, and when failures occur on one pair, the other set in a different position can mitigate. Making a small deposit will help you control an immense contract value. You will reap enticing profits as well as minimize risking capital. You can trade with substantial cash flow compared to your deposit. Choose a reasonable leverage size, which will translate to getting a potential profit as well as reducing the losses that you may incur.

You can access tools to aid you in trading

There are numerous trading platforms on tablets, mobile, web and many more. You can also access a specialist platform in case you want to take your trading on a higher level. There are a lot of trademarks designed to assist you in upgrading your trading and interactive charts as well as consolidated news feeds. Some of the features include stops as well as limits that are vital in managing risks. You will too access products that are designed to assist you in growing the Forex trading. You will be offered to help you practice trading as well as improve your skills. The demo accounts serve as a variable resource in case you are financially down, and you need to sharpen your trading techniques. You will establish whether it is safe for you to open a live marketing account.

Wide range of options

When you buy one currency, you are likely to sell the other, meaning that the transactions should be in pairs. There are numerous options you can put into consideration in Forex trading. You can trade in multiple pairs by choosing the set based on specific criteria. You can either decide to base on volatility patterns as well as the level of economic development. It is as well advisable to time when it is convenient. Embrace volatility, and this will help you to shift from on to another currency pair. When you speculate that the value of a particular currency will decline, you have to sell that and then buy one which to pair with it. Forex trading provides a wide range of opportunities to trade and not forgetting the budget as well as the risk factor. You sell one currency and buy the other. A Forex pair cost is similar to a unit of the money purchased and worth in the selling currency. You will make a profit or loss depending on the accuracy of the prediction you have made. In either case, you are subject to make a profit regardless of the deviation of the market.

There is no fixed amount for you to operate with

In many markets, the contract, as well as lot sizes, are regulated and supposed to be a certain amount. There are no such restrictions in the currency market, and you have the freedom to operate with the amount you are willing to. A reasonable cost is involved in providing you with a great option. It is pretty consistent when it comes to trading as well as investing. It is so because both the buyer and the seller are directly involved in eliminating any broker that can be required.

The cost is low

There are typically considerate transaction costs involved under usual market conditions. The Forex trading is associated with a little expense since there are rare cases of brokerage as well as commissions given. It is more reliable compared to any other type of trade where you take into account brokerage fees. The cost you are supposed to pay to the Forex broker is relatively small compared to what is paid to get into trading other securities. There are no clearing as well as government fees that need to be deducted.

Individual control

One of the critical advantages of Forex trading is that any trader has total control in either buying or selling. You are not forced to make a trade that you are not in agreement with. You as well have the freedom to make the final decision whether you are willing to get into trading. You will get a chance to access to the extent you are ready to risk for you to earn money.

Chapter 20

Trading Errors and Mistakes

When you trade options, you generally get profit when the stocks go sideways, up, or down. Option strategies are a great way to get good gains and protect them while avoiding losses as well. You can control significant parts of stock with small cash outlay, but all of this sounds too good to be true, as there is a catch associated with this.

You can lose more than what you invested initially in little to no time while trading options. This is why it is crucial to move forward with adequate care and caution. Many times, even expert traders make simple errors that lead to grave results.

It is clear that options and trading them can help people gain a lot of profit. It is necessary to trade the options correctly and avoid any potential mistakes that can lead to a considerable loss. It is recommended to have a list of common errors that happen when you try to become an advanced trader. Many of these mistakes are similar to the ones that are made by new traders. This is why many traders tend to lose their entire account right after they start. But most of these errors are simple enough to avoid them. Let us have a look at the variety of errors and mistakes that you should avoid while trading options. You should always keep these things in mind, as they will help you to earn a lot of profit while avoiding loss as well.

Avoid Short Time Frames

In recent years, many options brokers have started offering a wide range of terms. Today, many brokers offer users extremely short contact period options; in fact, many brokers also offer a one-minute contact period. These periods generally attract new users who are inexperienced in trading. But they can also attract seasoned traders looking to get rich quick. Looking closely at the statistics, it is clear that this novel approach is a fad that can create big problems. The markets are impossible to predict and no one can deduce what the market will do in the next minute or so. That is why these contact options should be avoided at all times. Don't go after them, as they will surely lead you to a loss.

The market is difficult to predict even in the broader frames such as months and weeks, but in the case of longer time frames, traders can generally assess the dominant trends. They can also make a stance that understands and reflects the condition of the options market.

Use Conservative Leverage Levels

Another error that can be avoided with ease is using extreme amounts of leverage. This generally takes place in many variations. For instance, some traders who find themselves in a loss begin to look for new strategies that can make up for their losses. When traders add new positions at higher or lower levels (depending on the direction of the original trade), it is generally known as doubling-up. This term is often considered to be a polite and diplomatic version of 'adding to a loser,' which again describes the same phenomenon.

Many other mistakes can be observed when traders use very little margin in positioning. This brings out the potential for significant profits, but it can also make a trading account vulnerable to extreme losses if the market fails to move in the correct direction. These are some of the many reasons why it is always better to avoid chasing quick profits and work hard instead. It is recommended to use a conservative but functional approach that will limit the leverage levels on an average scale.

Use an Economic Calendar

Many trading failures can happen when the trader uses an economic calendar before creating and establishing new positions on the market. It is crucial to understand that for any tradable assets, there always exist relevant events that may result in shocking and surprising volatility in the prospective prices. These events generally change based on the type of asset that is currently being traded. For instance, the people who are trading stock options, or are dealing with stock benchmarks, need to a have proper understanding of when the major earning reports come out. In most cases, this results in volatility inequities. It can be quite impossible to point out the direction in which this volatility works and towards which direction it will move in the future. Due to this, it is generally a smart plan to wait for important news events to go away before you decide to establish positions on the market. Normally, most of these events are scheduled in advance, so it is recommended to have an economic calendar handy. It will prove to be a great asset for all traders if you use it proactively.

Focus on Liquid Assets

This is contentious advice for some people, but it is recommended to focus on liquid assets. There are many options traders that seek opportunities in assets that are not as frequently traded as others. It is possible to make a significant profit using these types of trades. But if you want to continue with a conservative outlook and reduce the chances of risks, you should consider liquid assets. Liquid assets will help you avoid risks and still gain profit. Liquid assets are the most commonly and frequently traded assets. These include stock benchmarks, blue-chip stocks, silver, gold, oil and forex majors such as EUR/USD, USD/GBP, USD/JPY, and AUD/USD, etc.

Always Have an Exit Strategy

When you enter the world of finance and trading, you need to learn how to control and manipulate your emotions. This does not mean that you should forget all your emotions and become a fearless entity. Instead of doing that, you need to create a plan and stick to it as much as possible. You need to have an exit plan.

It is necessary to have a plan B or an exit strategy before you decide to start trading. If you plan to put a lot of money into trading and do not have an exit plan, you may suffer monumental losses. It is crucial to have an exit strategy for people who use American-style options trading. It is necessary because, in this style, the traders are allowed to close the position before the expiration of the contract happens automatically. No trade can provide your 100% chances of success because the market changes all the time and is volatile. This means that traders need to prepare themselves for all kinds of scenarios, especially when the markets do not follow the planned or expected trajectory.

It is possible that you have never used an exit strategy before and have still fared well in the past, but there is nothing worse than losing a lot of money just because you cannot get out of the market. The most successful options traders are the ones who have a plan prepared for every possible scenario. To begin this, you need to check and develop an exit strategy before the market starts to work against you.

You need to create a downside exit point, an upside exit point, and all your timeframes for all other exits when things are going your way.

It is recommended to form an upside exit plan and a worst-case scenario downside exit plan as well. If you reach your upside goals, you should clear your positions immediately. Do not act too greedy. If you reach your downside loss step, clear your positions immediately. Do not let yourself suffer more losses by gambling your options by waiting for the price to come back.

Many people tend to avoid this advice because the circumstances change frequently. But do not do it. Make a plan and stick to it as much as possible. Many traders make a plan and then forget it and follow their emotions instead. It may work a couple of times, but it may eventually lead to huge losses.

(OTM) Call Options

Purchasing OTM or out of the money calls outright is a difficult way to earn money through options trading, while this option may sound great for beginners and some experts because they are extremely cost-effective and seem efficient. Buying them cheap allows you to put money on a lot of things. Many people think that this is a safe option because it coincides with the pattern that people who indulge in equity trade are used to this. This pattern, i.e., buying low and selling high, is present almost everywhere. But if you plan to use only this strategy, you will limit yourself significantly and may start losing money on a regular basis.

Try selling the OTM call option on a stock that you already have. This should be your first strategy. In trading terms, it is known as a covered call strategy.

The best thing about the covered call strategy is that the risk factor is not a result of selling the option when the option is covered by a stock position. It also has a lot of potentials to help you earn money on stocks when you want to sell the stock when the price of the stock goes up. This strategy is great because it can allows you to 'feel' how OTM option contract prices fluctuate all the time, especially when the expiration is approaching rapidly. In such cases, the stock prices fluctuate as well.

A drastic risk is situated in reinvesting the stock, though. Selling the call option does not produce capital risks as such, but it will limit your upside. This means that it will create an opportunity risk. Another risk is when you plan to sell the stock upon the assignment when the market rises. Your call then becomes exercised.

Misunderstanding Leverage

You will be surprised to know that even a lot of advanced traders fail to consider the leverage factor option. Many people tend to misuse this option that the contracts offer because they do not realize how much risk they are taking due to it. They often tend to buy short-term calls.

It is recommended to become a master of leverage. It should be your priority, especially for beginners who are looking to enter the advanced strategy. If you generally trade 100 share lots, instead of considering a lot of shares, stick to one share only. Similarly, if you generally trade 400 share lots, stick to 4 contracts. This is a decent starting amount. If you fail to succeed in these sizes, then you will surely fail in the bigger sizes as well.

Not Being Open to New Strategies

Change is necessary and accepting change can help you become an overall successful person. Many options traders believe that buying options out-of-the-money or never selling options in-the-money is a bad thing, it should never be done. These may seem like a childish strategy until you get caught in a trade that is moved against you.

All experienced options traders have gone through this in the past. This scenario can be quite difficult, which is why many people try to break their personal rules and work against it.

Chapter 21
Strategies for Making the Best of a Bad Situation

When it comes to trading options successfully in the long-term, the secret is not being able to make the right trades at every juncture. After all, that is impossible. No, the true secret to long-term success is learning to recover when a surefire trade suddenly goes sideways on you at the last moment. The faster you can get your trade back on track, the faster you can get back to making a profit.

Long call repair strategies

This contains strategies designed to increase the profit potential of long call positions that have recently seen a quick, unrealized loss. Remember, having a great plan is extremely important, but there is more to making a profit in the long-term than that. In trading, the best offense is often a good defense.

Who should run it: This strategy is suitable for veterans.

When to run it: This strategy is effective in a bullish market.

Details: It is common for new traders to buy a simple put or call, only to find out that they were ultimately wrong about the way the underlying asset moved when everything was said and done. For example, a long call that is out of the money would see sudden unrealized losses if its underlying asset dropped. To understand the best course of action in this situation, a second example is required. For this example, assume that it is the middle of February, and you believe that Microsoft, which is currently sitting at 93.30, is about to make a move that puts it above its resistance levels and ends at about 95. You can then easily jump in with a near the money call for July, leaving you roughly six months until expiration and plenty of time for the related movement to occur.

From there, however, things do not go according to plan, and the stock drops to below $90 instead. The price of your July call would now be worth only about $1.25, down from about $3 thanks to the time decay, creating an unrealized loss of $175 per option purchased. As there is still a fair amount of time left until expiration, it is possible that the stock could still make the option profitable, but waiting also has the potential to generate additional losses or other opportunity costs, which could also result in a loss of profit.

One way to mitigate this loss is through the process of averaging down and purchasing additional options, though this only increases your risk if things continue to not go your way. Instead, a simple and effective means of lowering your breakeven point, while also increasing the possibility of turning a profit is to roll the position down into a bull call spread. The concept of rolling it simply means to replace an existing option with a new option that is similar in most ways except that one has a lower strike price than the other. Utilizing this practice means you do not have to exercise the initial option as the time is extended until the end of the second option.

To use this strategy in the above example, you would start by placing an order to sell a pair of calls at the July expiration date at your target price of $95 for $1.25, which is essentially going short on the initial call option. At the same time, you would want to buy an additional July 90 call and sell it for roughly $2.90. The result of this process is a bull call spread that improves the odds of success while only adding a small amount of additional risk. What's more, the breakeven point decreases dramatically from $98, all the way to $93.25.

From there, assuming that the Microsoft stock continued to trade even higher, past the original starting point, then your bull call spread would be strong enough to break even with a potential profit for the target of $95, though the maximum amount of profit for each option is going to be $175 due to the way it was constructed.

Alternate Repair Style

Who should run it: This strategy is suitable for veterans.

When to run it: This strategy is effective in a bullish market.

Details: Alternately, you could roll down into a traditional butterfly spread, when the underlying stock drops to $90. When using this strategy, you would instead want to sell a pair of July $90 calls, which would sell for about $4 each, while also hanging on to the July $95 long call. You would also need to purchase a call for the July date at $85 as well that sells for around $7.30 after time decay has been taken into account.

You will see that the total risk decreases on the downside in this scenario as the total debit amount drops to $230, and there is also a limited upside risk if the stock moves back towards the breakeven point. If the stock goes nowhere, the trade still turns a profit as well.

Combined Repair Strategy

Who should run it: This strategy is suitable for all-starts.
When to run it: This strategy is useful in a bullish market

Determining strike price: One of the most important facets of using the repair strategy effectively is setting the correct strike price for the options in question. This price will ultimately determine the cost of the trade as well as influencing your breakeven point. The best place to start is by considering the magnitude of the unrealized loss that you are coming off. For example, if you purchased a stock at $40 and it is now at $30, then your paper loss is $10 per share.

In this case, you would want to purchase at the money calls while at the same time writing out of the money calls with a higher strike price that is above the strike price of the purchased calls by half of the stock's loss. This means you would want to start with three-month options before moving forward from there as needed. Generally speaking, the greater the loss you have already experienced, the greater the amount of time that you will have to spend repairing it.

It is also important to keep in mind that it will not be possible to repair all mistakes for free as the worst offenders will require a small debit payment to set up the position in a potentially profitable manner. If your loss is over 70 percent, then it is likely not going to be possible to repair it at all.

Unwind the Position

While breaking even after the hypothetical situations might sound good now, when you find yourself in a similar situation in the real world you may find yourself wanting to more than just breakeven, you will likely want to make an additional profit as well. As an example, assume that the Microsoft stock that previously dropped now rose to $60, which means that you are now interested in keeping it rather than selling when it hits $70.

Unwinding becomes an even more advantageous proposition if the volatility in the underlying stock has increased to such a point that you decide you want to hold onto the stock. You will be able to find your options priced much more attractively in this scenario as long as you remain in a good position with the underlying stock.

Problems can arise in this scenario if you make an attempt at exiting while the stock is trading at or above the break-even price as this will cost you as the total value of the option in question will be negative. As such, you should generally only consider unwinding an existing position if the price remains underneath the original breakeven price, and the prospects look promising. Otherwise, you are typically going to be better off simply establishing a new position in the same stock at the current market price.

Synthetic Short

Who should run it: This strategy is suitable for veterans.

When to run it: This strategy is effective in a bearish market

You can think of this strategy as being similar to the short stock position as a whole as there is no maximum for profit as long as the underlying stock price continues to drop. Furthermore, credit is typically taken when entering this scenario, as calls are almost always going to be more expensive than puts. This means that even if the underlying stock price remains relatively unchanged for the length of the expiration time, there will still be a potential for profit based on the amount of the initial credit that was taken.

Chapter 22

Finding a Suitable Market

One of the hardest parts of swing trading, especially for a beginner, is finding the best market. This includes what types of financial instruments you want to focus on when it comes to trading. There are a variety of financial instruments, such as ETFs, futures, options, currencies, cryptocurrencies, and stocks. As a beginner, it is important to try to find a financial instrument that you are comfortable with. The different types of financial instruments, so you can get a better idea of which device is best for your business lifestyle. As I discuss the various types of financial instruments, I will also give you some of the pros and cons of these instruments. It will help you decide whether to focus on stocks, currencies, ETFs, or other financial instruments.

Of course, while you want to pick one financial instrument, this does not mean that you cannot do more research to see if you have chosen the right instrument. For example, you might feel that stocks are your best option because you hear the most about them. However, once you start trading with stocks, you begin to think that you might be better of trading currencies. You can then switch your financial instrument to see if currencies are a better fit for you.

Sometimes, following the guideline of trial and error is the best way to help you develop yourself as a trader. It is important to realize that you should establish your trading personality. While you will follow the advice of others, such as people in your online community and your broker, you should still make sure to take time to figure out what is right for you. Many beginners have felt uncomfortable as a swing trader because they were following what other traders were doing instead of learning about their trading personality. If you want to become a successful swing trader, you will focus on developing your trading personality instead of following someone else.

Selecting a Financial Instrument to Trade Stocks

Stock is probably the most common financial instrument that people think of when they start their trading career. In fact, most people probably believe that this is the financial instrument they will be trading. Part of this is because of its popularity. However, another part is because they do not realize how many financial instruments there are when it comes to trading.

When people talk about stocks in the trading community, they will often refer to them as shares. There are several ways you can handle shares. Of course, you can decide to trade shares using the swing trading technique or you can decide to invest your stocks with the buy and hold method. Whatever you choose to do (you might change your mind once you truly start trading), it is essential to remember that you need to continue your research and get to know as much as possible about trading stocks in the market. This not only means that you have to learn about stocks, but it also means that you have to learn about the stock market in general. In reality, this goes for any type of financial instrument you decide to focus on.

Because stocks are so popular, it is important to look carefully at your research. For example, you might find valuable information about a stock but realize the website is focusing on investing stocks instead of trading them. While you can learn about the details of a stock through this resource, you will not want to spend your time focusing on investing stocks when you are looking into trading. The main reason for this is because, as I have mentioned earlier, trading and investing are two different pieces of the stock market. When you invest, you hold the stock for a long period of time. In fact, there are many investors who focus on holding the stock for the rest of their life. But, when you are a swing trader, there is only a small window of time, you will hold your stock. Therefore, you want to make sure that you are reading about the correct strategies and information to help you along your swing trading journey.

One of the biggest examples of running into information about stocks that will not be important to you as a swing trader is reading that you should not pay attention to the daily prices of the stock market. While this is valuable information for an investor who focuses on the buy and holds strategy, this is not valuable information for someone who is taking on swing trading. While you will not need to focus on every single price dip and rise as day traders do, unless you are trying to analyze a chart, you will need to pay close attention to the daily stock prices you have in your portfolio.

At the same time, you want to make sure that you are focusing on stocks that are within your target companies. For example, you might want to focus on blue-chip stocks. Therefore, if you find a stock that is not considered blue-chip, you will want to move on.

One of the biggest downsides to choosing stocks is that each stock you take on will carry its individual risk. This means that no matter what type of negative news comes about the company for a stock you hold, such as Google or Twitter, you will have the risk of losing money due to the negative news. However, there is a way to trade stocks without having to think of each stock carrying it is a risk, and this is through ETFs.

ETFs

ETFs are known as Exchange-Traded Funds. When you think of ETFs, you can picture a bunch of stocks in one basket. Whatever group of stocks or other securities you decide to trade, analyze the underlying index of the fund. There is a variety of ETFs. For example, you can choose an ETF that follows more of a target, such as retail companies, or you could choose an ETF that has more variety within its basket. While you are looking at different ETFs, you want to keep in mind the same rules and guidelines for yourself that you do for stocks or any other type of financial instrument. While ETFs used to be focused more towards stocks, they can now focus on bonds, currencies, and even looking into cryptocurrencies.

One of the biggest pros to ETFs is you can have variety through purchasing one ETF because it is made up of different securities. Many people believe that this can save you money because if you decided to purchase the stocks in the ETF separately, you would be spending more money. For example, if you are interested in stocks that focus on space, you can look for an ETF that has this target instead of having to purchase a dozen or more separate stocks. In fact, most ETFs can hold hundreds of stocks.

Another positive of ETFs is you do not have to worry so much if one of the company's securities starts to fall because of negative press as the other securities will help balance out the fall. Therefore, you might not even notice that price drop from one security. Because of this, many traders feel that ETFs are a good risk management instrument.

The price also tends to be more positive when it comes to ETFs. While most people believe that they will be expensive because they hold so many securities from different companies, this method of thinking is not true. In fact, you might find that many ETFs are cheaper than some of the most popular blue-chip stocks on the market.

On top of this, some ETFs might have a blue-chip stock within them.

Diversification is one of the terms that you will often run into as a trader. Diversification basically means that you have a variety of stock or whatever type of financial instrument you decide to trade. This is another reason why many traders look at ETFs as they will offer diversification through their variety of stocks. However, many traders and investors feel that diversification can also be negative in the stock world. While it is highly debated, some people feel that if you have too much diversification in your account, then you can find yourself struggling to manage some risks.

Currencies

Trading currencies is just like trading money when you go on a vacation. For example, if you live in Canada and you decide to travel to Europe, you will have to trade your Canadian money in for Euros. In a sense, trading currencies in the stock market works the same way. You will always need to have two different currencies to trade. You will also want to watch to see what the value of the money is through comparison. For example, some currencies receive a higher value compared to others, while other currencies receive a lower value.

Currency trades are completed in the Foreign Exchange Market, which is known as forex. While this is a different market, you will still want to make sure to follow the same risk management techniques that you do when trading in the stock market. For example, you will want to make sure that you only trade a certain percentage of your account amount, such as 1%. You will also want to make sure that you take all the time you need to learn about trading currencies and the foreign exchange stock market.

One crucial piece of advice from many experienced swing traders is that most of them agree that you should not start out trading using currencies as your financial instrument. They believe that after you use simulation trading, you should turn your attention to stocks as these are often considered to be a base in the trading world. Stocks have been around an incredibly long time, which often helps beginners as they are learning the guidelines, rules, and how to trade in general.

Cryptocurrencies

Cryptocurrencies are one of the newest types of financial instruments available to trade. They are similar to currencies; however, they are often having a variety of different coins. Some of the types of cryptocurrencies are Ethereum, Ripple, Bitcoin Lite and Bitcoin.

Just like currencies, nearly every experienced trader will tell you that beginners should not start with cryptocurrencies. Most would probably see a beginner start with currency over cryptocurrencies. There are a couple of main reasons for this one, both of them dealing with how risky these types of financial instruments are.

First, cryptocurrencies are newer, and this means that there is not as much research completed on them. One of the main things that experienced traders who are including cryptocurrencies in their portfolio are working hard to make sure they note everything about their trades so they can help expand the research on this type of financial instrument.

Second, cryptocurrencies are known to have high risk. In fact, many believe that they are the most high-risk financial instruments that you can trade and invest in. They tend to suffer more than any other instrument when it comes to negative press, governmental regulations and is even more likely to be hacked. Because of this, many traders feel it is important that the people who take on cryptocurrencies are comfortable with high risk, will not allow their mental state to be affected by the risk, and can remain calm under stress so they can continue to think rationally when having to make a quick decision to trade.

Chapter 23
Money Management

As a trader, you have to develop specific skills, and one of these is money management. Learning how to trade is important, but money management is equally important. Money management is simply all about keeping as much of your money as possible and not losing any of it unnecessarily.

As a trader, you do not have any control over the markets, but you can control your money and reduce your losses and any wastage. Money management is just as important as your trading skills. No matter how impressive and on-point your trading skills are, without money management skills, you will not thrive and will be a huge risk. Therefore, learn and understand all the essential aspects of money management.

The main purpose of money management is to ensure that each risk you take is a calculated risk and not guesswork. Every move that you make on the trading platform should be well researched, well informed, and guided by your analysis. Never make any guesswork or blind moves as you risk losing your money. It is better to hold out a little longer from entering a trade rather than lose money blindly.

As the experts say, the key to winning at the stock market losing as little money as possible If you are not right. Some of the key considerations that you should make as a trader are the number of shares you should buy and the amounts to spend per trade.

Importance of Proper Money Management Skills

As a trader, one of the most important skills you will need to develop is how to manage your money properly and how to keep as much of it as possible. You need to learn how to save as much of your money as possible and avoid entering trades where you risk losing money. If you are unsure about a strategy, then do not implement it.

Your most crucial goal as a trader should be to preserve and protect your trading capital. This will enable you to last longer and grow your wealth and make big wins. For instance, there is a general rule that you should never spend more than 2% of your trading capital on a single trade. This means that if your trading capital is $100, 000 then no single trade should take more than $2,000. This way, should things not work in your favor, then you stand to lose as little as possible.

Also, no matter how enticing or attractive a position seems, never place a larger amount than initially planned. Market positions on charts sometimes seem way too appealing, and we are inclined to invest more money for higher returns. However, the markets can be unpredictable and chances of losing money or trades not working out as desired are always high. Therefore, avoid such temptations and stick to your trading plan.

Also, check your account balance each month and then work out the amount that makes 2% of the total. For instance, if your account balance is $50,000, then 2% is equivalent to $1,000. As a swing trader, you cannot afford to lose more than this amount. This kind of approach will enable you to hold onto most of your money as well as stay safe even as you trade. Keep in mind that the premise of the swing trading strategy is to collect profits on half of each position's amount as soon as the stock moves and gains an amount that is equivalent to the original stop loss.

Maintain Proper Cash Flow Management

Always have a very sound and well-thought-out cash flow process. This is probably one of the most crucial elements of long-term investment planning. It is a very simple approach. All you need to do is to deposit money regularly into your accounts. This money can be used to buy more shares for long-term benefits.

Setting Target and Stops

We can define a stop-loss as the total amount of loss that a trader is willing to incur in a single trade. Beyond the stop-loss point, the trader exits the trade. This is basically meant to prevent further losses by thinking the trade will eventually get some momentum. We also have what is known as a take-profit point. It is at this point that you will collect any profits made and possibly exit a trade. At this point, stock or other security is often very close to the point of resistance. Beyond this point, a reversal in price is likely to take place. Rather than lose money, you should exit the trade. Traders sometimes take profit and let trade continue if it was still making money. Another take-profit point is then plotted. If you have a good run, then you can lock in the profits and let the good run continue.

Always Have a Trading Plan

The single most crucial aspect of your trade should be risk management. Without it, your whole trading life will be in jeopardy. Therefore, start all your trading ventures with a plan that you intend to stick by. Traders have a saying that you should plan your trades and then trade your plan. This means to come up with the best plan possible and then implement it and stick by it. Trade is very similar to war. When it is well planned, it can be won before it is executed.

Some of the best tools you will need as part of your risk management plan are take-profit and stop-loss. Using these two tools, you can plan your trades in advance. You will need to use technical analysis to determine these two points. With this information, you should be able to determine the price you are willing to pay as well as the losses you can incur.

Risk versus Reward

A lot of traders lose a lot of money at the markets for a very simple reason. They do not know about risk management or how to go about it. This mostly happens to beginners or novice traders. Most of them simply learn how to trade, then rush to the markets in the hope of making a kill. Sadly, this is now how things work because account and risk management are not taken into consideration.

Managing risk is just as important as learning how to trade profitably. It is a skill that every trader needs to learn, including beginners and novice traders. As it is, investing hard-earned funds at the markets can be a risky venture. Even with the very best techniques and latest software programs, you can still lose money. Experts also lose money at the markets occasionally. The crucial aspect is that they win a lot more than they lose, so the net equation is profitability.

Since trading is a risky affair, traders should be handsomely compensated for the risks they take. This is where the term risk vs. reward ratio comes in. If you are going to invest your money in a venture that carries some risk, then it is good to understand the nature of the risk. If it is too risky, then you may want to keep away, but if not, then perhaps the risk is worth it.

Financial Dashboards

A financial dashboard is a management tool commonly used by swing traders and other traders as well. It is mostly used for a fast comparative analysis of major indicator data visually.

The data is often in the form of trend diagrams that are in series form, usually side-by-side. This tool is among the many useful tools that all traders should have if they need to compare market information fast.

A financial dashboard can accommodate huge amounts of data and organize it in such a way that it is easy to visualize it and make fast decisions based on the visualization. A wide variety of data can be formatted and presented to you as you prepared to trade and even as you trade. You will be able to proceed with more accuracy and make informed decisions.

Major Indicators for Stock Traders

As a stock trader, you will need to use a whole bunch of tools. Most of these tools will help to guide you in your stock trading ventures. Some of the best trading indicators or tools are those that will help in the identification of suitable stocks for trading. They include tools that will enable you to identify best market entry points, management of your market positions, and also for-profit collection and market exit.

Fibonacci Retracement

One of the best tools used by most traders, including swing traders, is the Fibonacci retracement pattern. This pattern is used mostly to identify resistance and support levels. When these support and resistance levels are known, it is possible to determine the reversals and hence, appropriate market entry points.

Stocks generally retrace their path a short while after trending either upwards or downwards. The market entry point is often deemed best as soon as the retracement is over, and the trend is resumed. The retracements are generally measured as percentages. Swing traders usually watch out for the 50% market, which is rather significant even though it does not exactly fit in with the Fibonacci pattern. Fibonacci is often at ratios ranging from 23.6% and 38.2% all the way to 61.8%.

Pullbacks

By their very nature, pullbacks always generate a variety of different trading opportunities after a trend moves lower or higher. Profiting through this classic strategy is not as easy as it sounds. For instance, you may invest in a security or sell short into a resistance position, and these trends can continue so that your losses are considerable. Alternatively, your security or stock could just sit there and waste away, even as you miss out on many other opportunities.

There are certain skills you need if you are to earn decent profits with the pullback strategy. For instance, how aggressive should a trader be, and at what point should profit be taken? When is it time to pull out? Basically, these and all other important aspects should be considered.

For starters, you require a strong trend on the markets such that other traders' timing pullbacks get to line up right behind you. When they do, they will cause your idea to become a profitable one. Securities that ascend to new heights or falling to new lows are capable of attaining this requirement, especially after the securities push much farther beyond the breakout level.

You will also need persistent vertical action into a trough or peak for regular profits, especially if the volumes are higher than usual, mainly because this results in a fast price movement once you attain the position. It is imperative that the stock in question turns a profit quickly after either bottoming or topping out but with no sizable trade range or consolidation. It is also crucial that this happens. Otherwise, the intervening range is likely to oppose profitability during the resulting subsequent rollover or bounce.

Resistance and Support Triggers

There are lines known as support and resistance points that form the core of the technical analysis. It is easy to build a trading plan using these indicators. The first one is the support line, and it is a good indicator of the price level. It also indicates areas below prevailing market prices on the chart with strong buying pressure.

Chapter 24

A Project for Success

Remember, when your real money is at stake, there are several mental and emotional factors that are also at play. Fear and greed can take over your decision-making process and may push you towards incorrect decisions. No scenario-playing can prepare you for the emotional turmoil most traders face, yet this will help you in understanding the practicalities of the process.

The best way to avoid getting emotionally burdened is to trade in a limited quantity and never let your risk increase beyond a limit. If you feel that your risk is enhanced by a percentage point, be prepared to square off your position no matter what the result may turn out to be later on.

Planning and Strategizing

This is the most important part of the process. This is the part where you will do your homework. On stock selection. The most important part of stock selection is looking at the technical indicators and chart patterns. You will have to do this planning and strategizing part at least a day before you are going to trade the stock. As you get more acquainted with the trading process and stocks, you can make such decisions more quickly, but for now, the planning should be done at least on the night prior to trading.

Your focus should be on specific segments or industries that are performing well in general. This is one of the safest strategies as the stocks that are moving in correlation with the indices or the market, in general, are more predictable for the beginners.

Look at the charts and candlestick patterns. Try to identify the bullish or bearish trends that might be forming. Initially, you should only enter the stocks that have clear bullish or bearish trends. Do not go for indecisive stocks or the stocks that are moving sideways as you may not be able to predict their movement properly.

The second part is to form a strategy that you would follow. You must be clear on that outright, and changing your strategy in the middle can be confusing.

Stock Selection

Once you have identified the segment or industry, look for a few stocks that look promising to you. It is better to have a couple of stocks singled out. Do not rely on a single stock. Remember is a gap of a few hours between planning, strategizing, and market opening. You cannot predict which stock is going to give a good opening and which is going to open flat.

Therefore, pick a few stocks that are passing your technical scrutiny within your selected segment. You can also add these stocks to your watch list so that as soon as the market opens up, their movements remain in your prime focus and you do not have to look here and there.

Risk Assessment

Risk and reward ratio calculation is an essential thing that you must do much before the markets have opened. There is no doubt that you might have to recalculate this again when the markets open, but doing a basic calculation before the market frenzy begins is always good.

You must look at the highs and lows made by the stocks. Look at the volatility shown by them. This will help you in understanding the kind of stop losses you can put. It is crucial to understand that even if a stock is bullish before it reaches your target price, it might make several smaller up and down movements. Your stop loss should be such that it does not get triggered by such movements. Yet, you should not select stocks that are highly volatile and are making more than 2% upward and downward moves as they can be very difficult to predict. In the beginning, select stocks that are making normal moves.

Your risk-reward ratio should be 1:2 or 1:3. Do not keep a risk-reward ratio higher than that even if you expect the stock to go up much higher. Remember that you are just starting out in the market, and the more calculated risks you take, the longer you will be able to survive in the market. In the 1:2 ratio, if you expect to book your profits at 40 cents, then your stop loss should be 20 cents lower than your purchase price. In a 1:3 ratio, you can expect a target price 60 cents higher and keep your stop loss 20 cents lower than your purchase price.

These are hypothetical figures as the price of stocks would vary, and along with that, price-rise would also change. The figures are simply to help you understand the difference you need to keep between your target price and stop loss.

Managing the Spread

At the time of trading, you must look at the spread very carefully. The stocks with high liquidity generally have a very thin spread. This means that generally, the difference between the bid price and the asking price would be meager. However, if you trade in stocks with poor liquidity or volume, the spreads can be very wide.

At the beginning of your trading career, stay away from stocks with poor liquidity.

Remember, the bid price would be the highest the price the buyers are ready to pay for that asset. The asking price is the lowest price the seller is ready to accept for that asset.

The price that you should be interested in is the bid price. This is the price you are going to put.

Trading Long or Short

Once you have selected your stock, you will have to choose your bias towards that stock. You can go long or short as per your assumption about that stock. This is going to be an important decision as to your whole trading strategy, and the outcome of the day would depend on this decision.

In case you have a positive bias on the stock, you will go long. You will have to fill out a BUY order.

In case you have a negative bias on the stock, you will go short. You will have to fill out a SELL order.

Placing a Limit or Market Order

In this step, you will have to select the order type.

You can select two order types:

Market Order: In this order, the order quantity would get filled at the prevailing rate at that time. You will have no control over the price, and the order may get filled at a slightly higher rate. This type of order should only be placed when you want the order to get filled immediately. Beginners should avoid this order type as your price calculations can fluctuate.

Limit Order: In this type of order, you simply fill out the price at which you want your order to get filled. In case the stock comes down to that price, your order will get filled, or else it will get canceled by the expiry time set out by you.

Understand the Risks and Placing the Stop Loss and Target Price

This is a very important part of understanding your risk carefully. The stop-loss should be clear in your mind as it is going to be an important part of your risk assessment process.

Fill out the stop-loss carefully. Do not think twice before placing the stop-loss. Failing to place a stop-loss at the time of placing the order can be very risky.

At the same time, also place your target price. It is another component of your risk-reward assessment. Like your stop-loss, your target price should also remain fixed in the beginning. When you develop a better understanding of the market, you can extend your target price as per the momentum in the stock.

Things to Watch Out For

Once you have placed your order, you will have to observe the market. Remember that in the initial phases, this is important so that you understand the way market moves. This is not important for the execution of your trades as the orders will now get filled on their own. If the prices are going up, as soon as the target price is hit, the order will get filled, and you will have your profit.

In case the stock moves in the opposite direction, the stop loss will get hit, and you will book some loss. If you go as per the plan, neither the profit nor the loss would be higher than expected.

Keep Control over Your Emotions

This is another very important thing. When your money is at stake, the market moves can make you feel anxious. You may feel that you have waited long enough, and still, the price target has not been achieved, and you would feel like changing it. In case there is quick movement, you may also feel compelled to change the prices. When the stock is moving up, people who have set limit order also start feeling anxious as they feel that they may not get the order.

Remember that you have to get over such feelings and simply sit as an observer. In the beginning, if you develop the tendency of changing too many things too many times, this habit will stick with you, and trading would become very difficult for you. Just learn to sit tight and let things take their course.

Set the Cover Order

This is the final step in case your target price or the stop loss is not hit, and the stock is moving within a range. You have to cover your position with the same day, and hence in the last session of the day, if the stock is trading above your purchase price but lower than your target price, book whatever profit it is giving you. In case it is in the negative, take the losses, and cover your position.

If you had taken a long position, you would have to sell the number of stocks you currently hold.

In case you had taken a short position, buy the number of shares you sold earlier.

Make a Journal Entry

This is the final but essential part of your trading routine.

Always make a journal entry of:

- Your bias on the stock
- The number of stocks traded
- The purchase price
- The selling price
- The turnaround time of trading
- The profit or loss booked

Conclusion

Options trading is most suitable for a certain personality type and mindset. But if you are intrigued by the concept of options, but you simply have not had a chance to develop the correct mindset before, there are a few tips that we can rely on to get in the right frame of mind.

You can weather the storm

Options prices can move a lot over the course of short times. So, someone who likes to see their money protected and not losing any is not going to be suitable for options trading. Now, we all want to come out ahead, so I am not saying that you have to be happy about losing money to be an options trader. What you have to be willing to do is calmly observe your options losing money, and then be ready to stick it out to see gains return in the future. This is akin to riding a real roller coaster, but it is a financial roller coaster. Options do not slowly appreciate the way a Warren Buffett investor would hope to see. Options move big on a percentage basis, and they move fast. If you are trading multiple contracts at once, you might see yourself losing $500 and then earning $500 over a matter of a few hours. In this sense, although most options traders are not “day traders,” technically speaking, you will be better off if you have a little bit of a day trading mindsct.

You do not make emotional decisions

Since options are, by their nature, volatile, and very volatile for many stocks, coming to options trading and being emotional about it is not a good way to approach your trading. If you are emotional, you are going to exit your trades at the wrong time in 75% of cases. You do not want to make any sudden moves when it comes to trading options. As we have said, you should have a trading plan with rules on exiting your positions, stick to those rules, and you should be fine.

Be a little bit math-oriented

To understand options trading and be successful, you cannot be shy about numbers. Options trading is a numbers game. That does not mean you have to drive over to the nearest university and get a statistics degree. But if you do understand probability and statistics, you are going to be a better options trader. Frankly, it is hard to see how you can be a good options trader without having a mind for numbers. Some math is at the core of options trading, and you cannot get around it.

You are market-focused

You do not have to set up a day trading office with ten computer screens so you can be tracking everything by the moment, but if you are hoping to set up a trade and lazily come back to check it three days later, that is not going to work with options trading. You do need to be checking your trades a few times a day. You also need to be keeping up with the latest financial and economic news, and you need to keep up with any news directly related to the companies you invest in or any news that could impact those companies. If the news does come out, you are going to need to make decisions if it is news that is not going to be favorable to your positions. Also, you need to be checking the charts periodically, so you have an idea of where things are heading for now.

Focus on a trading style

As you can see, there are many different ways that you can trade options. In my opinion, sticking to one or two strategies is the best way to approach options trading. I started off buying call options, but now, I focus on selling put credit spreads and iron condors. You should pick what you like best and also something that aligns with your goals. I moved into selling put credit spreads and iron condors because I became interested in the idea of making a living from options trading with regular income payments, rather than continuing to buy calls and hope that the share price would go up. There is no right or wrong answer, pick the trading style that is best suited to your personal style and needs.

Keep detailed trading journals

It is easy to fool yourself when trading options, especially if you are a beginner. I hate to make the analogy, but this is kind of like going to the casino. If you have friends that gamble at casinos, then you are going to notice that they tend to remember the wins, and they will forget all the times that they gambled and lost. I had a cousin that won a boat, and she was always bragging about how she won a boat at the casino. I remember telling her that yes, she won a boat, but she paid $65,000 more than the boat was worth to the casino over the years. You do not want to get in the same situation with your options trading. It can be an emotional experience because trading options are active and fast-paced. When you have a profitable trade, it will be exciting. But you need to keep a journal to record all of your trades to know exactly what the real situation is. That does not mean you quit. If you look at your journal and find out you have a losing record, what you do is figure out why your trades are not profitable and then make adjustments.

Made in the USA
Coppell, TX
01 February 2021